MW00364093

It Starts
with Veg

It Starts *with* Veg

100 Seasonal Suppers *and* Sides

Ceri Jones

PAVILION

Contents

When Life Gives You Lemons...

When life gives you lemons, you make lemonade. A useful analogy for making the best of a sour situation, but what happens when life gives you a stick of rhubarb, a kohlrabi or a cabbage? What do you make then?

Whether you subscribe to a veg box and have stared blankly at the vegetables in your weekly box, or you're interested in exploring a wider variety of vegetables that have caught your eye, this book will be your trusted toolkit as I (re)introduce you to 40 seasonal vegetables commonly found in British veg boxes and farmers markets – most will be available in supermarkets, too. You'll find information on different varieties, the best ways to prepare them, ideas for tasty flavour pairings, as well as 100 vegetable-led simple supper and side recipes.

This book is divided into 8 chapters with vegetables grouped together in families; brassicas, bulbs and stems, fungi, pods, roots, squashes, and summer vegetables. The family groupings aren't always strictly by botanical classification; they're also categorized according to looks, seasons, and how they can be similarly used in recipes. Amongst each recipe you will find tips on how to switch your vegetables around within each chapter, and in some cases further afield, giving you flexibility and licence to get creative and avoid any languishing vegetables ending up in the bin.

Approximately two-thirds of the dishes are vegetarian, with fish, seafood, and meat making up the remainder. Meat and fish are sometimes only used as a seasoning rather than a main ingredient – perhaps a little bit of prosciutto, anchovies, or 'nduja. Where possible, I give suggestions for how to turn a meat-based dish vegetarian because I enjoy that flexitarian approach.

All the recipes in this book are scaled to feed two people. Most recipe books give recipes to feed four, and without a family to feed, I've always found this made me less inspired to try them. The beauty of recipes for two is that they can be doubled to serve four without drastically affecting the cooking times or intensity of spices used. Due to the small batch size of these recipes, you'll discover that most recipes focus on one to two vegetables to keep you from having multiple halves of leftover vegetables to deal with.

Why Vegetables?

Yes, they're good for you – it's a given that we should all be eating more of them – but I find them utterly delicious when fresh and prepared in exactly the way that lets them shine. Plus, they're quick and easy to cook; way more forgiving than the technicalities of meat and fish cookery, and require far less precision than baking, which I don't have quite enough patience for.

I didn't always love vegetables – they're an ingredient I came to appreciate the more I learnt to cook. I grew up in a very Welsh household in the northern tip of Surrey, observing how to make the perfect Welsh cake from my Mum, and the joy of eating cockles straight from the bag in Swansea market from my dad. I mostly turned my nose up at Mum's insistence to eat vegetables, which were always served on the side as a 'must eat for good health' rather than as a celebrated part of any dish.

I've always had an interest in eating but my interest in cooking grew once I'd left home and had my own kitchen to experiment in. When farmers markets started popping up all over London, it inspired me to pick up things I'd never cooked before such as courgette flowers and radicchio, and I taught myself what to do with them. After university, I spent 10 fun years working in orchestral management in London (I have a bachelor's degree in music and still keenly play the clarinet) but gradually found myself becoming more excited about coming home to cook my dinner. It wasn't until my thirties that I decided to undertake my chef training after a very difficult period when both my parents fell ill and passed away. It's still a surprise to me that the creative juices I spent my whole life passionately channelling into music making could also be passionately channelled into cooking, teaching, and writing about food.

After I cemented my cooking knowledge with my Natural Chef training at Bauman College of Holistic Nutrition and Culinary Arts in Berkeley, California, it was time to get to work. I've done many different jobs in food including working for a vegetarian café, teaching cooking classes, writing recipes, cooking for retreats across the UK and Europe, and working as a Food Educator at The Garden Museum in London, all the while creating my own library of useful recipes. I'm so happy to be sharing some of them with you here for the first time in print.

When a new local veg box scheme popped up in my area, I soon found myself with a weekly box and spent five years writing their weekly customer newsletters full of recipe ideas to suit what was in the box each week. I was told that the reason most people end up cancelling their subscription was because they were wasting vegetables as they didn't know what to do with them. Everyone loves springtime asparagus or a summer tomato, but in Britain, veg-box-land means root vegetables and cabbages. I believe these are all vegetables that can be met with the same excitement – even kohlrabi – you just need the right recipe. I personally found that getting a veg box each week amped up my own relationship with vegetables. I too, was dealing with the ennui of muddy carrots every week and was learning to be creative with vegetables like cabbage that I'd usually skip past in the veg aisle.

I'm often asked where the inspiration for my recipes comes from. What to do with a vegetable is always the starting point, hence 'It Starts with Veg' became the perfect title for this book. I take an ingredient, think about the best way to cook it, what it goes with, what's already in my cupboards or fridge, and build everything else around that. Consciously, or sometimes subconsciously, I might recall an aspect of a dish I've eaten in a restaurant, at home, or whilst travelling, from street food stalls, or other people's houses. Recipes I've cooked from my collection of cookbooks or from the web, or watched being made on the wide variety of cooking programmes we have at our disposal. I've learnt a lot about flavour pairings from great books that have gone before, such as the excellent *Flavour Thesaurus* series and *The Flavour Bible*, but when it comes to food and cooking, you never stop learning and will always discover new ideas.

Most importantly, I create recipes I know I'll love to eat, not just because I'm greedy, but because that's the best way for me to pump my creative passion into them. If I don't want to shout from the rooftops about how good a recipe is, how can I persuade you to cook it? This curated collection of my vegetable recipes is here to guide and inspire you rather than to exist as a set of rules you must follow. Play around, experiment, and most of all, have fun. And when you've found some more kohlrabi recipes, please send them my way.

Ingredient Notes

BLACK PEPPER
I generally use cracked black pepper or freshly ground from a grinder.

BREADCRUMBS
Coarse breadcrumbs are best for all of these recipes. You can buy
breadcrumbs coarsely ground, but it's easy to make your own. Blitz
day-old bread in a food processor until broken down into coarse crumbs.
I keep sourdough bread in my freezer, defrost and blitz one slice at a time
for fancy breadcrumbs on demand.

BUTTER
I use unsalted butter and add my own salt as needed.

DAIRY
I always recommend using full fat dairy – whether that's crème fraîche, Greek
yoghurt or pouring cream. This is for flavour, and also the higher fat content
means they won't split when added hot to your dishes.

EGGS
It doesn't really matter what size they are for the purposes of these recipes.
I usually buy boxes of mixed sized eggs.

LEMONS AND OTHER CITRUS
Use unwaxed citrus fruits where possible.

OLIVE OIL
I use extra-virgin olive oil for almost all my cooking, even roasting and
sautéing. I might save a more expensive extra-virgin for cold dressings but,
in general, extra-virgin olive oil is the one. In the recipes you will just see olive
oil written unless I have specified otherwise – for example, a light olive oil if
I don't want the pepperiness of olive oil. I use coconut or rapeseed where it
makes more culinary sense.

LEFTOVERS
- Due to the portion sizes of the recipes, it is inevitable there will be the odd
  bits of ingredients leftover. The biggest culprit of my cooking is lemons. I
  never throw half lemons away though – any spare lemons go straight into
  my glass of water. Alternatively, you can slice into wedges and freeze, ready
  to add cold to drinks.
- Most cooked foods will keep for at least 3 days, if not 5. Use your common
  sense when eating up leftovers. Repurposing leftovers into new dishes is
  often a good way to come up with new ideas.
- Any leftover pesto, wine, or stock can be frozen in ice-cube trays.

- If you've bought a carton of cream and only need a couple of tablespoons for your recipes, then the leftovers can go into a frittata, be swirled into soup or tossed into a pasta sauce.
- If you don't use a whole pack of puff or filo pastry, don't panic. Any offcuts of puff pastry can be cut into bite-sized pieces with a cookie cutter, brushed with egg and topped with Parmesan cheese. Bake until crispy. Spare filo pastry can be kept well wrapped in the fridge for a few days.
- If you end up with lots of whisked egg leftover after glazing pastry, keep in a sealed container, and add to tomorrow's scrambled eggs. Spare egg whites from making mayonnaise can be used in exactly the same way.

SALT

Salt is used in all of my recipes and is measured using my preferred choice of flaked sea salt. In the UK I use Cornish or Maldon®. If you use fine salt, adjust your quantities down. 1 teaspoon of flaked salt is a lot less than 1 teaspoon of fine salt. Also, my pinches of salt are quite big – it's a chef thing.

Cooking Terms

Here's a more in-depth explanation for some of the terms referred to throughout the recipes:

AL DENTE
Italian for 'to the tooth'. A useful term for describing how cooked pasta, rice and vegetables should taste. Firm, but not hard, retaining a little bite. How *al dente* these items are cooked is up to you, as long as they are no longer raw.

BLANCHING AND SHOCKING
Most greens will require blanching and shocking. This is when vegetables are briefly cooked, or until al dente in hot water (always salted), then shocked in cold water to lock in the colour and stop the cooking process. You might be encouraged to shock in a large bowl of iced water, but I know that is not practical for the home cook, so a good rinse under cold water is fine for small quantities.

Blanching and shocking is useful for when the ingredient is going into a salad, to be cooked fully in the rest of the dish, or needs peeling (broad beans). Different ingredients require different blanching times. This is different to boiling, which is usually for cooking an ingredient until it is completely soft (such as potatoes).

DEGLAZING
I use this term quite a lot when making stews. You'll be instructed to deglaze with liquid – usually wine or vinegar. After searing meat or vegetables at high heat, little caramelized bits get stuck to the pan. Adding the liquid will dissolve these so you can scrape and stir them back into your dish for full flavour.

EMULSIFY
This is when two liquids that have different densities (such as an oil and vinegar) are forced together until smooth, with the help of an emulsifier (egg, honey, mustard), by a gradual mixing process. Usually referred to when making a salad dressing or mayonnaise.

EQUIPMENT
On top of the basic equipment such as pots and pans, mixing bowls, and a sharp knife, these will come in handy for a veg-centric kitchen:
• High speed blender or strong hand blender (above 600W)
• Cast-iron griddle pan
• Casserole dish with lid that goes on the hob and in the oven
• Food processor or mini chopper
• Pestle and mortar for pesto and crushing spices

- Vegetable scrubbing brush for all those dirty carrots and Jerusalem artichokes
- Vegetable peeler and julienne peeler
- Mandoline for thinly slicing vegetables
- Pastry brush for egg washes

JULIENNE
Fancy word for a matchstick cut, useful for vegetables (*see* knife skills, below).

KNIFE SKILLS
Food prep will become less daunting with solid knife skills. A knife doesn't need to be expensive but it does need to be sharp. A basic chef-style knife that feels comfortable to hold is a good place to start your journey. A honing steel is useful for keeping your knives sharp on a daily basis. Most cooking schools offer the basics in knife skills and I really recommend treating yourself to this. You'll learn about keeping your fingers tucked under in a claw and using your thumb and first finger as a bridge. Fast chopping is for show-offs.

PAN-FRYING FISH
Pan-frying can be a bit tricky at first. Make sure your fish is patted dry, you've got a cast-iron or non-stick pan, and plenty of room for manoeuvre in the pan. If the fish sticks, which happens to the best of us, it's likely because the pan isn't hot enough, or there is not enough oil. When the fish is ready to be flipped it should easily come away from the pan.

SEASONING TO TASTE
After knife skills, learning how to season to taste was the best thing I learnt at cooking school. In my classes I encourage participants to taste their food throughout the cooking process to learn the way I did. But why aren't seasoning quantities written in a recipe? Ingredients, especially vegetables, can vary hugely in their quality, flavour, and water content, and all of this will have an impact on how much seasoning is required.

But what does 'season to taste' mean? What you are looking for is for the dish to 'sing', to taste well rounded but not taste of salt. If it tastes dull, your first job is to add a pinch of salt, then taste again. Seasoning isn't just about salt and pepper. You will notice I also add lemon juice or other acids such as vinegar, as well as fat in the form of olive oil or butter to alter the taste. In order to consistently make great tasting dishes, learning to alter your seasoning as required is the best thing you can do to improve your cooking. The only way to get better at this is to practise.

Salt doesn't just sit on the dish at the end – onions and other aromatics are seasoned as they cook, vegetables are seasoned before roasting. This all helps build layers of flavour. Adding salt also helps bring the moisture out of onions so they cook quicker.

SUPREME
A term for segmenting an orange. Slice the top and bottom off the orange, then glide your knife just under the peel to remove it along with the pith. To segment hold the orange in your hand, over a bowl to catch the drips. Choose one segment to remove, cut along the line of the pith into the centre, and do the same on the other side of the segment – you should now be able to remove the segment. Continue this same pattern until all the orange is cut. If easier, you can just slice the peeled orange into thin rounds.

TOASTING NUTS, SEEDS AND WHOLE SPICES
Toasting is used throughout the book and usually written as a pre-prepared ingredient. Toasting releases natural oils in these ingredients and with it flavour. In small quantities, toasting should be done in a hot, dry frying pan. Add only when the pan is hot and toss frequently until golden brown (timings vary but are generally short). Spices will smell fragrant. Remove from the pan immediately to prevent them from cooking in the residual heat.

BRASSICAS

Bouquets of broccoli and cauliflower, leaf-like cabbages and kale, bulbous kohlrabi and rooty radish, these exceptionally good-for-you family of vegetables are also known as 'cruciferous' veg. Brassicas can have a whiff of sulphur if overcooked but don't let this put you off – you might just find a recipe here that will change your mind!

Broccoli

CALABRESE – YEAR-ROUND (BEST SUMMER TO AUTUMN)
PURPLE SPROUTING BROCCOLI – LATE WINTER TO SPRING

A bouquet of broccoli was known as 'trees' in the Jones' household (and others too I imagine). It's entirely edible from its crunchy stem to its clusters of tiny trees. In the years I've been teaching family cooking classes, I have discovered it's universally liked by kids when other seemingly 'normal' vegetables are pushed aside. Fortuitous then, that it's incredibly nutritious.

Calabrese is the variety of broccoli that's most popular, but not the original. It was developed from purple sprouting broccoli (PSB) for its tighter cluster of trees on one head. With its purple florets and longer thinner edible stems, I can't be alone in saying I actually prefer PSB. It reigns supreme in the UK during the harvesting hungry gap of early spring, when there really isn't much else about. Supermarket popular Tenderstem® broccoli was developed as recently as the 1990s as a hybrid of broccoli and Chinese kale.

All types of broccoli can be steamed or blanched, this is reliable and tasty if done briefly, but don't miss out on the joy of roasting. It doesn't take long in the oven for the stalks to soften and the florets to crisp up. The purple colour of PSB is near impossible to maintain once cooked, but roasting will give you the best chance. Broccoli can also be charred on a griddle pan or blitzed into a soup which is infinitely better with blue cheese. As with all blanched greens, if using cold in a recipe, shock with cold water as soon as you've lifted them out of the boiling water to lock in the green.

The tiny florets of calabrese will spray all over your kitchen if you slice straight through them. Another approach is to slice through the stalk, then gently pull apart the florets.

The edible stalk requires peeling, then can be diced and cooked along with the base or onion part of a dish. It can also be thinly shaved into ribbons, marinated and eaten raw or tossed into a dish towards the end of cooking (*see* Broccoli Gratin, page 20).

Tasty flavour pairings for broccoli you'll already find in my recipes are: almond, capers, chilli, cream, garlic, lemon, olives, olive oil, parsley, and Parmesan. Others to try include: anchovies, mustard seeds, pasta, sesame, and tarragon.

RECIPE IDEA Toss blanched and shocked broccoli florets with olive oil and thin slices of red onion soaked in lemon juice for an easy side dish.

TOP TIP
Use purple sprouting broccoli
as a dunker for dippy eggs.

Purple Sprouting Broccoli Puff Pastry Tarts with Ricotta and Olive Tapenade

Purple sprouting broccoli spears are the perfect length for individual-sized puff pastry tarts. A standard shop-bought sheet of puff pastry is an awkward size for a tart for two – it's just a bit too big – so I recommend making three tarts and keeping the spare one for lunch tomorrow. Leftovers keep brilliantly, just warm through in the oven for 10 minutes before serving. Serve with a simple side of dressed leaves.

This ricotta and olive tapenade tart combo will work with a host of different vegetables; try asparagus, slices of slightly overlapping tomato, slim wedges of glazed beetroot (*see* page 168), or roasted squash cubes.

SERVES 3 | TIME TO PREPARE – 35 MINUTES

FOR THE TART
320g/11½oz ready-made puff pastry sheet
1 egg, lightly whisked
200g/7oz purple sprouting broccoli
250g/9oz ricotta
zest of ½ lemon, plus extra for garnish
olive oil
salt and pepper

FOR THE TAPENADE
50g/1¾oz pitted Kalamata olives
1 heaped tbsp chopped parsley
1 tbsp capers
2 tbsp olive oil
½ tbsp lemon juice

Remove the pastry from the fridge 10 minutes prior to using and preheat the oven to 200°C fan/220°C/425°F/gas mark 7.

Open out the pastry and divide into 3 even rectangles. Transfer these onto a lined baking tray. With a dinner knife, score a 1cm/½ inch inside border on each one, prick all over with a fork and give an egg wash. Bake in the oven for 8–10 minutes, until starting to puff up and turn golden brown. Leave to cool for a few minutes.

Meanwhile, prepare your toppings. Prepare the broccoli by trimming, so the spears fit across the tart lengths. Slice any fatter spears into half lengthways. Blanch the broccoli by boiling in a large saucepan of salted boiling water for 2–3 minutes until cooked but still firm (al dente). Drain, rinse under cold water until completely cold and leave to drip dry in the colander. Whisk the ricotta with the lemon zest and season to taste.

Put together your rustic tapenade by roughly chopping the olives, parsley and capers together on a chopping board (a food processor would create brown sludge). Scrape into a small bowl and stir in 2 tablespoons of olive oil and ½ tablespoon lemon juice. Season to taste, bearing in mind the olives and capers are already salty.

When the pastry is cool to the touch, push down the centre of each tart if it has puffed up, and spread over the ricotta. Arrange the blanched broccoli spears on top in a head-to-toe fashion. Lightly drizzle with olive oil and sprinkle over a pinch of salt. Put the tarts back in the oven for 10–15 minutes, rotating the tray halfway if your oven doesn't cook evenly. The tarts will be done when the crust is browned, the broccoli crispy, and the base crisp. Remove from the oven, dot over the olive tapenade, add a smattering of lemon zest and serve warm.

Almond Crumbed Broccoli Gratin, with Chilli, Capers and Crème Fraîche

This easy-to-put-together gratin makes use of the whole of the vegetable. The broccoli stalk is shaved with a peeler and tossed into the creamy sauce with the cooked florets. It's spiked with broccoli's best mates – fiery chilli and salty capers. Serve as a light lunch for two, or as a side dish.

Try replacing the broccoli with purple sprouting broccoli, Tenderstem, romanesco or cauliflower.

SERVES 2 | TIME TO PREPARE – 35 MINUTES

500g/1lb 2oz broccoli (approx. 2 medium-sized heads of broccoli)
1 tbsp olive oil
2 garlic cloves, finely chopped
2 tbsp capers
¼ tsp chilli flakes
4 heaped tbsp full-fat crème fraîche
3 tbsp ground almonds
3 tbsp finely grated Parmesan cheese
salt and pepper

Preheat the oven to 200°C fan/220°C/425°F/gas mark 7.

Separate the florets from the broccoli stalk and chop them into small bite-sized pieces. Keep the leaves. Square off the broccoli stalk, removing the knobbly bits, then using a peeler, peel the stalk into thin strips.

Blanch the broccoli florets in salted water for 3–4 minutes until tender, then drain, rinse under cold water and set aside.

Heat 1 tablespoon of olive oil in a frying pan big enough to take all the broccoli to a low-medium heat. Sauté the garlic, capers, and chilli flakes for around a minute. Keep on the heat and add in the broccoli stalk strips, broccoli leaves, crème fraîche, and stir. Finally, toss in the cooked florets and mix so that everything is coated in the cream. Season to taste with salt and pepper.

Tip everything into a baking dish about 18 × 22 cm/7 × 8½ inches in size. Mix together the ground almonds and Parmesan, and scatter over the top of the broccoli. Bake the gratin in the oven for 15–20 minutes until the cheese has melted and the top has just caught brown.

All types of broccoli can be steamed or blanched, this is reliable and tasty if done briefly, but don't miss out on the joy of roasting.

Cabbage

YEAR-ROUND FOR MOST VARIETIES, BUT BEST IN WINTER

Cabbage possibly delivers the best value for money of all the vegetables. It's usually one of the cheapest to buy and produces an endless volume once shredded. To get over my dread of the never-ending cabbage in the fridge, the recipes in this chapter have been designed to use up as much cabbage as is physically possible to eat in one sitting without exploding – literally, cabbages can be quite gassy.

Varieties of cabbage include crunchy white and red, softer Savoy, January King, spring greens, and those that fall somewhere in the middle such as pointed sweetheart cabbage (hispi) and Chinese (or napa) cabbage. Mini green cabbages AKA Brussels sprouts are also included here.

As well as being good for making coleslaw, shredded raw cabbage can be fermented into kimchi (Chinese cabbage) or sauerkraut (white or red cabbage). Cabbage can also be steamed, braised, stir-fried, grilled or roasted. Roasting works particularly well for wedges of larger cabbages or Brussels sprouts. More versatile than you thought? I'd choose any of these methods over boiling, because the nutrition and flavour escape into the cooking water, along with the sulphurous smell, which will subsequently waft through your house.

For all cabbages you'll need to slice out and discard the core unless you're using it to hold a wedge together; halve, quarter, then slice it out. Thinly shredding is a good opportunity to practise your knife skills, but you could always dig out the relevant attachment of your food processor. With the softer big leaf cabbages, I prefer to separate into leaves, slice out the stalk, stack, roll, and then slice into ribbons – this is known as a *chiffonade* in the business. Savoy, January King or spring greens have huge leaves once opened out and can be used instead of vine leaves as a parcel wrapper.

Brussels sprouts trees also produce sprout tops. These are tough green leaves that can be shredded, cooked and used like spring greens or kale.

Tasty flavour pairings for cabbage you'll already find in my recipes are: anchovy, orange (kumquat), cumin, chicken, onions, and thyme. Others to try include: apple, carrots, bacon or pancetta, potatoes, caraway seeds, cream, raisins, and walnuts.

RECIPE IDEA A trickle of double cream stirred through steamed cabbage, leeks, and kale makes an excellent winter side.

Griddled Sweetheart Cabbage Wedge with Anchovy Crumb

Salty, spiced, anchovy-flavoured breadcrumbs elevate charred sweetheart cabbage in this side dish that uses an entire cabbage in one go – hurrah. Any leftover anchovy crumbs can be tossed through spaghetti. To turn the griddled cabbage into a main course, serve over a pool of celeriac mash, whipped ricotta, or hummus.

A pointed sweetheart or hispi cabbage works best in this recipe, as if you slice carefully through the core, it will hold together in a wedge. A Savoy sliced into wedges would also be good. Try the breadcrumb topping scattered over a pile of roasted halved Brussels sprouts.

SERVES 2 AS A SIDE | TIME TO PREPARE – 20 MINUTES

olive oil
1 pointed sweetheart cabbage, cut into quarters through the core
1 x 50g/1¾oz can anchovies in olive oil
½ tsp chilli flakes
100g/3½oz coarse breadcrumbs or day-old bread, blitzed into breadcrumbs using
    a food processor
1 lemon
salt

Preheat the oven to 200°C fan/220°C/425°F/gas mark 7. Heat a griddle pan over a high heat. Drizzle olive oil all over the cabbage and cook for 2–3 minutes on each side until sufficiently charred (start with the cut side, then flip over to the curved side. Adjust heat as necessary – once the cast-iron pan gains enough heat it can be a scorcher. Transfer the charred cabbage to a baking dish with the cut sides pointing up. Season with salt and bake in the oven for 10 minutes to ensure the deepest part of the cabbage has softened.

Meanwhile, make your anchovy crumb. Measure out the anchovy oil from the can and top up with olive oil from a bottle to make up 3 tablespoons. Heat up a frying pan to medium-high, add the oil and the anchovies. Break up the warm anchovies using a wooden spoon so they dissolve into the hot oil, then add the chilli flakes and breadcrumbs. Cook for 5–6 minutes, until golden and crisp, stirring intermittently so they don't stick (if you stir too much they won't crisp up), adjust the heat as necessary. Zest over the entire skin of the lemon, stir, and take off the heat. Cut the lemon in half and set aside.

Pull the cooked cabbage out of the oven and squeeze over one of the cut halves of lemon. Transfer to a serving plate, top with as many of the anchovy crumbs as you are hungry for, and serve.

Brussels Sprouts and Paneer Stir Fry with Grated Coconut and Nigella Seeds

A Keralan thoran is a dry curry that combines shredded cabbage with fresh coconut. I must have had this in the back of my mind when one dreary winter's day I had a wave of inspiration to grate some coconut from my freezer into some shredded Brussels sprouts sautéed with garlic and ginger. To make this more substantial, I now add paneer and nigella seeds – I love their oniony flavour with sprouts. Serve alongside brown rice.

Shredded Savoy, spring greens, or Kalettes® would work well as a substitution for the sprouts.

SERVES 2 AS A MAIN, 4 AS A SIDE | TIME TO PREPARE – 30 MINUTES

2 tbsp rapeseed oil or coconut oil
200g/7oz paneer, diced into 2.5cm/1 inch cubes
1 red onion, thinly sliced
1 tbsp apple cider or white wine vinegar
25g/1oz fresh coconut, grated (or use creamed coconut from a block, also grated)
1 garlic clove, finely chopped
1 small red chilli, seeded and finely chopped
a thumb tip of ginger, peeled and finely chopped
300g/10½oz Brussels sprouts, tough base removed and finely shredded
2 tsp nigella seeds
juice of 1 lime
salt and pepper

Warm 2 tablespoons of rapeseed oil over a medium-high heat in a medium-sized frying pan. Add the paneer and fry for about 10 minutes, turning regularly with tongs until crispy and browned on all sides. The paneer shouldn't stick if the pan is hot enough and you allow it to form a crust before turning it. Transfer the paneer to a side plate, leaving the oil in the pan.

Turn the heat down to low-medium, and sauté the red onion with a pinch of salt. Cook for around 5–8 minutes, stirring regularly to avoid sticking or too much colouration. Deglaze with 1 tablespoon of vinegar – use your wooden spoon to scrape any small crispy bits of paneer back into the onions. When the vinegar has evaporated add the coconut, garlic, chilli, and ginger, and cook for a minute more, then add the shredded sprouts along with 4 tablespoons of water. Stir well so everything is coated. Cover the pan with a lid, and cook for 5 minutes or until the sprouts have softened, stirring every so often to avoid any sticking. Add the paneer back in to warm through, then finish with the nigella seeds and lime juice, and season to taste. Serve straight away.

Chicken Thighs Braised with Red Cabbage and Kumquats

Braising red cabbage in stock transforms this crunchy vegetable into a soft, tender, sweet bite. Braised along with chicken thighs it becomes a simple one pot. Kumquats add a contrasting note of sweet-sour. They're small citrus fruits that can be eaten whole, skin and all, and you should be able to find them at any good greengrocer. This braise will need to be cooked in a casserole or deep cast-iron dish with a lid (or one fashioned out of tin foil) you can use on the hob and in the oven. Serve with some cooked grains and seasonal salad leaves.

Try this dish with white cabbage, or segments of orange instead of kumquats (no need to char, just pop them in along with the cabbage).

SERVES 2 | TIME TO PREPARE – 1 HOUR

1 tbsp olive oil
4 skin-on, bone-in chicken thighs
1 red onion, finely sliced
125g/4½oz kumquats, split in half lengthways, any large pips removed
1 garlic clove, finely chopped
3 sprigs of thyme, leaves stripped
1 tbsp cumin seeds
2 tbsp apple cider or white wine vinegar
250g/9oz red cabbage, thinly shredded
125ml/4fl oz chicken stock
2 tsp butter
salt and pepper

Preheat the oven to 190°C fan/210°C/415°F/gas mark 6½.

Heat the olive oil in a casserole dish over a medium-high heat. Season the chicken with salt and pepper and place skin-side down in the hot pan. Cook for 5–6 minutes until the skin is crispy. Keep an eye on the heat and respond accordingly to avoid burning the chicken skin. When the chicken is ready to be turned, it will easily come away from the pan. Flip over and cook for a further 3 minutes until the underside is also browned. Remove the chicken from the pan, leave all the chicken crumbs and around 1 tablespoon of fat in the pan.

Turn down the heat to low-medium. Add the sliced onion into the fat, along with a pinch of salt, and sauté for around 5 minutes, until starting to soften.

Add the kumquats and char undisturbed in the heat of the pan for a couple of minutes. Next add the garlic, thyme, and cumin seeds, and cook briefly until fragrant. Deglaze with 2 tablespoons of vinegar – use a wooden spoon to scrape any brown bits from the bottom of the pan back into the dish and cook until the vinegar evaporates. Tumble in the cabbage, pour over the chicken stock, stir, then nestle the chicken back in, keeping the skin exposed. Cover the pan with a lid (or tin foil) and transfer to the oven to cook for 25 minutes.

After 25 minutes, take the dish out of the oven. Remove the lid, add the butter to the cabbage, and return to the oven uncovered for 10 minutes to crisp up the chicken skin and for any excess liquid in the cabbage to evaporate. To check that the chicken is cooked, the juices should run clear and the flesh no longer be peachy. Season to taste then serve the braise straight to the table.

Cauliflower

AVAILABLE YEAR-ROUND, BEST IN WINTER

My first introduction to cauliflower was boiled and drenched in cheese sauce and served as one of our Sunday lunch sides. I didn't like it much, the texture of the boiled cauliflower wasn't too appealing. Since then, cauliflower has had a resurgence as chefs and food writers have opened our eyes to a variety of cooking techniques. Cauliflower has been saved by the 'steak', spiced crispy-edged florets and roasting whole as a plant-based centrepiece – I now love it.

Purple, yellow, and orange cauliflowers are, on first look, beguiling, but in reality, a swindle. They taste much the same as their white sisters and, sadly, the colour tends to disappear once cooked. A better choice is the romanesco, with its fractal patterned conical pine-tree-like florets. It's a cross between a cauliflower and broccoli, and I find it works better as a sub in cauliflower recipes. Like cauliflower it is marvellous roasted with chilli and lemon.

Cauliflower can be steamed or boiled, pickled, charred, and roasted. It has a high water content so is suited to puréeing, and makes the silkiest of soups. I once had a savoury puréed cauliflower panna cotta as a restaurant starter that was so convincing, years later I am still wondering how it was made. Roasting is best – either whole (you'll need to par-boil it first), in wedges, bite-sized florets, or as seen on every plant-based menu in the land, cut into a steak (*see* page 31 for instructions on how to do this).

It can also be grated or processed into tiny bits to serve as a low-carb rice substitute. Contrary to my former beliefs, it tastes nothing like rice and is the messiest thing to prepare. Due to the fact the smaller cauliflower is chopped, the more sulphurous it gets, it smells utterly horrendous if left in the fridge.

Cauliflower leaves are not to be wasted – they are insanely good when baked into crisps with olive oil and salt. The huge outer leaves have a thick stalk and are a bit too tough, it's the inner leaves that are best for roasting. I never serve a cauliflower dish without them now (*see* page 31 for the recipe).

Tasty flavour pairings for cauliflower you'll already find in my recipes are; puy lentils, parsley, capers, chillies, coriander, garlic, lemon, curry powder and turmeric, sultanas, and watercress. Others to try include; anchovies, apple, blue or strong hard cheeses, cream, dill, orange, and potatoes.

RECIPE IDEA Easy cauliflower soup: add raw cauliflower florets and vegetable stock to a pan of sautéed onion, celery, and garlic. Add spices if you like. Simmer until soft, blend smooth with a touch of cream. Serve with anchovy breadcrumbs (*see* page 24).

TOP TIP

Cauliflower can be pickled. For a quick pickle, simmer a pickling liquor
of equal volume vinegar and caster sugar, drop in your choice of spices
(for example coriander seeds, mustard seeds, peppercorns, turmeric),
then cool, strain, and pour over chopped cauliflower florets. Toss
regularly for 30 minutes–1hour, until crunchy and pickled.

Cauliflower Steaks with Puy lentils and Salsa Verde

This 'cauliflower is the hero' dish is one of my retreat catering favourites. A roasted steak smothered in fragrant herby sauce, served piled on top of warm puy lentils cooked with flavourful bay leaf, celery, and mustard. You will generally get two steaks out of an average-sized cauliflower, so I always roast the spare cauliflower to have alongside, as well as baking the leaves into crisps for a fabulously crunchy garnish. Alternatively, cut the cauliflower into quarters to roast and there won't be any spare. In summer, serve this dish with a sharp tomato salad on the side, in autumn honey roasted roots.

Replace the cauliflower with a romanesco steak.

SERVES 2 | TIME TO PREPARE – 40 MINUTES

1 medium-sized cauliflower
olive oil
salt and pepper

FOR THE LENTILS
2 banana shallots, finely chopped
2 celery sticks, finely chopped
1 garlic clove, finely chopped
1 bay leaf
1 tsp Dijon mustard
140g/5oz dried puy lentils, rinsed
60ml/2fl oz white wine (optional, or add the equivalent in extra stock)
350ml/12fl oz vegetable stock
2 heaped tbsp finely chopped parsley

FOR THE SALSA VERDE
15g/½oz parsley
15g/½oz basil
1 garlic clove
2 tbsp capers
½ tsp Dijon mustard
juice of ½ lemon

Preheat the oven to 180°C fan/200°C/400°F/gas mark 6.

Prepare your cauliflower steaks. Remove the leaves from the cauliflower. Turn the cauliflower stalk facing up. Slice off the florets either side of the stalk, leaving you with one gigantic steak, then divide this into two to leave you with two 2-cm/¾-inch thick steaks. Brush the cauliflower steaks all over using around 1 tablespoon of olive oil, season both sides with salt and pepper, and place on a baking tray. Break the remaining cauli florets into small pieces and put on a separate baking tray with 1 tablespoon of olive oil. Season with a little salt. In a small bowl, toss the leaves with enough oil to lightly coat them. Season and set aside.

Next, start the lentils. Add 1 tablespoon of olive oil to the saucepan and sauté the shallot and celery for 5 minutes, until softened but not coloured. Add the garlic, bay leaf, and mustard, and cook for 30 seconds. Add the lentils to the pan along with the wine and then the stock. Bring to the boil, then reduce to a simmer and cook for 25 minutes.

Whilst the lentils simmer, roast the cauliflower steaks in the oven for 25 minutes or until browned all over and a knife glides through the stalk like softened butter. When there are 15 minutes remaining on the clock, pop in the tray with the smaller florets. When 6 minutes remain, scatter in the leaves with the florets – cook until just crisp but not burnt.

Meanwhile make your salsa verde. Remove the stalks from the parsley and basil, and chop them finely together on your chopping board. Finely chop the garlic, then scatter it over the herbs with the capers and rustically chop everything together. Slide into a bowl and stir in the mustard, lemon juice, and 3 tablespoons of olive oil. Season to taste. The sauce should be strongly tangy and herby.

When the lentils are al dente and will have absorbed most, if not all, of the water, take off the heat. Fish out the bay leaf, stir in the chopped parsley, and season to taste with salt and pepper, and a drizzle of olive oil.

To plate up, split the lentils between 2 plates, top each with a steak, smother with 1 tablespoon of salsa verde, then add the crispy leaves as garnish. Serve the florets on the side with the remaining salsa verde.

Curry Roasted Cauliflower Florets with Sultana Studded Quinoa

Dried fruit is often paired with cauliflower; chopped apricots, dates, and sultanas are all good. This warm salad gives me hints of the flavours of coronation chicken combining the flavour of curry powder with sweet sultanas and the crunch of toasted almond flakes. It's a dish I make often on a retreat as part of a lunchtime spread of seasonal salads, and if two of you don't manage it all for dinner, it will keep well for tomorrow's lunch box.

This dish works beautifully with romanesco and also regular broccoli – just reduce the cooking time to 15 minutes as it will inevitably char faster.

SERVES 2 | TIME TO PREPARE – 35 MINUTES

125g/4½oz quinoa, well rinsed
250ml/9fl oz vegetable stock
a pinch of ground turmeric
olive oil
1 tbsp medium curry powder
½ tsp ground cinnamon
1 medium-sized cauliflower, broken into small florets
2 spring onions, finely sliced on an angle
juice of 1 lemon
2 heaped tbsp sultanas
2 heaped tbsp finely chopped coriander
2 tbsp toasted flaked almonds
a handful of watercress (15g/½oz), to serve
salt and pepper

Preheat the oven to 180°C fan/200°C/400°F/gas mark 6.

Place the quinoa in a medium-sized saucepan that you have a lid for. Pour over the stock and add a pinch of turmeric. Bring to the boil, cover, turn to a low heat with only a very gentle bubble (I recommend moving to your smallest hob). Cook for 20 minutes, by which time the water should be absorbed and the quinoa soft. Turn off the heat and sit for 5 minutes with the lid on to absorb any remaining moisture. Transfer to a large mixing bowl to cool a little.

Meanwhile, in a small bowl, whisk together 2 tablespoons of olive oil with the curry powder and cinnamon, and season with salt and pepper. Lay out the cauliflower in one layer on a baking tray and toss with the marinade so that the florets are well coated. Roast for 22–25 minutes, until the stalks are fork tender, and florets crispy around the edges.

While everything cooks, place the sliced spring onions in a small bowl with the lemon juice to marinate for at least 10 minutes. This will take the oniony edge off.

When the quinoa has sufficiently cooled, toss in the spring onions with lemon juice, sultanas, and finely chopped coriander into the quinoa. Season to taste – if it lacks richness, drizzle in some olive oil.

Transfer the quinoa to a serving platter and top with the roasted cauliflower florets, scatter over the toasted flaked almonds, and garnish with the watercress and a drizzle of olive oil.

Kale

My kale consumption quadrupled when I moved to California for a short time, over ten years ago, to do my chef training. There, I discovered people walking down the street wearing 'kale' university sweatshirts and tasted an abundance of health promoting green kale-laden smoothies and massaged kale salads. I've since learnt that kale also tastes fantastic with cream, butter and cheese, which sounds to me like the perfect balance for a health promoting vegetable.

There are many varieties of kale. The easiest to source – which you should be able to find in larger supermarkets across the autumn and winter – are curly kale and cavolo nero. Cavolo nero, or black cabbage, isn't black at all, but very dark green with long flat leaves. Look out for it in Italian recipes such as the Tuscan ribollita stew. It's also called Tuscan kale, lacinato kale or dinosaur kale thanks to the scaly surface of the leaves. You might also come across purple varieties of curly kale, or the purple-red Russian kale. There are also Kalettes®, or flower sprouts, a relatively new hybrid of Brussels sprouts and kale.

Kale can be cooked a number of ways; sautéed, stir fried, steamed, blanched, roasted until crispy, blitzed into soups and smoothies, or braised in the final minutes of a stew. It even works in pesto. It can be eaten raw if the fibres are broken down by massaging with a dressing (*see* Curly Kale, Celeriac, and Apple Salad with Crumbled Stilton on page 39 and Warm Delicata with Black Rice, Cavolo Nero, and Za'atar Dressing on page 236).

Always remove the stalk of the leafy kales as it's too tough to eat. If you buy curly kale already shredded you'll have a tedious time picking out the shredded stalks which are not removed in the packaging process, so ideally buy it in a bunch. To shred cavolo nero into ribbons, de-stalk, stack the leaves, roll them up, then slice. Curly and Russian kale don't need to see a knife and can be roughly torn with hands before using if you prefer.

Tasty flavour pairings for kale you'll already find in my recipes are; garlic, blue cheese, lemon, Parmesan, chilli ('nduja), and tomatoes. Others to try include; anchovies, mustard seeds, pasta, sesame, and tarragon.

RECIPE IDEA For a simple dinner add a handful of kale sautéed with chilli to spaghetti with olive oil and finish with Parmesan.

TOP TIP
For excellent kale chips, massage a little olive oil into the whole leaves, season, and roast for 8 minutes at 200°C fan/220°C/425°F/ gas mark 7 until crispy. They burn easily, so watch like a hawk.

Kale and Walnut Pesto Green Lasagne

My mum used to make a simple vegetarian lasagne with béchamel sauce and basil pesto. I've created a brassica version, by layering the lasagne sheets and sauce, not only with homemade kale and walnut pesto, but also with finely sliced softened leeks and kale. The smell of this baking in the oven alone makes me salivate. It's hard to make this pesto in smaller quantities, so keep any leftovers and freeze or stir through spaghetti later in the week.

The pesto or filling of the lasagne can be made with whichever kale you have to hand.

SERVES 2 GENEROUSLY | TIME TO PREPARE – 1 HOUR 15 MINUTES

FOR THE KALE AND WALNUT PESTO
125g/4½oz kale, woody stems removed and leaves shredded
30g/1oz walnuts, toasted
1 garlic clove, finely chopped
6 tbsp olive oil
juice of 1 lemon

FOR THE LASAGNE
1 tbsp olive oil
2 large leeks, shredded in half moons
2 celery sticks, finely chopped
75g/2½oz kale, woody stems removed and leaves shredded
9 sheets dried lasagne (approx. 175g/6oz)
30g/1oz finely grated Parmesan cheese

FOR THE BÉCHAMEL SAUCE
50g/1¾oz unsalted butter
50g/1¾oz plain flour
600ml/1pint semi-skimmed milk
nutmeg
salt and pepper

You will need a deep baking dish that holds approx.
   1 litre/1¾ pints of liquid (approx. 24 x 18 cm/9½ x 7 inches)

Preheat the oven to 180°C fan/200°C/400°F/gas mark 6.

First make the pesto. Blanch the kale in a saucepan of salted boiling water for around 2 minutes until wilted. Drain, and cool under the cold tap, then wring it out using your hands to remove the excess water. Use a food processor to pulse together the toasted walnuts and garlic until broken down. Add in the wrung out kale, 6 tablespoons of olive oil, lemon juice, and season with salt. Blitz until broken down into a chunky paste. Taste and adjust seasoning.

Next get on with the filling. Warm 1 tablespoon of olive oil in a large frying pan over a medium heat and sauté the leeks and celery with a good pinch of salt until completely soft, at least 10 and up to 20 minutes. Add a lid during cooking to keep the leeks soft, stir regularly. In the final moments, add the shredded kale and cook until wilted.

While the leeks soften, make your béchamel sauce. Melt the butter in a medium saucepan over a low heat. Add the flour and stir constantly for 2 minutes as it thickens to a doughy paste – this is your roux. Slowly add the milk, stirring constantly with a wooden spoon, so that the roux loosens into a thick sauce. Bring to a simmer and cook whilst stirring regularly on a low heat for 5–10 minutes, or until thickened – it should coat the back of a spoon. Season with a pinch of freshly grated nutmeg, add salt and pepper to taste.

Construct your lasagne. Start with a layer of the béchamel sauce – use a quarter of the sauce to cover your baking dish, then top with 3 sheets of pasta, slightly overlapping (you may need to break them to fit). Top this with 2 tablespoons of the pesto, half of the cooked leeks, then another quarter of sauce. Then add a second layer of pasta, another 2 tablespoons of the pesto, cooked leeks, and another quarter of sauce. For the third layer add the final 3 sheets of pasta, and the remaining white sauce making sure it covers all the pasta. Sprinkle over the Parmesan cheese and bake in the oven for 45 minutes until browned and crispy and the pasta has cooked through. Stand for 5–10 minutes for the layers to set before serving.

Cavolo Nero, 'Nduja, and Butter Bean Stew

Not for the faint-hearted, 'nduja packs a fiery punch. This spicy sausage paste from Calabria in southern Italy has risen in popularity in the UK in recent years; most often found dotted across sourdough pizzas in trendy neighbourhoods, which is where I first tried it. I was inspired to pair it with kale after cooking a gnocchi version of Nigella Lawson's Pappardelle Pasta, Cavolo Nero & 'Nduja in *Cook, Eat, Repeat* – do try that too. On the table in just 20 minutes this is a great midweek supper option. Serve with bread, or alongside a bowl of lemony steamed couscous.

Try this recipe with other varieties of kale, Kalettes, shredded spring greens or Savoy cabbage.

Tip: If you end up with leftover 'nduja, try it with my recipe for Griddled Leeks and Spring Onions with Yoghurt and 'Nduja Butter Sauce (page 74)

SERVES 2 | TIME TO PREPARE – 20 MINUTES

1 heaped tbsp butter
40g/1½oz 'nduja
1 x 400g/14oz can chopped tomatoes
a pinch of sugar
1 x 400g/14oz can butter beans, drained and well rinsed
125g/4½oz cavolo nero, leaves stripped from the stalk and shredded
1 tbsp finely chopped parsley
juice of ½ lemon
finely grated Parmesan cheese
salt and pepper

Melt the butter over a medium-high heat in a deep frying pan that you have a lid for. When it has melted and is starting to froth add the 'nduja, and break it down with the back of your wooden spoon until it melts into the butter. Add the chopped tomatoes, half fill the empty can with water (200ml/7fl oz), and add that in too. Add a pinch of sugar. Bring to a gentle bubble and simmer uncovered for 10 minutes.

Add the butter beans into the stew, and the shredded cavolo nero. Cover with a lid and cook for 4–5 minutes until the beans have warmed through and the cavolo has completely wilted. Stir in the chopped parsley, squeeze in the juice of half a lemon and season to taste. The 'nduja is so flavourful that a little salt and pepper will be plenty. Serve in pasta bowls with a shower of finely grated Parmesan cheese on top.

Curly Kale, Celeriac, and Apple Salad with Crumbled Stilton

In autumn and winter, unseasonal salad leaves just don't feel right, so a massaged kale salad is something I make to complement a lunchtime buffet of soup or a warm tart. Sticks of celeriac, sweet apple, and Stilton add flavour and texture to the kale. Curly kale needs to be massaged in its dressing for at least 3–4 minutes for the fibres to be broken down so it can be enjoyed raw – do not skip this stage!

You can replace the curly kale with cavolo nero, but reduce the massaging time to 1 minute as it will break down quicker.

SERVES 2 AS A MAIN | TIME TO PREPARE – 15 MINUTES

100g/3½oz (¼ small) celeriac, peeled and chopped into matchsticks
100g/3½oz curly kale, stalks removed and torn
1 red-skinned eating apple
60g/2¼oz Stilton blue cheese, crumbled
2 tbsp toasted pumpkin seeds

FOR THE DRESSING
1 tsp wholegrain mustard
1 tsp honey
1 tbsp lemon juice
3 tbsp olive oil
salt and pepper

First make the dressing. In a small bowl or jar stir together the mustard, honey, and lemon juice until combined. Add the oil, then whisk (or, add the jar lid and shake) together to emulsify. Season to taste.

In a small bowl toss the celeriac with 1 tablespoon of dressing and an extra pinch of salt. Gently massage and leave to marinate for 10 minutes. In a larger mixing bowl, toss the torn kale leaves with 1 tablespoon of the dressing. Use your hands to massage the dressing into the kale leaves for 3–4 minutes until they start to soften and break down. Taste test the kale to check the progress.

When ready to put the salad together, matchstick or thinly slice the apple with its skin on (discard the core). Toss the kale with the apple, marinated celeriac, crumbled blue cheese, and toasted pumpkin seeds. Taste for seasoning then transfer to a serving bowl and serve with the rest of the dressing drizzled across the top. Alternatively, leave in the fridge for a few hours before serving to soften the kale and celeriac in their marinade.

Kalette Tartine with Soft Goat's Cheese, Six-Minute Eggs, and Balsamic Glaze

Kalettes lean into their kale, rather than Brussels sprouts gene, for their flavour pairing with eggs and creamy goat's cheese. My preferred way to cook Kalettes is to briefly fry for flavour, then add a little water and a lid to finish cooking in their own steam. A winning combination with toast for a 'start the day as you mean to go on' veg-loaded breakfast.

Try switching up the Kalettes for any other variety of kale.

SERVES 1–2 (MAKE 2 SLICES OF TOAST)
TIME TO PREPARE – 15 MINUTES

2 eggs, at room temperature
2 tsp butter
175g/6oz Kalettes, rough ends trimmed, and split in half
1 garlic clove, finely chopped
2 slices of sourdough bread
85g/3oz soft goat's cheese
balsamic glaze
1 tbsp toasted pine nuts (optional)
salt and pepper

Bring a small saucepan of water to the boil, carefully submerge your eggs, and set a timer for 6 minutes. Remove with a slotted spoon and rinse under cold water until cool to the touch. Peel and set aside.

Melt the butter over a medium-high heat in a small frying pan that you have a lid for. Add the halved Kalettes to char for a minute or so, tossing regularly. Add 1 tablespoon water to the pan and quickly cover with a lid to trap in the steam. Lower the temperature a little and cook for a further 2–3 minutes, until the centre of the Kalettes are just soft. Stir in the chopped garlic to briefly cook, then season to taste.

Toast your bread, then spread with a decent layer of softs goat's cheese. Top with the cooked Kalettes. Slice the eggs in half and nestle them on top of the Kalettes. Add a zig zag drizzle of balsamic glaze, a scatter of toasted pine nuts (if using), and add pepper to the gooey tops of your soft-boiled eggs. Devour while still warm.

Kale also tastes
fantastic with
cream, butter,
and cheese, which
sounds to me
like the perfect
balance for
a health promoting
vegetable.

Kohlrabi

LATE SUMMER TO AUTUMN

Kohlrabi is known for its unique, instantly recognizable looks. It's a thick-skinned tennis-ball sized bulb that comes in green or purple, with spindly thin stems shooting upwards towards edible green leaves. The flesh is crisp and crunchy, denser than a radish, mildly cabbagey and tasting similar to the stem of a broccoli. It's rarely a supermarket vegetable, but a favoured crop for farms that supply veg box schemes and farmers markets in the UK. If you've ever let an untouched kohlrabi languish at the bottom of your fridge (although it keeps well, which is one of its redeeming features) simply because you didn't know what to do with it, keep reading.

There is no discernible difference in flavour between green and purple skinned varieties of kohlrabi. The colour is only skin deep, and since it should be removed before eating, it makes no difference for your recipes. Kohlrabi can be eaten raw or cooked. The crunch of raw kohlrabi is ideal for coleslaws, remoulades (*see* page 44) and crunchy salads. It can be steamed, roasted, stir fried, or thinly sliced and layered in a dauphinoise-type dish. You may find recipes for kohlrabi soup but I prefer crunchy matchsticks or roasting in butter. These were the methods that convinced me kohlrabi didn't need to be neglected in my fridge until there was nothing else to cook.

Kohlrabi needs to be peeled before use. It can then be diced or cut into wedges. A mandoline will come in handy for uniformity in making thin carpaccio slices (*see* page 45) or a julienne attachment for matchsticks. If you don't have either, a sharp and steady knife will do. For perfect matchsticks, cut with a knife, peel, and square off your kohlrabi, cut thin square slices about 2mm/⅛ inch thick, stack a couple on top of each other, then carefully slice these into matchsticks.

You may get the greens attached to your kohlrabi bulb. They can also be eaten. Use as you would any brassica leaf. Don't leave them stored with the bulb as they'll continue to feed off it, drying it out.

Tasty flavour pairings for kohlrabi you'll already find in my recipes are; apple, horseradish, lemon, mayonnaise, parsley, and sesame. Others to try include; butter, cream, garlic, Parmesan cheese, potatoes, fennel seeds, and soy sauce.

RECIPE IDEA Peel and dice kohlrabi, and roast at 180°C fan/200°C/400°F/gas mark 6 with plenty of butter, fennel seeds, and seasoning for around 45 minutes, or until completely soft and charred round the edges. Toss with dill and serve as a side.

TOP TIP
Kohlrabi is German for turnip cabbage and is popular in Northern and
Eastern European countries. Look to these cultures for recipe ideas.

Kohlrabi and Apple Remoulade with Horseradish Mayonnaise

Matchsticks of crunchy kohlrabi balanced with sweet crisp apple, creamy mayonnaise, and pleasantly up-your-nose horseradish sauce; a reliable and surprisingly quick go-to for kohlrabi. A good base recipe that can take you in many different directions – if you add toasted walnuts, grapes or sultanas, and a handful of crunchy lettuce leaves, you're leaning towards the flavours of a Waldorf salad. Or add carrot or onion and it's more of a coleslaw. Serve as is on the side of anything that goes with a creamy, mayonnaise-based salad; cold meats, smoked fish, breaded chicken escalope.

For a variation, add in some radish or substitute the kohlrabi for finely shredded white cabbage.

SERVES 2 | TIME TO PREPARE – 10 MINUTES

300g/10½oz kohlrabi (approx. 2 small or 1 medium-sized), peeled and sliced
   into matchsticks
1 red-skinned apple, skin on, sliced into matchsticks
1 tbsp finely chopped soft herbs (e.g. chives, parsley, or tarragon)
salt and pepper

FOR THE MAYONNAISE DRESSING
2 tbsp mayonnaise
1 tbsp Greek yoghurt
1 tbsp cream of horseradish sauce
2 tsp lemon juice

First make your dressing. In a small bowl mix together the mayonnaise, yoghurt, horseradish sauce, and lemon juice. Season to taste.

Place the chopped kohlrabi and apple into a medium-sized bowl and stir through the dressing to lightly coat. Scatter over the herbs and stir again. Adjust seasoning to taste.

Ideally leave to marinate for at least 30 minutes for the flavour to develop, but it can be eaten straight away, if you wish.

Kohlrabi Carpaccio with
Blood Orange, Avocado, and Chilli

Look who's had a glow up! For this good looking carpaccio-style dish, thin slices of pale green, steamed kohlrabi are dressed in lime juice and sesame oil, then beautified by blood orange, avocado, and flecks of chilli. Steaming transforms kohlrabi from crunchy to buttery soft. Use a mandoline if you have one for refined, even slices. Enjoy as a side dish or a dinner party starter.

Try this same flavour combination with thin slices of steam roasted beetroot (*see* page 168).

SERVES 2 AS A SIDE OR STARTER | TIME TO PREPARE – 15 MINUTES

1 medium-sized kohlrabi (approx. 300g/10½oz)
2 tsp toasted sesame oil
1 tbsp lime juice (approx. ½ lime, or more to taste)
2 blood oranges, peeled and sliced into rounds or segmented (*see* page 13)
1 medium avocado, halved, flesh scooped out with a spoon and thinly sliced
chilli flakes
salt

Remove any stems or leaves from the kohlrabi. Top and tail, and peel the kohlrabi leaving curved smooth edges. Thinly slice into 2–3 mm/⅛ inch rounds using a knife or very carefully on the finest setting of a mandoline.

Set up a steaming basket and when boiling, add the kohlrabi slices. Steam for 5–6 minutes, or until the kohlrabi is translucent and soft enough to bend without snapping. Remove from the steamer and rinse under cold water until cool to the touch. Shake off the water and spread out to air-dry on a plate or board, dab with kitchen paper to speed this up.

Put the cooked kohlrabi circles in a bowl and toss with the sesame oil and lime juice, so it is well covered on both sides. Season.

Arrange the kohlrabi rounds over two side plates or one large serving platter (keep any dressing left in the bowl). Arrange the blood orange and avocado slices on top, and sprinkle over as much chilli as you can handle. Finish with a crumble of sea salt on the top, paying special attention to the avocado. Drizzle over any remaining kohlrabi dressing left in the bowl and eat straight away before the blood orange juice bleeds.

Radish

LATE SPRING TO EARLY AUTUMN

I have a photo album of pink recipes on my phone. It is populated by radish, beetroot and radicchio, but mostly peppery radish with its varying shades of candy through hot pink, which I serve sliced into salads or roasted. Yes, roasted. The first time I roasted radish, and tasted how different it now was, I felt like I'd gained a whole new vegetable to explore. Radishes are also roots, and can grow in a matter of weeks in relatively shallow soil. Radishes range in flavour from mild to peppery – this may depend on the variety or who's grown them.

There are white tipped French breakfast radishes, dark shades of purple radish, the more unusual black radish, plus daikon/mooli, which is a key ingredient in kimchi. There is also the watermelon radish, a daikon variety with its fairly average looking grey-green outer skin and stunning watermelon-coloured flesh.

Radishes can be eaten raw with no preparation other than a wash, or quickly pickled in something acidic. Just a handful blended will add a peppery flavour to a raw savoury cucumber gazpacho. Plus, as I've already mentioned, they can be cooked – ideally roasted, but charring on a hot griddle pan, or stir fries are a possibility.

If preparing for a salad or to pickle, top and tail, then thinly slice, halve, or quarter. Given their size, I find a mandoline too risky if you value the tips of your fingers, so stick to using a sharp knife and a steady hand. If not too ginormous, roast whole.

Soft radish leaves are edible and best eaten as soon as possible after buying or harvesting. They may taste a little peppery. Wash well and add in small quantities to salads, wilt, or blitz into pesto. Detach leaves from the radish as soon as you buy them and – similarly to herbs to keep them fresh – wrap in damp kitchen paper in the fridge until you have time to use them.

Tasty flavour pairings for radish you'll already find in my recipes are; feta, cucumber, lemon, and fish (mackerel). Others to try include; avocado, butter, blue cheese, celery, chives, lettuce, spring onions, and thyme.

RECIPE IDEA Grab a packet of room temperature butter, dip in your radish, and sprinkle salt on top. That's it!

Roasted Radishes with Whipped Feta on Toast

One or two radishes in a salad – no, try harder! To use the whole bunch in one recipe, roasting is the way to go as roasting mellows radishes pepperiness. Here, roasted radishes look more like baby pink balls of candy, than a member of the brassica group as they take their leading role as a toast topper, supported by whipped feta.

Whipped feta is such a useful recipe to have in your back pocket. This spreadable version of beloved feta cheese is brilliant for sticking a whole host of vegetables onto toast – try roasted carrots, ribbons of griddled courgette and blistered cherry tomatoes for starters.

SERVES 2 | TIME TO PREPARE – 25 MINUTES

300g/10½oz radishes, topped, tailed, and sliced in half
1 tbsp olive oil
½ tsp cumin seeds
2–4 slices of sourdough bread (depending on size and appetite)
butter
salt and pepper

FOR THE WHIPPED FETA
200g/7oz feta cheese
100g/3½oz Greek yoghurt
1 tbsp finely chopped soft herbs (e.g. parsley, dill, mint, or oregano),
    plus a little extra for garnish
1 lemon

Preheat the oven to 180°C fan/200°C/400°F/gas mark 6.

Toss the radishes onto a baking tray with the olive oil and season with salt. Roast in the oven for 15–20 minutes until tender, are just starting to char, and their colour has mellowed to a baby pink.

Meanwhile, make the whipped feta. Use a small food processor or mini chopper. Crumble in the feta, scoop in the Greek yoghurt, and blitz into a smooth-ish paste. Add the herbs, a little lemon zest, and 1 teaspoon of lemon juice. Season with salt and pepper. Briefly blitz again to combine.

Toast your cumin seeds until fragrant in a dry, hot pan, and prepare your toast. Spread with a little butter then top with a decent smoosh of whipped feta and the roasted radishes. Garnish with the cumin seeds, a sprinkle of herbs (or a handful of radish leaves if you have them). Best eaten while the radishes are still warm.

Chopped Radish Chaat Masala Salad with Pan-Fried Mackerel and Rice

The mango powder in chaat masala gives it a unique sweet-sour taste – the spice mix is often used in Indian cuisine for a boost of flavour. Sprinkle it over this kachumber-inspired salad to balance the richness of oily mackerel. Perfectly pan-fried fish is a learned skill but one worth persevering with. If the skin of the fish is sticking, it will either be because your pan wasn't hot enough, or because it's not ready to flip over just yet.

You can also try this salad with halved cherry tomatoes instead of radish.

SERVES 2 | TIME TO PREPARE – 25 MINUTES

FOR THE CHOPPED RADISH CHAAT MASALA
175g/6oz radishes, topped, tailed and thinly sliced
1 banana shallot or ¼ red onion, thinly sliced
juice of 1 lime
a pinch of caster sugar
¼ cucumber, seeds removed and cubed
a handful of pomegranate seeds (approx. 2 tbsp)
1 tbsp finely chopped coriander or parsley
½ tsp chaat masala powder, or more to taste

FOR THE DISH
150g/5½oz basmati rice (brown, white or a wild rice basmati mix)
2–3 tbsp rapeseed or other neutral oil
2 x fresh mackerel fillets (approx. 175g/6oz each)
salt and pepper

Mix the radishes and shallot in a medium bowl with the lime juice and sugar, and season with a pinch of salt. Leave for at least 15 minutes to pickle. Just before serving, add the cucumber, pomegranate, coriander, and chaat masala. Season to taste. Cook the rice according to type and/or packet instructions.

Cook the fish. Heat 2–3 tablespoons of rapeseed oil to a medium-high heat in a heavy-bottomed cast-iron or non-stick pan. Pat dry your mackerel fillets with kitchen paper and season all over. When the oil is hot, lower the mackerel fillets into the pan, skin-side down, and hold down with a spatula to stop the fish from curling up. Cook for around 5 minutes, until the skin is crispy and the fillet will easily come away from the pan. Adjust the heat as necessary to avoid burning. Flip over to sear the flesh for a final 1 minute.

Plate up individually starting with a pool of rice, followed by the salad, and then the mackerel fillets, skin-side up. Eat straight away.

BULBS & STEMS

A catch-all chapter for vegetables that have a bulb, stem, or both. The aromatic bulbs and stems of celery, fennel (umbellifers) leeks, onion and shallot (alliums), have strengths diced and used as base flavour, but are also entirely convincing as a star vegetable. Neither asparagus nor rhubarb have a vegetable family of their own but, looking like stems, are welcome here.

Asparagus

LATE SPRING

Bright skinny green spears of asparagus usually appear towards the end of April, and the season lasts around 6 weeks. As the season progresses, asparagus spears get thicker and more abundant. The rest of the year we import asparagus from South America but I generally avoid it as I believe the thing that makes asparagus so exciting and desirable is its limited availability. You might find purple varieties lurking at your farmers market but, like other purple versions of green veg, the colour quickly dissipates once cooked. Northern European countries are keen on white asparagus – it's grown under cover to prevent green chlorophyll from forming.

The best way, hands down, to cook whole spears of asparagus is to use high heat from a frying pan, griddle pan, grill, BBQ, or oven, and cook with olive oil or butter. Asparagus can also be steamed or blanched for a softer texture. You can purée for soups but I find this a waste of the spears – in my unblended minestrone style Asparagus, Spring Vegetable and Fregola Soup (*see* page 54) the pieces are left whole to mingle amongst aromatics and stock. Asparagus can also be eaten raw, this works best with fresh, tender spears, shaved into thin ribbons with a peeler, then marinated in oil and lemon juice.

Asparagus spears require little prep other than removing the tough ends. Gently bend the spear towards the stalk end, snap, and discard. If rough ends bother you, trim slightly to neaten off. This produces quite a lot of wastage, so instead, try taking your asparagus spears to the asparagus barbers. You'll still need to remove around 2.5cm/1 inch from the bottom with a knife, but then use a peeler to shave off the fibrous looking skin about 2.5cm/1 inch up from the cut edge to reveal tender asparagus underneath. If slicing asparagus to use in a sauté or soup, slice off the tips and leave whole, then cut the stalk into whatever size you need. I always cut mine on an angle to be aesthetically pleasing. Instead of throwing away the discarded ends, be a zero waste hero. Briefly simmer in liquid (usually stock or cream) and by the power of osmosis you'll have an asparagus flavoured ingredient to use in your recipes.

Tasty flavour pairings you'll find in my recipes are; butter, carrots, feta, dill, garlic, parsley, dill, tarragon, prawns, and sesame. Others to try include; ricotta, goat's cheese, capers, eggs, leeks, mushrooms, pasta, and tomatoes.

RECIPE IDEA Sauté tips and thin rounds of asparagus in a little butter or olive oil with garlic until soft, add cream and pasta water to loosen into a sauce. Season and serve with ribbons of tagliatelle topped with Parmesan cheese.

> **TOP TIP**
> Asparagus likes eggs. Serve asparagus spears instead of toast soldiers to dip into your gooey boiled eggs.

Asparagus, Spring Vegetable and Fregola Soup

A hint of asparagus with every slurp in this light minestrone-style brothy soup. Usually destined for the compost bin, snapped off asparagus ends are cleverly used to infuse your stock. This stock becomes the base for your soup along with an always flavourful combination of shallot, carrot, celery, and garlic and the best bits of asparagus. Fregola, a Sardinian pasta similar to giant couscous, provides body. Serve with bread for dunking.

If you can't find fregola, use giant couscous or any other small pasta shape suitable for minestrone-style dishes. The variation in grains, or size of grains will affect the cooking time. If unsure on timings, taste at regular intervals until just tender.

The base of this soup can be made with whichever aromatics you have to hand – onions, shallots, leeks, celery, carrots, etc. Instead of asparagus, you can try adding peas or beans.

SERVES 2 | TIME TO PREPARE – 30 MINUTES

250g/9oz asparagus
600ml/1 pint chicken or vegetable stock (homemade or good quality shop-bought)
olive oil
1 banana shallot, finely chopped
1 small carrot, peeled and finely diced
1 celery stick, finely diced
1 garlic clove, finely chopped
a splash of white wine or white wine vinegar
60g/2¼oz fregola or giant couscous
70g/2½oz frozen peas, green beans chopped into 1cm/½ inch pieces, or pre-cooked
    and double podded broad beans
2 tbsp finely chopped soft herbs (e.g. parsley and/or dill, mint, tarragon)
finely grated Parmesan cheese
salt and pepper

Snap off the woody ends of the asparagus, and place into a small saucepan with your stock. Simmer for 15 minutes for the asparagus flavour to infuse your stock, then strain, reserve the stock, and discard the ends. To prepare the rest of the asparagus, separate the stalks and the tips. Leave the tips whole, then slice the spears on the diagonal into 1 cm/½ inch pieces.

Meanwhile in a medium-large saucepan, heat 1 tablespoon of olive oil over a medium heat and sauté your finely diced shallot, carrot and celery with a good pinch of salt for around 10 minutes until softened. Add the garlic for a further minute, then splash in the wine and cook until evaporated. Add the asparagus stock to the soup base. Bring to a simmer, then add the fregola and cook for around 10 minutes, or until just al dente. Add the sliced asparagus stalks, tips, and peas (or beans) to simmer for a further 2–3 minutes until cooked through. Depending on how much the stock has reduced during the simmering time, you may wish to add a little extra water to your soup – you're after a brothy consistency.

Stir through the herbs and season to taste with salt and pepper. Serve the soup warm, or slightly cooled, in pasta bowls. Garnish with a drizzle of olive oil and a shower of finely grated Parmesan.

Sautéed Asparagus, Borlotti Beans, and Seafood

Inspired by a squid, bean, and asparagus dish I once had at a tapas bar in Barcelona that was so good, I had to ask the waiter what was in the sauce – "just a touch of balsamic vinegar" he replied. Squid and asparagus aren't always in season at the same time in the UK (yes, seafood has seasons too!) so I now make this dish with prawns if I can't get hold of squid. Luckily the cooking times are similar, so can be easily switched around or used in combination. Serve tapas-style alongside bread, or another dish such as roast potatoes, blistered padrón peppers or a salad.

Green beans are a good substitute for asparagus.

SERVES 2
TIME TO PREPARE – 15 MINUTES (SLIGHTLY LONGER IF PREPARING SQUID)

175g/6oz raw peeled king prawns or 2 medium-sized squid (ask your fishmonger to prepare for you)
olive oil
250g/9oz asparagus spears, woody ends snapped off and chopped into 2.5cm/1 inch pieces
1 garlic clove, finely sliced
1 x 400g/14oz can borlotti beans, drained and rinsed
1 tbsp balsamic vinegar
1 tbsp chopped parsley
salt and pepper

If using squid, dry with kitchen paper, cut into rings 2cm/ 3/4 inch wide and leave the tentacles whole, but trim to a reasonable length. Prawns can be cooked whole. Season with salt and pepper.

Heat 1 tablespoon of olive oil in a large frying pan over a medium-high heat and add the asparagus pieces. Fry for 2–3 minutes tossing regularly until starting to char. Lower the heat a little, then add the sliced garlic for a few seconds before adding the beans to warm through for another 2–3 minutes. Scrape everything out of the pan, onto a plate, and set aside.

Put the pan back on the heat, turn up the heat to high and add 1 tablespoon of olive oil. Add the prawns or squid rings and tentacles and cook for 90 seconds–2 minutes, until pink and cooked through (prawns) or until translucent and softened (squid). Add the bean and asparagus mix back into the pan. Splash in the balsamic vinegar, toss well and wait for it to evaporate. Remove from the heat, stir through the parsley and season with salt and pepper to taste. Finish with a drizzle of olive oil. Take the pan straight to the table.

Blistered Asparagus with Feta and Dukkah Inspired Mix

Asparagus blistered over a high heat is my first craving when it comes into season. I like to top it with creamy salty feta and the flavour bomb of a crunchy spiced dukkah inspired mix. Dukkah's origin is in Egyptian cuisine. There are ways to make it with different combinations of nuts and spices but I prefer to keep it simple using just four ingredients. For a more substantial serving, add a self-saucing gooey soft boiled egg on top.

Try the feta and dukkah combo with purple sprouting broccoli or griddled spring onions instead.

SERVES 2 AS A LIGHT LUNCH | TIME TO PREPARE – 15 MINUTES

FOR THE DUKKAH
30g/1oz blanched skinned hazelnuts
1 tsp sesame seeds
½ tsp coriander seeds
½ tsp cumin seeds

FOR THE DISH
2 tbsp olive oil
500g/1lb 2oz asparagus, tough ends snapped off and trimmed
juice of 1 lemon
80g/2¾oz feta cheese
salt and pepper

You will need a pestle and mortar to make this dish.

For the dukkah, heat a dry frying pan to a medium-high heat. Toast the hazelnuts for 2–3 minutes until they start to brown and release their oils, slide out of the pan. Set aside. Next, add the sesame seeds to the frying pan – they will toast and start to dance around the pan in a matter of seconds – transfer into your mortar bowl. Lastly, toast the coriander and cumin together, until they start to smell fragrant. Transfer to your mortar with the sesame seeds. Using your pestle, roughly break all the seeds down, leaving a little texture. Roughly chop your hazelnuts then add these into the spices. Gently pound the hazelnuts into the spices, again leaving a little texture.

Wipe out the pan, and put back on a medium-high heat with 2 tablespoons of olive oil. Add your asparagus and cook for 5–7 minutes (depending on the thickness of the spears), tossing regularly until blistered on all sides. Transfer to a serving platter, season with salt and pepper, and squeeze over the juice of a lemon. Crumble over the feta and top with as much dukkah as you fancy.

Celery

AUTUMN TO SPRING

Crunchy, savoury celery doesn't get as much credit as it should. It's often relegated to the crudité course, where I'm not sure even a dollop of the creamiest hummus does it any favours. Celery has, sadly, spent a lot of time rolled up in diet culture. I remember reading in a magazine that eating celery uses up more calories than those you gain from eating it and that celery juice is the answer to eternal life. Neither of these facts are verified and distract from how important it is as a base vegetable.

Celery ranges in colour from deep green to paler white, and the sticks are held together around a central heart. The vegetable celeriac, or celery root (*see* Roots Chapter) is the root of a different variety of celery to the one that is grown for its sticks.

Celery can be eaten raw or cooked. The most familiar use of celery is sautéeing to add flavour at the start of a dish. It more than pulls its weight alongside onions and carrots in the trio known as a *mirepoix* – the base to many stews, soups, and sauces. Celery can also be braised in larger pieces, stir fried, added to gratinée, or puréed into a soup. Perhaps the only acceptable way to eat it raw is in the famous Waldorf salad – drowned in mayonnaise alongside apple, walnuts, and grapes, it is saved.

Celery is an easy ingredient to prepare. Gently pull the sticks apart and run under the tap to remove any dirt. Top and tail to remove any dry ends, and use a sharp knife to thinly slice into moons, or chop into smaller sticks and dice. If thinly slicing celery to toss into a salad, a mandoline might come in useful. But, what about the fibrous stringy bits? If you have the time and inclination, these can be peeled away – I have neither.

Celery leaves are edible and have a strong flavour similar to the herb lovage. Its seeds are crushed with salt to produce celery salt, which can be used to add celery flavour to your dishes, especially boiled eggs.

Tasty flavour pairings for celery you'll find in my recipes are; butter, feta, garlic, shellfish, parsley, thyme, and tomatoes. Others to try include; carrots, blue cheese, onions, dill, grapes, mayonnaise, potatoes, rice, and walnuts.

RECIPE IDEA Take 250g/9oz diced celery and sauté this with a little onion and garlic, simmer in 400ml/14fl oz stock along with 250g/9oz potato, then blend with a hunk (60g/2¼oz or thereabouts) of blue cheese, and you've got a flavourful soup.

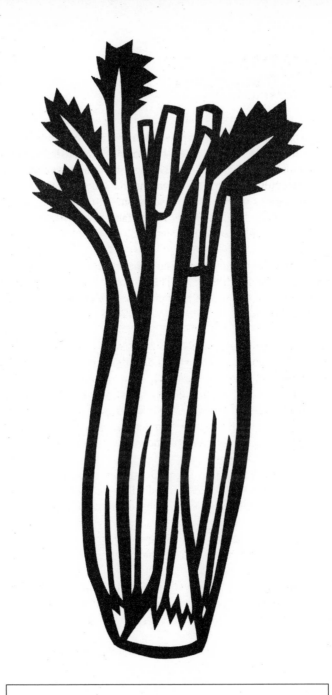

Mussels Steamed in White Wine with Celery and Mustard

In my former career working in orchestral management I took many 24-hour trips to Belgium for concerts. Always rather stressful, but the bonus was a steaming bowl of moules marinière for supper. It always felt like such a treat, but they're surprisingly easy to prepare at home. 1kg looks like a lot of mussels but bear in mind you'll need to discard those that are broken, don't close (dead), or don't open after cooking (also dead). Celery usually takes a supporting role alongside its *mirepoix* pals onion and carrots, but by focussing on them in this dish, you'll discover that the flavour is one to be enjoyed in its own right. For the full Brussels effect, serve with a portion of your favourite oven chips, or slices of baguette.

For a variation, replace the celery with finely diced fennel or leeks, or add spring onions, a little red Thai curry paste and coconut milk instead of the wine, mustard and cream.

Top tip: Skip the cutlery and use an empty mussel shell as a pincher to pick out the meat from other shells to eat.

SERVES 2 | TIME TO PREPARE – 40 MINUTES

1kg/2lb 4oz mussels
1 heaped tbsp butter
200g/7oz celery, finely chopped
1 banana shallot, finely chopped
1 garlic clove, finely chopped
2 sprigs of thyme
1 dry bay leaf
175ml/6fl oz white wine
1 tsp Dijon mustard
2 tbsp crème fraîche or double cream
1 tbsp finely chopped parsley
salt and pepper

First prepare your mussels – allow a good 10–15 minutes for this in your schedule. Give them a good rinse under a cold tap, and scrub the shells to remove any barnacles. Carefully pull out the beardy bits. Discard any with broken shells. If any mussels are already open give them a tap and wait to see if they fizz and close. If they don't they're dead and you should also discard them.

In a large, lidded, deep-sided frying pan that is big enough to take all the mussels, melt the butter over a medium heat. When frothy, add the celery, shallots, a little salt and sauté for 10–15 minutes or until softened to your liking, but not coloured. Stir in the garlic, and drop in the thyme sprigs and bay leaf. Gently tumble in the mussels, and pour in the wine. Bring to a bubble, cover the pan and cook for 3–4 minutes, giving the pan an occasional shake until all the mussels pop open.

Using a slotted spoon, scoop out the mussels into two wide deep serving bowls. Add the Dijon mustard and cream to the celery and wine left in the pan and stir until combined. Discard the bay leaf and thyme, and season to taste. Ladle the celery sauce over the two bowls of mussels and garnish with parsley. Discard any mussels that don't open.

Tomato Braised Celery and Beans with Grilled Feta

A Mediterranean inspired one-pot rich tomato braise with celery and beans. Rather than finely dicing the celery, diagonally slice larger chunks to take pride of place alongside the beans. It takes quite a long time for the celery to fully soften when braised like this, but do persevere – the buttery soft celery rewards are worth it. Top with chunks of feta, and grill until golden for a creamy melt-in-the-mouth finish. Serve the dish straight to the table with toasted pitta bread.

Instead of celery, use wedges of fennel.

SERVES 2 | TIME TO PREPARE – 55 MINUTES

olive oil
200g/7oz celery (approx. 4 sticks), sliced on the diagonal into 3cm/1¼ inch pieces
3 garlic cloves, finely sliced
1 x 400g/14oz can chopped tomatoes
a pinch of sugar
1 tbsp tomato purée
1 tbsp red wine vinegar
1 tsp dried herbs (e.g. oregano/thyme)
a pinch of chilli flakes (or more, to taste)
1 x 400g/14oz can butter beans or chickpeas, drained and rinsed
1 tbsp finely chopped oregano
1 tbsp finely chopped parsley
100g/3½oz feta cheese, broken into chunks
salt and pepper

Cook in a medium-sized frying pan that can also go under the grill or transfer everything into a baking dish for the grill part (more washing up – sorry).

Heat 1 tablespoon of olive oil over a medium heat in the frying pan. Add the celery pieces and sauté for around 4–5 minutes, until the skin is starting to brown, tossing regularly. Add in the garlic and cook briefly, then add the chopped tomatoes with a pinch of sugar, half fill the empty can with water (200ml/7fl oz) and add that in too, plus the tomato purée, red wine vinegar, dried herbs, chilli flakes, and then season with salt. Bring to the boil, then add the beans or chickpeas, cover the pan with a lid and lower to a simmer. Cook for around 45 minutes, stirring intermittently, until the celery is tender, buttery soft and no longer tastes fibrous.

While the celery is in its last stage of simmering, preheat the grill to medium-high.

Remove the lid from the braise and cook uncovered for a few minutes to reduce the sauce so that it just clings to all the ingredients. Season to taste (with salt, pepper, chilli, and/or a splash more red wine vinegar) and stir through the fresh oregano and parsley. Top with the chunks of feta. Drizzle olive oil over the top, and place under the grill for around 5 minutes, or until the feta has browned. Serve warm.

Fennel

SUMMER TO AUTUMN

An aromatic, aniseed-flavoured bulb that is stronger when raw, yet mellowed and sweetened when cooked. Fennel fronds could be easily mistaken for dill (they're actually related). Fennel is a vegetable that many people I cook for tell me they thought they didn't like, but having it prepared a different or new way, has changed their mind. How you slice, dress, and cook fennel will dramatically change its popularity.

Aside from the fennel bulbs we eat as vegetables, there is herb fennel grown for its pretty yellow flowers. These produce fennel seeds which sit in our spice cupboards; their sweet aroma adds a liquorice-like flavour to dishes. Fennel can be eaten raw, but if so, it needs to be shaved very thinly, and marinated for at least 10–15 minutes to soften any strong aniseed flavour. Methods for cooking fennel include roasting, braising, stewing, griddling or BBQ-ing or sautéing as an aromatic with your *mirepoix*. Any method with strong direct heat will char or caramelize fennel (*see* Braised Fennel, Sausage and Butter Beans with Olives, page 66) adding another flavour dimension. Sautéed fennel can be a lovely addition or star flavour of a puréed soup.

To prepare fennel for a raw salad, remove the stalks then slice in half lengthways. Carefully slice out the triangle core, then slice as thinly as you can with a knife or mandoline. If preparing in wedges for roasting or braising, remove any rusty bits on the base, then slice in half lengthways and quarter, or slice into wedges. Leave the core in as it will hold the layers together. The stalks are too fibrous to eat but can be added to your freezer stock bag.

Fennel fronds are usually removed for ease of storage and travel. If yours has plenty of fronds still attached, lucky you. I like to use fennel fronds instead of herbs – especially dill – to garnish my fennel dishes. Any kind of herb sauce from pesto to chimichurri will be all the better for a handful of finely chopped fresh fennel fronds.

Tasty flavour pairings for fennel you'll already find in my recipes are; butter, cucumber, lemon, pork (sausages), mint, olives, orange, and parsley. Others to try include; almonds, apple, beetroot, carrot, blue cheese, chicken, fish, potatoes, rocket, tomato, and watercress.

RECIPE IDEA Raw fennel likes sweet fruit. For a summer salad try mixing slices of marinated raw fennel with charred apricots, a handful of rocket or watercress, and crumbled blue cheese. Add a simple dressing.

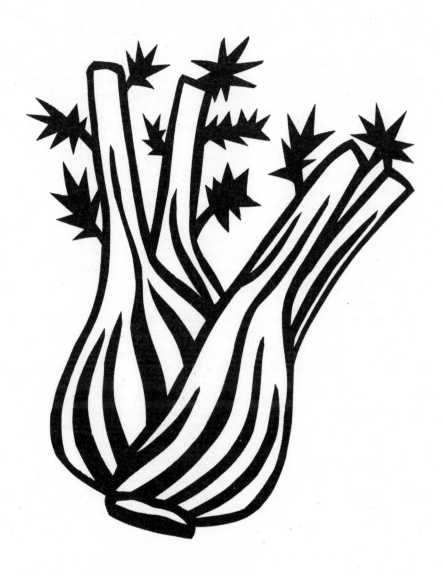

TOP TIP
Chop fennel fronds with parsley, lemon zest,
and raw garlic for a fennel-flavoured gremolata.

Braised Fennel, Sausage, and Butter Beans with Olives

Braising fennel in stock softens it until buttery soft to eat, and mellows its aniseed flavour. It gets along very well with pork, butter beans, and salty olives in this one-pot on-the-hob braise. For this, I use good old English sausages, an occasional meaty treat which will always remind me of my childhood. Serve on its own, or if hungry with some rice, steamed couscous or bulgur wheat.

For a vegetarian version, omit the sausages, use vegetable stock and increase the beans to a 400g/14oz can. Or, try replacing some or all of the fennel with wedges of onion or chunky slices of celery.

SERVES 2 | TIME TO PREPARE – 45 MINUTES

1 tbsp olive oil
4 good quality, high per cent pork sausages
2 tsp butter
2 small or 1 large fennel bulb (approx. 375g/13oz), halved and sliced into wedges, reserve the fronds
1 banana shallot, quartered lengthways
1 x 200g/7oz can butter beans, rinsed and drained
2 garlic cloves, finely sliced
1 tsp fennel seeds
a splash of white wine (approx. 2 tbsp, optional)
150ml/5fl oz chicken stock
50g/1¾oz pitted Kalamata olives, halved
1 tbsp finely chopped parsley
zest and juice of 1 lemon
salt and pepper

Heat the olive oil to medium-high in a wide deep frying pan that you have a lid for. Brown the sausages on all sides, cooking for around 5–7 minutes. Use tongs to transfer the sausages to a plate.

Take the pan off the heat to cool down a little. When safe to do so, add the butter to the pan and put back on a medium heat. Add the fennel wedges and shallot quarters cut side down, season with salt. Cook for 10 minutes, turning over every few minutes, until the fennel and shallots have started to caramelize on all sides. Add in the butter beans, the browned sausages, sliced garlic and fennel seeds. Give the pan a good shake. Pour in a splash of wine (if using) and enough chicken stock so that the vegetables and sausages are half submerged. Bring to a gentle simmer, cover and cook for 18–20 minutes, occasionally giving the pan a gentle shuffle to make sure nothing is sticking.

After 20 minutes, remove the lid, add the olives and cook uncovered for another 3–5 minutes, until the stock has sufficiently reduced and is just clinging to, rather than drowning, the ingredients. Check that the sausages are cooked through with no pink flesh remaining inside, and the fennel cores are buttery soft.

Finely chop the fennel fronds, and add these to the pan along with the chopped parsley. Season to taste (salty olives and stock might already be enough), and add lemon zest and lemon juice to lift the flavours. Serve straight away.

Shaved Fennel, Orange, and Harissa Salad

Side salads can offer an explosion of flavours, perhaps even stealing the limelight from the main course. In this one, smoky spiced harissa and sweet oranges give the oomph, while helping to calm the aniseed flavour of the fennel. If making this ahead of time, it will get juicy, so strain before plating up, and add the mint and pine nuts to serve. Serve on the side of a whole roasted sea bass. It's also great with the Chickpea Stuffed Aubergine recipe (*see* page 242).

Make this with or without the cucumber or try replacing the fennel with ribbons of carrot.

SERVES 2 | TIME TO PREPARE – 20 MINUTES

1 large fennel bulb (approx. 250g/9oz)
juice of ½ a lemon
¼ cucumber
a large handful of mint leaves
2 tsp rose harissa paste
1 tsp olive oil
2 oranges, segmented (*see* page 13)
1 tbsp toasted pine nuts
salt and pepper

First, prepare the fennel. Remove the stalks and slice in half from the stalk end down to the root. Carefully slice out the firm triangle core, then use a mandoline or knife to slice the fennel as thin as possible. If there are any fronds attached to your stalks, finely chop, and set aside.

Transfer the sliced fennel to a medium-sized bowl, squeeze over the lemon juice and season. Toss together and leave the fennel to sit in the juice for 10–15 minutes to soften up. While the fennel softens, halve your cucumber, scoop out the seeds, and finely slice. Stack your mint leaves, roll up, and run your knife across to shred into ribbons.

In a small bowl or ramekin, mix together 2 teaspoons of rose harissa paste with 1 teaspoon olive oil and pour over the fennel. Add in the cucumber slices and toss everything together so that the harissa covers all of the ingredients. Gently fold in the orange segments, shredded mint, and reserved fennel fronds, and season to taste. Transfer to a serving dish – leave any excess liquid in the bowl – and scatter over the toasted pine nuts.

Fennel fronds are usually removed for ease of storage and travel. If yours has plenty of fronds still attached, lucky you. I like to use fennel fronds instead of herbs – especially dill – to garnish my fennel dishes.

Leek

AUTUMN TO SPRING

The vegetable of my ancestors in Wales, although the explanation for this is best suited to history class, rather than home economics. This mild, sweet allium is a resourceful vegetable to have around, shredded, and lending itself in place of or as well as onion in the base of many a dish, or served whole as an impressive side. Long stems of leeks are whiter towards the root, and increasingly green and tough as you get to the top 'flag' leaves.

Baby leeks are just regular leeks, harvested before they've had time to grow. These are sweeter, less fibrous, and with smaller tough green leaves. They look more like a fat spring onion and can be kept whole.

Leeks, like onions, I think, are at their best when thinly sliced and sautéed in oil or butter and used as the base aromatic ingredient for soups such as the famous vichyssoise soup, stews, hearty rice-based dishes like risotto or pilaf, or baked with eggs into a quiche or frittata. They add a different flavour to onions, somewhat milder and softer in texture. Leeks can also be steamed, roasted in chunks or added to a tray bake, left whole or in larger pieces and braised, or briefly steamed and finished on a griddle pan or BBQ.

Getting dirt out of the leeks is a bit of a pain, as it gets trapped in between the tightly wrapped layers. There are two ways to clean leeks. If finely slicing for a dish, do so, then submerge the slices in a bowl of water, give a good jiggle, and pray any dirt sinks to the bottom of the bowl. The fresh clean leeks float on the surface and can be scooped out. Alternatively, leave the leek whole, split the green end in half and fan out. Stand this in a large jug of water, and wait for the grit to float out. Rinse under a cold tap to be sure.

The tough green flags of the leaves can be added to your stock pot.

Tasty flavour pairings for leeks you'll already find in my recipes are; butter, hard cheese, chilli, chives, garlic, shellfish, pasta, and red peppers. Others to try include; bacon, carrot, chicken, fish, mushrooms, mustard, potatoes, and tarragon.

RECIPE IDEA Cut leeks into 3cm/1¼ inch chunks, steam until tender, stir through a batch of homemade béchamel sauce, top with cheese and breadcrumbs, and bake until crispy for an alternative take on cauliflower cheese.

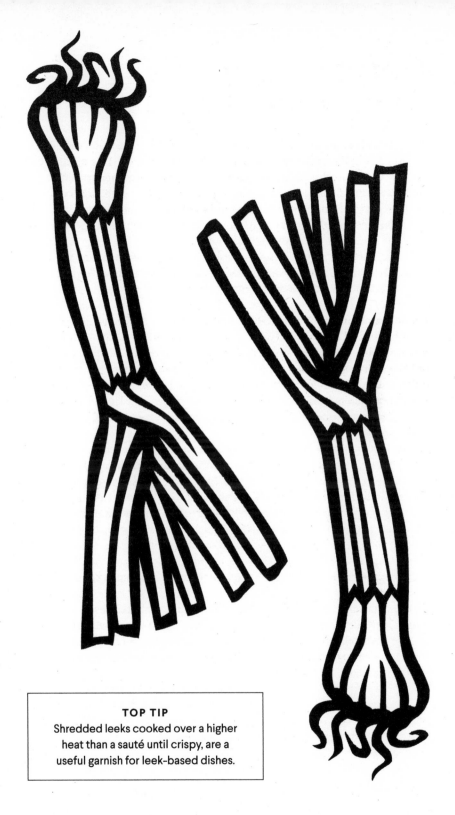

TOP TIP
Shredded leeks cooked over a higher
heat than a sauté until crispy, are a
useful garnish for leek-based dishes.

Leek and Clam Spaghetti

Shredded leeks, cooked in olive oil until soft and melty take on a real buttery quality, even when there is no butter. Leeks pair well with seafood, so I've chosen to weave them into a version of *spaghetti alle vongole*. This is one of my absolute favourite dishes, preferably enjoyed under the Mediterranean sun, but equally joyful in my south London kitchen. You may need to ask your local fishmonger for clams, but like mussels, they're very quick and easy to cook by steaming in a pan with white wine.

Try replacing the leeks with a smaller amount of softened spring onions – they'll be ready in 4–5 minutes rather than 10 minutes.

SERVES 2 | TIME TO PREPARE – 25 MINUTES, PLUS SOAKING THE CLAMS

500g/1lb 2oz clams
180g/6½oz spaghetti
olive oil
250g/9oz leeks, split and finely sliced into half moons
2 garlic cloves, finely chopped
¼ tsp chilli flakes
100ml/3½fl oz white wine
1 tbsp finely chopped parsley
salt and pepper

First prepare your clams. Soak in heavily salted water (35g/1¼oz salt per 1 litre/1¾ pints water is ideal) for around 20 minutes. This will encourage any sand hiding in the clams to escape and sink. Scoop out the clams without disturbing the sand at the bottom of the bowl, rinse in cold water, and discard any with broken shells or those that don't close when tapped. Set aside.

Bring a large saucepan of salted water to boil for the spaghetti. Try to time putting your spaghetti on to cook when you're midway through sautéing the leeks (the next step) so everything is ready at the same time. Cook the pasta according to packet instructions; usually 10–12 minutes. For the leeks, heat 2 tablespoons of olive oil over a low-medium heat in a wide, deep frying pan that you have a lid for. Sauté the sliced leeks with a pinch of salt for around 10 minutes, stirring frequently until the leeks are completely soft and buttery. Add the garlic and chilli to the leeks, and stir for 30 seconds or so. Add the clams, pour in the wine, and cover the pan with a lid. Cook for 3–4 minutes until the clams pop open. Give the pan a shake every once in a while.

Drain the spaghetti and add into the leek and clam sauce, toss to coat the pasta with the clam juices. Scatter over the parsley, season with lots of black pepper and add a slick of olive oil. Serve the pan straight to the table. Remember not to eat any clams that haven't popped open.

Leek, Roasted Pepper, and Cheese Toastie

I used to earn a living making toasted sandwiches. When I say living, I mean enough to pay for a new scrunchie or pair of earrings, as those were my needs aged 16. During my weekly Saturday morning shift in my local village bakery, people would order all sorts of fillings – a full English or ham, cheese and marmite – there are no rules in toastie land. Inspired by the pairing of leeks and the flavours of Catalan romesco sauce, this no-rules toastie combines roasted peppers from a jar, hot smoked paprika, soft sautéed leeks, and cheese to stick it together. I prefer to use a sandwich toaster maker and multigrain sandwich loaf to make mine, but you can also use sourdough and cook a toastie on a pan, if you like.

Try replacing the leeks with a smaller amount of softened spring onions – they'll be ready in 4–5 rather than 10 minutes.

SERVES 2 | TIME TO PREPARE – 20 MINUTES

2 tbsp olive oil
2 medium-sized leeks (around 150g/5½oz), finely chopped
2 garlic cloves, finely chopped
butter, softened to room temperature (needs to be easily spreadable)
4 slices of medium-to-thick slice soft sandwich loaf bread
85g/3oz hard cheese (e.g. mature Cheddar, Gruyère, Comté, or manchego), grated
2 roasted red peppers from a jar, roughly sliced
½ tsp hot or sweet smoked paprika
salt

Heat 2 tablespoons of olive oil in a frying pan over a low-medium heat. Add the leeks with a pinch of salt, and sauté for 8–10 minutes, until softened but not coloured. Add the garlic, and cook for a final minute. Set aside to cool off.

Heat up your toastie maker.

Butter both sides of your bread slices – be careful not to tear it. Top the slices of bread with half of the cheese, the softened leeks, sliced peppers, and sprinkle over the smoked paprika. Add the remaining cheese and top with the other slices of bread. Cook in your toastie maker until the bread is golden brown and cheese is oozy, this should be about 3–4 minutes.

Griddled Leeks and Spring Onions with Yoghurt and 'Nduja Butter Sauce

Spring onions are wonderfully sweet when griddled, which is a welcome element, along with cooling yoghurt, to tame down the fiery hot 'nduja sausage paste. Partnering leeks alongside gives you the opportunity to appreciate their similarities as well as differences. A double hit of alliums, triple if you garnish with chives. Serve as a light main with a side of couscous, bulgur wheat, or with bread for mopping up the sauce.

Try griddled fennel instead of the leeks. No need to blanch before cooking, but you should cook for a little longer on each side, or until the fennel is tender. Asparagus or slices of griddled aubergine are also good with these flavours.

SERVES 2 | TIME TO PREPARE – 30 MINUTES

3 medium-sized leeks (approx. 300g/10½oz), washed
1 bunch of spring onions (approx. 8 spring onions)
olive oil
250g/9oz Greek yoghurt
½ tbsp chopped chives, or parsley
1 tbsp toasted flaked almonds (optional)
salt and pepper

FOR THE 'NDUJA BUTTER SAUCE
1 tbsp butter
40g/1½oz 'nduja paste

Preheat the oven to 180°C fan/200°C/400°F/gas mark 6.

To prepare the leeks, trim in length so that they will fit on your griddle pan, around 20cm/8 inches is a good length. Trim off the hairy roots, and neaten the base, but make sure they're still held together. Split the leeks in half lengthways, inspect for any remaining dirt and rinse again if required. Trim off the hairy roots of the spring onions and cut down in length so they also fit on your griddle pan. Split in half lengthways if the white part is particularly bulbous.

Bring a large saucepan of salted water to the boil, and blanch the leeks for 4–5 minutes, or until tender and floppy. Drain and pat dry.

Heat your griddle pan to medium-high. Toss the leeks with 1 tablespoon of olive oil and cook on the griddle pan for around 3–4 minutes each side, until tender and charred with dark tram lines. Depending on the size of your griddle pan, you will need to cook in batches. Use tongs to carefully transfer to a baking tray and into the warm oven. Drizzle the spring onions with a couple of teaspoons of oil to just coat, then cook on the griddle pan, also for around 3–4 minutes each side until the white bulb part of the spring onion feels tender. Transfer onto the tray with the leeks, season all over, and return to the oven to keep warm while you cook the sauce.

To make the sauce melt the butter in a small frying pan, when it starts to froth add the 'nduja and break it down with the back of your wooden spoon until it melts into the butter. Cook until bubbling, then take off the heat.

To serve, spread the yoghurt over a sharing plate or individual plates, top with lines of the leeks and spring onions. Drizzle over the 'nduja butter, then garnish with the chopped chives and toasted almonds if using. Serve hot.

Onions and Shallots

The smell of sautéed onions is comfortingly familiar, it's the start of every good home-cooked dish, the smell of a stock pot at culinary school, or of a hotdog stand at a car boot sale I went to with my Dad. From the tang of raw pickled onions to the intense sweetness of caramelized or roasted onions, we bow down to the ways they add texture, flavour, and sweetness to our dishes.

Brown onions are the most dependable, and similar in use to white or large Spanish onions. Red onions are milder and sweeter. Spring onions aren't as harsh when eaten raw. If you've not immediately jumped to this chapter in the book, you'll have noticed that I use shallots a lot. I enjoy the more delicate onion flavour they offer – they're easier to chop and they're smaller than onions, which is handy when only cooking for two. I prefer the elongated banana or echalion shallots to the tiny round ones, the size is perfect.

How long does it take to properly sauté an onion? If you want to build flavour, 4–5 minutes isn't going to do it – 10 minutes is better, and fully caramelized onions can take up to 40. Onions or shallots can also be roasted, stuffed, grilled or braised in halves/wedges, or deep fried in batter for an onion ring or bhaji. Raw, they are best pickled which takes away some of their bite. Raw diced shallots appear in some salad dressings, or as thinly sliced garnishes. Soak in iced water before using to reduce the harshness.

Successfully dicing an onion or shallot is a skill once mastered you'll use for life. With the skin on, chop the onion in half from root to tip. Peel. Leave the root intact (it will hold your onion together while you chop). With one half flat on your board, slice off the tip and make one or two horizontal cuts through the body of the onion towards (but not through) the root. Next, make a number of downwards cuts across the onion. Finally, turn it 90 degrees, make more vertical cuts through the onion half – little bits of diced onion will fall away and all you will be left with is the hairy root. To thinly slice, cut in half, remove root and tip, and then carefully slice into thin crescents. Practice makes perfect, and speed is not as important as safety.

Tasty flavour pairings for onions and shallots you'll find in my recipes are; butter, chicken, cream, garlic, rosemary, thyme, and vinegar. Others to try include; any other vegetable! Chilli, cinnamon, cumin, mustard, paprika, and sage.

RECIPE IDEA For a tasty garnish, toss thinly sliced onion in seasoned gram flour and oniony nigella seeds. Fry in oil until golden. Use on top of soups, salads, and curries.

Creamy Onion and Chicken Fricassée

In this creamy French-style fricassée, onions are the absolute star of the sauce. You'll need some patience for the onions to gorgeously caramelize, but it is absolutely worth it! I specifically use skinless boneless chicken thighs in this recipe to reduce the cooking time and compensate for the time it takes for the onions. Serve with a side of rice or crusty bread and freshly blanched green vegetables.

Instead of onions, try the equivalent weight of leeks and/or shallots with celery. For a vegetarian version, replace the chicken with a can of drained butter beans and start with the second step. For a summer twist, add 175g/6oz cherry tomatoes into the sauce at the same time as the garlic.

SERVES 2 | TIME TO PREPARE – 50 MINUTES

4 skinless boneless chicken thighs (approx. 400g/14oz)
1 tbsp butter
1 tsp olive oil
2 large brown onions (approx. 375g/13oz total), thinly sliced
½ tsp caster sugar
2 garlic cloves, finely chopped
3 sprigs of thyme, leaves stripped
½ tbsp plain flour
4 tbsp white wine
250ml/9fl oz chicken stock
3–4 tbsp double cream
2 tbsp finely chopped parsley
salt and pepper

Season the chicken thighs with salt and pepper. In a lidded, large, wide frying pan, melt the butter with the oil over a medium-high heat. When frothy and sizzling add the chicken thighs and sear for 2 minutes on each side, until just browned. Remove the chicken to a plate, leaving all the fat in the pan.

Add the onion to the pan and season with salt. Turn the heat down to low-medium and cook for around 20 minutes, until the onions are fully softened and starting to darken, but not char. Stir regularly to stop them from catching on the pan. Add the sugar, garlic, and thyme, and cook for 5 minutes more.

Sprinkle over the flour, stir well until it's absorbed by the onions, then add the wine. Once that is also absorbed, slowly add the stock and keep stirring as it slowly absorbs into the flour to thicken the sauce. Bring to a simmer, pop the chicken back in, and cook with the lid on for a further 8–10 minutes, until the chicken has cooked through (cut open to check there is no pink flesh remaining). Stir in the cream and parsley. Season to taste. Serve immediately.

Red Onion and Rosemary Farinata

Farinata is an Italian thin, unleavened flatbread made from a chickpea flour batter and baked in a hot tin of sizzling olive oil. A large batch often ends up on my retreat lunch buffets, especially when I'm 20 miles from the nearest bakery. I like to top farinata with softened sweet red onions and rosemary. The onions aren't fully caramelized in this method, as that would take a lot longer, but sweetened with balsamic and soft enough to make a tasty topping for the farinata.

Instead of the red onions, try topping the farinata with other alliums such as leek and shallots, or roasted fennel wedges.

SERVES 2–4 AS A SIDE
TIME TO PREPARE – 45 MINUTES, PLUS FLOUR SOAKING TIME

125g/4½oz chickpea flour
250ml/9fl oz water
olive oil
1 large red onion, thinly sliced
1 tsp caster sugar
1 tbsp balsamic vinegar
3–4 sprigs of rosemary, needles picked
salt

Mix the chickpea flour together with the water and ½ teaspoon salt. Whisk until well incorporated into a smooth batter, cover and leave at room temperature for at least 1 hour (or overnight in the fridge).

Preheat the oven to 200°C fan/220°C/425°F/gas mark 7.

Heat 1 tablespoon of olive oil in a small frying pan over a low heat, and cook the onion, stirring regularly, for around 20 minutes until completely softened, but not crispy. After 20 minutes add the sugar, balsamic vinegar, and cook for a couple more minutes until the onions are gooey.

Prepare the rosemary by lightly coating the needles in olive oil, this stops them from burning in the hot oven.

Pour 2 tablespoons of olive oil into your baking tin (a square baking tin around 23cm/9 inch is ideal) and place in the hot oven for 5 minutes to heat up. Carefully remove the tin from the oven and work quickly to pour in the batter and scatter over the cooked onions and rosemary. Bake in the oven for 20 minutes, until lightly browned and firm on top. Remove from the oven and leave to cool for at least 10 minutes before slicing up to eat.

Shallot and Pesto Puff Pastry Tartlets

Shallots can be given the tarte tatin approach, this pairing with buttery puff pastry is largely the inspiration for my tarts, except I've turned the tart back the right way round. I mostly make my own pesto, but thick shop-bought pesto has the texture we need to support the buttery shallots on the pastry. Use green or sun-dried tomato pesto in this recipe, both are an excellent pairing for the caramelized shallots. Serve with a simple side salad.

Onions or fennel sliced into wedges would also work in this tart recipe.

SERVES 2 | TIME TO PREPARE – 45 MINUTES

6 banana shallots (approx. 280g/9¾oz total)
1 x 320g/11½oz sheet ready rolled puff pastry
olive oil
1 egg, lightly whisked
1 heaped tbsp butter
a splash of white wine
2 tbsp green or red pesto
20g/¾oz feta or goat's cheese, crumbled
a handful of herb leaves for garnish (e.g. oregano, parsley, or basil)
salt and pepper

You will need 2 individual loose-bottomed tart tins, about 12cm/4½ inch diameter for this recipe. If you don't have any you can make square tarts – follow a similar method to my purple sprouting broccoli tart (*see* page 18).

Preheat the oven to 200°C fan/220°C/425°F/gas mark 7.

Place the whole shallots in their skins in a small bowl, and cover with boiling water. Sit for 10 minutes.

Meanwhile, open out your pastry, and cut out two circles 2cm/¾ inch larger than the diameter of your tins. Brush the insides of your tart tins with olive oil, then push your pastry circles into the base and up the sides. Prick the bases all over with a fork, brush with an egg wash and bake in the oven for 8 minutes until just starting to brown. The pastry will rise quite considerably in the oven, don't panic. Remove the tarts from the oven to cool, then use a teaspoon to gently push down the lifted centres to make room for your filling.

Back to the shallots. Drain from their water bath, peel, halve, and carefully remove any hairy root so that the shallot layers are still held together. Melt the butter in a medium-sized frying pan over a medium heat then sear the shallots cut-side down for around 5 minutes on each side, until starting to caramelize. Add a splash of wine and water, and cook for around 5 minutes more until the largest shallot is tender enough for a knife to glide through the core. Season and remove from the pan.

Spread 1 tablespoon of pesto over the bottom of each tart, and nestle in a layer of cut-side-up cooked shallots, alternating the direction of the tips. Bake the tarts in the oven for 10 minutes until the pastry is cooked through and golden brown all over. Cool for a few minutes, then use an upturned small glass under the tart tins to push them out. Crumble over the cheese, and add a few herb leaves to garnish.

Rhubarb

FORCED RHUBARB – WINTER
OUTDOOR RHUBARB – MID SPRING TO EARLY SUMMER

Long pink or reddish-green stalks of rhubarb usually mean a sweet crumble is on the cards, but botanically speaking, rhubarb is a vegetable not a fruit, so why aren't we using it in savoury recipes more? Rhubarb is sour, quite intensely so, and however it is prepared it will need sugar. It's perfectly acceptable for savoury dishes to have a balanced sweet note, though not as much as a crumble demands. Rhubarb as a vegetable needs outside-the-box thinking, not just a pair for oily fish as typically suggested. The Forced Rhubarb, Fennel and Chickpea Traybake with Soft Herb Cream Cheese in this section is some of my best outside-the-box thinking. The rhubarb as a vegetable revolution is on its way...

Early in the calendar year, from late January onwards, forced rhubarb is ready. It is grown in dark sheds, or under a cloche, which forces the rhubarb to grow without the aid of photosynthesis. The leaves are paler in colour, with white flesh and magenta pink stalks, and sweeter as a result. By mid spring, outdoor rhubarb is ready. Stalks are red, fading to green, tarter, and can be stringier once cooked. I have a tendency to prefer forced rhubarb for its colour, but outdoor rhubarb does have a stronger rhubarb taste. I use them interchangeably in my recipes, though sometimes fiddle with the cooking time and quantity of added sugar.

Rhubarb can be stewed into a compote or added to a savoury stew – look out for the Iranian rhubarb khoresh. It can also be poached, roasted and, once cooked, puréed into sauces or savoury ketchups. Rhubarb can also be eaten raw if pickled or macerated (*see* rhubarb salsa on page 86). When cooking, I prefer to roast rhubarb over poaching, and there is more wiggle room in timings before it is over cooked into a stewed mess.

Rhubarb is easy to prepare, and chop. Make sure all pieces are chopped to a similar size, this means they'll cook and soften at the same rate. Don't eat the leaves, they are poisonous.

Tasty flavour pairings for rhubarb you'll find in my recipes are; fennel, ginger, maple syrup or honey, lemon, lime, onions, and orange. Others to try include; almonds, cinnamon, hazelnuts, oily fish (salmon or mackerel), and pork.

RECIPE IDEA For a small batch of rhubard-infused gin, place 200g/7oz chopped rhubarb with 150g/5½oz sugar and cover with 400ml/14fl oz gin. Keep in a sealed sterilized jar in a dark cupboard for 2–3 weeks then strain and enjoy. Will keep well.

TOP TIP
Roast the rhubarb as per the rhubarb tartine on page 87, keep a batch to serve with yoghurt and granola or porridge for breakfast.

Rhubarb, Fennel, and Chickpea Traybake with Garlic and Herb Cream Cheese

Whilst brainstorming savoury ideas for rhubarb, I was reminded of an Iranian rhubarb khoresh stew I once cooked. It had a tonne of herbs, a surprising combination for a vegetable usually destined for crumble. I've used the idea of rhubarb and herbs together in this tray bake, along with chickpeas, fennel, and soft herb cream cheese for the prettiest and tastiest way to serve rhubarb away from the patisserie counter. Enjoy the tray bake as a simple supper served alongside some couscous, or some good bread and butter.

Outdoor rhubarb will also work in this bake, the pinker stems are best. You may need to increase the sugar slightly to compensate. Replace the fennel with onions, or leave out the rhubarb entirely (if so, no need for the sugar but keep the orange juice).

SERVES 2 | TIME TO PREPARE – 30 MINUTES

1 x 400g/14oz can of chickpeas, drained and rinsed
1 large or 2 small fennel bulbs (approx. 400g/14oz), stems removed and sliced
    into thin wedges (reserve the fronds, shred, and add to your herb pile)
olive oil
½ tsp ground allspice
2 garlic cloves, left whole and bashed
2 sticks of forced rhubarb (approx. 200g/7oz), sliced diagonally into 1.5cm
    /⁵⁄₈ inch pieces
1 tsp caster sugar
juice of 1 orange
60g/2¼oz soft herb cream cheese (e.g. Roulé or Boursin)
15g/½oz mix of mint and dill, finely chopped
1 heaped tbsp pistachios, toasted and roughly chopped
salt and pepper

Preheat the oven to 180°C fan/200°C/400°F/gas mark 6.

Arrange the chickpeas and fennel in a deep sided baking dish (approx. 24 × 30cm/9½ × 12 inches) in one layer. Drizzle over 2 tablespoons of olive oil and sprinkle over the allspice and season with salt. Toss everything together, tuck in the garlic cloves, and roast in the oven for 15 minutes.

Meanwhile, toss the chopped rhubarb in the caster sugar, squeeze over the orange juice and leave to macerate.

When the fennel has had 15 minutes, pull out of the oven, the cores should be starting to soften. Scatter over the chopped rhubarb and all the orange juice, slice or scoop the cheese into around 6 blobs, and dollop over the dish. Return to the oven for a final 10 minutes, or until the rhubarb has cooked through.

Taste and adjust seasoning, then finish the dish by topping with the chopped herbs, they should almost entirely cover the dish. Finally add the chopped pistachios and a drizzle of olive oil.

Rhubarb Salsa with Seared Halloumi

Rather surprisingly, rhubarb can be eaten raw if marinated or pickled. In this recipe, the lime juice and honey pickle the rhubarb, and – along with a hint of chilli and coriander – remind me of the flavours used to cure fish in Peruvian ceviche. As well as squeaky halloumi, the rhubarb salsa will complement anything fatty; pork belly, lamb, mackerel either baked whole or pan-fried fillets. Serve this halloumi dish as a small plate alongside one or two other sides.

This recipe will work with either forced or outdoor rhubarb.

SERVES 2 | TIME TO PREPARE – 5 MINUTES, PLUS MARINATING TIME

FOR THE SALSA
100g/3½oz rhubarb (approx. 1–2 sticks), finely diced into 5mm/¼ inch cubes
1 banana shallot, finely diced
1–2 limes, depending on juiciness
1 tbsp honey
1 tsp finely chopped fresh red chilli (approx. ¼ of an average-sized chilli), or more to taste
2 tbsp finely chopped coriander
½ tsp salt

TO SERVE
olive oil
225g/8oz block of halloumi cheese, cut into 6 rectangle slices
a handful of deep green salad leaves (e.g. watercress, rocket, baby spinach)

Combine all the ingredients for the salsa in the order above – use just enough lime juice for the ingredients to be paddling rather than swimming in it. Leave for at least 30 minutes to marinade, tossing regularly to make sure everything pickles equally. Taste and adjust seasoning when ready to serve.

Use a heavy-bottomed frying pan or griddle pan to cook the halloumi. Heat 1 tablespoon of olive oil to a medium-high heat. Fry for 2–3 minutes on each side, until nicely browned.

Working quickly as halloumi needs to be eaten warm, scatter some fresh green leaves over a serving plate, then top with the halloumi with as much salsa over the top as you'd like. The salsa keeps well in an airtight container in the fridge, so any leftovers can be enjoyed for up to 3 days.

Maple Roasted Rhubarb and Brie Tartine

If brie is a good enough companion for tart cranberry, it's good enough for tart rhubarb. If you have the odd stick of rhubarb left over from any other recipe, then roasting until tender with maple syrup and a little ginger is a good way to use it up. The shallot and mint are optional but do elevate the appearance and taste. Serve with a side salad for a quick lunch.

This dish works with forced or outdoor rhubarb and the difference in flavour is subtle. If using outdoor rhubarb, make the pieces a little smaller than 1cm/½ inch to avoid any potential stringiness. It may take 1 or 2 minutes more to roast.

MAKES 2 LARGE PIECES OF SOURDOUGH
TIME TO PREPARE – 10 MINUTES

150g/5½oz forced rhubarb (approx. 2 sticks), chopped on the diagonal
    into 1cm/½ inch pieces
1 tbsp maple syrup
½ tsp freshly grated ginger
a few very thin slivers of shallot (optional)
2 slices of sourdough bread
a little butter
100g/3½oz brie, sliced
4 mint leaves, stacked, rolled and shredded into ribbons (optional)
salt and pepper

Preheat the oven to 180°C fan/200°C/400°F/gas mark 6.

Arrange the rhubarb in one layer in a small baking dish, and toss together with the maple syrup and ginger. Season with a pinch of salt. Bake for around 8 minutes, until the rhubarb is tender but still holds its shape.

Meanwhile soak your shallot slivers (if using) for around 5 minutes in iced cold water to soften the pungent onion flavour. Drain and squeeze out excess water.

Just as the rhubarb is finishing, put on your bread to toast. Spread with a little butter, then top with the slices of brie. Pile on the cooked rhubarb and scatter over the slivers of shallot, the shredded mint leaves, and a good pinch of flaky sea salt and black pepper. Serve warm.

FUNGI

A family of edible brown toadstools.
There are thousands of varieties of fungi
which are either cultivated or found wild,
this chapter features recipes for; closed cup,
large flat, portobello, or wild mushrooms.
All are mushrooms that you can safely
forage for in a shop with the potential
to end up somewhere more enticing than
a classic English fry-up.

Closed Cup Mushrooms
90 – 97

Large Mushrooms
98 – 103

Wild Mushrooms
104 – 109

Closed Cup Mushrooms

IF CULTIVATED – AVAILABLE ALL YEAR ROUND

You'll only need to forage as far as your local shops to find a supply of closed cup mushrooms – labelled as baby button, white button, or chestnut. Available in varying shades of whitish grey and brown, these fungi are often the hero of a vegetarian recipe.

Small closed cup mushrooms can be thinly sliced and eaten raw in salads (most other mushrooms should not be eaten raw), but you'll most likely find me sautéing or frying them with garlic and parsley, then piling them on toast, using in risotto, stews, stir fries, or for toppings to tarts and pizza. If cooking a large batch at once, roasting is another option. Cooked mushrooms can be puréed into soup and add a meaty flavour to vegetarian pâté.

To prepare mushrooms, I don't recommend washing them, instead gently brush off the dirt with a brush or some kitchen paper. They don't need peeling. If the mushrooms are very small, use whole, otherwise slice. The stalks are edible too; leave attached to the cup, or remove, and dice.

Tasty flavour pairings for all types of mushroom you'll find in my recipes are; cream cheese, Parmesan, cream, garlic, ginger, miso, mustard, onions, parsley, soy sauce, and tarragon. Others to try include; bacon or pancetta, butter, chives, pasta, peas, rice, thyme, and tomatoes.

RECIPE IDEA Sauté mushrooms in olive oil until browned, add garlic and parsley. Toss through cooked tagliatelle and cover with a mountain of finely grated Parmesan.

TOP TIP
All mushrooms will release water as soon as they start cooking. When you add to a hot pan, let them sit for a few minutes before you stir as this will help them colour and reduce the likelihood of them getting soggy. Don't add salt until the end of cooking as this may also encourage sogginess.

Creamy Mushroom, Chicken, and Cannellini Bean One Pot

Mushrooms, chicken, and tarragon are a classic flavour combination, and they all love cream. The addition of cannellini beans is functional as well as nourishing in this recipe; they melt into the sauce giving creaminess and fill out the dish as a complete one pot. This dish will need to be cooked in a casserole-style dish with a lid (or one fashioned out of tin foil) you can use on the hob and in the oven. Serve with a little green veg on the side, if you like.

Most types of mushroom will work in this dish. The water content may vary, so adjust the added stock accordingly.

SERVES 2 | TIME TO PREPARE – 1 HOUR

1 tbsp olive oil
4 skin-on, bone-in chicken thighs
2 banana shallots, finely chopped
5 tbsp white wine
250g/9oz closed cup mushrooms (white, button, chestnut, or a mixture), thinly sliced
2 garlic cloves, finely chopped
1 x 400g/14oz can cannellini beans, drained and rinsed
4 tbsp chicken stock
2 heaped tbsp crème fraîche
½ tsp wholegrain mustard
1 tbsp finely chopped tarragon
salt and pepper

Preheat the oven to 190°C fan/210°C/415°F/gas mark 6½.

Heat the olive oil in a casserole dish over a medium-high heat hob. Season the chicken with salt and pepper. Place skin side down in the pan and cook undisturbed for 5–6 minutes until the skin is browned and crispy. Keep an eye on the heat and respond accordingly to avoid burnt chicken skin. When the chicken is ready to be turned it will easily come away from the pan. Flip over and cook for a further 3 minutes until the underside is also browned. Remove the chicken from the pan, leave all the chicken crumbs and around 1 tablespoon of fat in the pan.

Lower the heat and soften the shallots with a pinch of salt for 3–4 minutes, deglaze with 1 tablespoon of the wine, scraping all the chicken crumbs into the shallots. Tumble in the sliced mushrooms and garlic, cook for 4–5 minutes, until the mushrooms have all browned. Stir occasionally to avoid sticking. Add the beans, pour in the rest of the wine and the stock, and nestle the chicken back in, keeping the skin exposed. It won't look like a lot of liquid, but the mushrooms will produce more as they sweat. Cover the pan with a lid (or tin foil) and transfer to the oven to cook for 25 minutes.

After 25 minutes, remove the lid and cook uncovered for a further 10 minutes for the sauce to thicken and the chicken skin to crisp up. Remove from the oven, scoop out the chicken and check that the juices run clear, and that the flesh is white rather than peachy. Stir in the crème fraîche, mustard, tarragon, and season to taste. Serve the sauce with the chicken.

Chestnut Mushroom and Smoked Tofu Red Thai Noodle Broth

Mushrooms, smoked tofu, spinach, and rice noodles swim in a bath of red Thai coconut broth for this speedy supper. For quick home cooking, I am completely at ease with a good quality shop-bought Thai curry paste. White flat rice noodles usually come in nests within a pack, but the weight varies across brands. It's impossible to divide a nest, so go with what you think will suit your appetite and adjust the quantity of stock for your preferred liquid to noodle ratio. Do not eat this wearing a white t-shirt.

Any mushrooms will work in this recipe; sliced large flat, portobello, shiitake, or wild mushrooms. Replace the spinach with other leaves such as chard, curly kale, or pak choi, which will need slightly longer in the broth to wilt.

SERVES 2 | TIME TO PREPARE – 20 MINUTES

1–2 nests (approx. 100g/3½oz total, depending on brand) white flat rice noodles
150g/5½oz firm smoked tofu, diced into 2cm/3/4 inch cubes
2 tbsp soy sauce
3 tbsp neutral oil (coconut, light olive, or rapeseed)
250g/9oz chestnut mushrooms, thinly sliced
300ml/10fl oz vegetable or chicken stock
2 tbsp Thai red curry paste
200ml/7fl oz coconut milk
40g/1½oz baby spinach
1 heaped tbsp finely chopped coriander, plus a few extra whole sprigs for garnish
juice of 2 limes
2 tbsp roasted salted peanuts
salt

Prepare the noodles according to packet instructions. This usually involves placing in a jug or bowl, covering with boiling water to steep and soften for 3–4 minutes, then draining, rinsing with cold water, and draining again.

Toss the chopped tofu with 1 tablespoon of the soy sauce. Warm 2 tablespoons of neutral oil in a large frying pan over a medium-high heat. Fry the tofu for around 6 minutes until lightly browned all over. Scoop out using a slotted spoon – leave the soy sauce and oil in the pan. Repeat with the mushrooms, tossing regularly, rather than stirring, until lightly browned on both sides (about 4 minutes).

Meanwhile, simmer the broth. Heat 1 tablespoon of oil in a saucepan big enough to take all the ingredients, over a medium heat. Add the Thai red curry paste and 1 tablespoon of soy sauce and stir together. Cook for around a minute, until the paste is bubbly and fragrant. Pour in the coconut milk, stock and simmer gently while the tofu and mushrooms finish cooking.

Tip the cooked noodles, cooked tofu and mushrooms into the broth, then add the spinach and stir until wilted. Heat to serving temperature, then sprinkle over the coriander, and season to taste with lime juice and salt or soy sauce. If it's too spicy you can add a pinch of sugar. Plate up in two deep, wide bowls, and garnish with the peanuts and a few whole sprigs of coriander.

Miso Mushroom Pâté

Miso, soy sauce and mushrooms all have umami in common. The savouriness of these umami ingredients are complemented in this quick to make pâté by the sweetness of cream cheese. Enjoy slathered on toast topped with a fried egg for brunch, or on dark rye crackers with lightly pickled radish and cucumber for a quick lunch. The pâté will last in the fridge for 3 days in an airtight container.

Make with any mushrooms you have to hand.

SERVES 2+ | TIME TO PREPARE – 15 MINUTES, PLUS CHILLING TIME

1 tbsp butter
1 banana shallot, finely chopped
250g/9oz closed cup chestnut mushrooms, finely sliced
1 garlic clove, finely chopped
1 tbsp white miso paste
2 tsp soy sauce
125g/4½oz soft cream cheese
salt and pepper

Melt the butter in a large frying pan over a low-medium heat, and soften the shallot with a little salt for 4–5 minutes. Add the sliced mushrooms and cook for around 8 minutes until browned and cooked through, tossing from time to time. Add the chopped garlic, miso paste and soy. Stir to loosen and distribute the miso paste, cook for another minute or so, then remove from the heat and leave to cool for a short while, until no longer steaming.

Slide the cooled mushrooms into a food processor and blitz until broken down into a rough paste, stop and scrape down the sides as necessary. Add the cream cheese and blitz again until well combined, ideally leaving some texture. Season to taste using salt, pepper, and soy sauce. Scrape into a serving dish, cover and chill for 30 minutes or until cool to the touch before serving.

You'll only need to forage as far as your local shops to find a supply of closed cup mushrooms – labelled as baby button, white button, or chestnut.

Large Mushrooms

Here, I define large mushrooms to include portobello, flat mushrooms, or the king oyster. All of which offer a 'meatier' element to recipes, and are excellent for holding space on a plate where a piece of meat might have once been. The original vegetable 'steak', before cauliflower took over that trend. Portobello and large flat mushrooms are cup mushrooms that have grown and opened out. You may find other larger mushrooms out in the wild, but unless you're with a foraging expert, I would advise against picking and eating, some non-cultivated mushrooms can be poisonous to humans.

Whole portobello and large flat mushrooms can be marinated then roasted or grilled or cooked on a griddle pan. You can find my method in the Leaves chapter (*see* page 141), served with wild garlic chimichurri. These mushrooms can also be stuffed, once the stalks have been popped off (dice these to add to your filling), and the gills scraped back. Try my Portobello Mushrooms Stuffed with Black Rice and Pesto (*see* page 100), or get creative with other ingredients. They vary quite widely in size, and will always shrink when cooked, if in doubt go for two mushrooms per person. Larger mushrooms can also be thickly sliced and pan-fried alone, or added along with smaller mushrooms to stews and other recipes.

King oyster, also known as king trumpet mushrooms, have a more unusual mushroom shape, sporting a long thick stalk, and a smaller toadstool top. The stalk is the most useful element of these mushrooms and once cooked is firmer than a similarly cooked portobello, so is the king choice (pardon the pun) for meaty-textured recipes such as my Hoisin Bao Buns (*see* page 102). To prepare king oyster mushrooms, split in half from top to bottom, score the flesh with a tight diamond pattern, marinate, then cook on a heavy cast-iron pan. King oysters can also be shredded with a fork and used as a 'pulled meat' replacement, or the stalk can be cut, cooked and served as a scallop lookalike.

See Closed Cup Mushrooms (page 90) for ideas for flavour pairings.

RECIPE IDEA Marinate thick slices of flat mushrooms in a little soy sauce, maple syrup, and smoked paprika, then pan-fry or roast until browned for a breakfast alternative to bacon.

TOP TIP Use a large grilled portobello mushroom instead of a burger in a bun. Don't forget the sauces and gherkins. Use the grilled mushroom method in Wild Garlic Chimichurri with Portobello Mushroom Steak on page 141.

Portobello Mushrooms Stuffed with Black Rice and Pesto

Pop off the portobello mushrooms stalk and you're left with a cavity perfect for stuffing. This stuffing is made from black rice, pesto, and sautéed aromatics, then covered with breadcrumbs and Parmesan for a crispy top. Choose whichever flavour pesto you like, homemade, basil, or sun-dried tomato flavours will do just fine. I have served these black rice stuffed mushrooms at supper clubs and on retreats, choosing a celeriac or butternut purée for a base, and garnishing with roasted squash and a kale chip. That's quite a lot of work for the home cook, so instead keep it simple with a side of greens and or roasted potatoes.

You can stuff either portobello or large flat mushrooms, choose the biggest you can find, bearing in mind they do shrink in the oven.

SERVES 2
TIME TO PREPARE – 45 MINUTES, DEPENDING ON RICE VARIETY

85g/3oz black rice, such as Venus, Nerone, or Thai
4 large flat or portobello mushrooms
1½ tbsp olive oil
1 banana shallot, finely chopped
3 sprigs of thyme, leaves picked
2 tbsp green or red pesto
3 tbsp coarse breadcrumbs or day-old bread, blitzed into breadcrumbs using a food processor (approx. 25g/1oz)
3 tbsp finely grated Parmesan cheese
salt

Preheat the oven to 180°C fan/200°C/400°F/gas mark 6.

Cook the rice with timings according to variety and packet instructions, taste test well before the cooking time is up, the rice should be cooked through, al dente, but not mushy. Drain and give a good shake, to remove the excess cooking water.

Prepare the mushrooms, by popping out the stalk and scraping off the gills with a teaspoon. Finely chop the stalks and set aside. Place the mushrooms face side up on a baking tray, and drizzle 1 tablespoon of olive oil across the top. Bake for 10 minutes.

Heat ½ tablespoon of oil over a low-medium heat in a frying pan big enough to take all the filling. Sauté the shallot with a pinch of salt for 3–4 minutes to soften but not brown, then add the chopped mushroom stalks and two thirds of the thyme. Cook for another 3–4 minutes until everything is lightly browned. Stir in the cooked rice along with 2 tablespoons of pesto, or more if you prefer. Season to taste.

For the topping, mix together the breadcrumbs, remainder of the thyme and grated Parmesan cheese in a small bowl.

Remove the mushrooms from the oven and drain off any excess water that may have gathered in the mushroom. Generously pile in the rice filling, scatter over the breadcrumb topping, then pop the mushrooms back into the oven for a final 15 minutes until the breadcrumbs have browned on top.

Hoisin Griddled King Oyster Mushrooms in Bao Buns with Quick Pickled Veg

Bao buns have become a popular street food in London in recent years, and having never travelled to China, these are the only ones I know. I usually can't resist the combination of pork belly, sweet hoisin sauce, and lightly pickled veg stuffed into a pillowy bun, and this is my just as tasty vegetarian take. You could make the bao buns but the emphasis for this book is simple quick food at home, so I buy them. Look out for them in frozen or chiller sections of some larger supermarkets or in specialist Asian food retailers.

For this recipe, choose king oyster mushrooms as below or 200g/7oz (3–4) large flat mushrooms sliced into around 12 × 2cm/¾inch thick slices.

SERVES 2 | TIME TO PREPARE – 25 MINUTES

FOR THE MUSHROOMS
3 tbsp hoisin sauce, plus extra to serve
1 tbsp soy sauce
1 garlic clove, finely chopped
1 tsp finely grated ginger
3 king oyster mushrooms (approx. 200g/7oz), sliced in half and scored in a
    cross-hatch pattern at 5mm/¼ inch intervals
rapeseed or light olive oil for frying
salt

FOR THE QUICK PICKLED VEG
8cm/3¼ chunk of cucumber and/or carrot, cut into matchsticks
1 spring onion, sliced into 2 x 8cm/3¼ inch lengths and cut into matchsticks
1 tsp white wine vinegar or rice vinegar
½ tsp maple syrup, honey or sugar

TO SERVE
6 bao buns
½ tsp sesame seeds
a few sprigs of coriander

Preheat the oven to 180°C fan/200°C/400°F/gas mark 6.

In a medium-sized bowl, mix together the hoisin, soy, garlic, ginger, and season with salt. Toss in the prepared mushrooms and mix well so that all surfaces are covered. Leave to marinate for at least 10 minutes.

Meanwhile prepare your quick pickled veg. Toss the chopped cucumber and/or carrot and spring onion with the vinegar and maple syrup and set aside to marinate, also for at least 10 minutes.

Heat a griddle pan over a high heat, and add just enough cooking oil to coat the pan. Place the mushrooms flat-side down onto the pan, turn down the heat a little and cook for 2–3 minutes each side until charred and starting to caramelize. Pop the griddle pan with the mushrooms in the oven for 5 minutes to make sure the centres on the larger mushrooms are cooked through.

Heat up your bao buns according to packet instructions. When cool enough to handle, open out and stuff with 2 slices of mushroom or half a king oyster, top with the quick pickled veg, a drizzle of any leftover marinade or hoisin sauce, a sprinkling of sesame seeds and a sprig of coriander. Serve immediately.

Wild Mushrooms

IF CULTIVATED – AVAILABLE ALL YEAR ROUND
IF WILD – AUTUMN

Since I don't recommend foraging for mushrooms in the actual wild unless you are under expert supervision, this definition of wild mushrooms includes all those sold or labelled as wild or specialty mushrooms from the safe space of the veg aisle.

Wild mushroom selection boxes usually include oysters (not to be confused with king oysters), maitake, and shiitake. In this category you could also add chef's favourites morels, chanterelle, black trumpets, or truffle, but these can be pricey and this book was written during a cost of living crisis! Truffle or truffle-infused oil can be a more economical way to bring in a rich truffle flavour, but some are made with truffle flavouring that can taste synthetic. I once accidentally spilt a full bottle on my carpet which stunk so much I had to replace the carpet. A waste of truffle oil and a waste of carpet.

Wild mushrooms are daintier than cup mushrooms, and so require the lightest of sautéing. Tear, rather than slice, any large ones, keep small ones whole, and cook very gently in oil or butter with lots of room in the pan and without much movement for 3–4 minutes until browned. Once cooked, add to tarts, risottos, pizza, or pasta. These are not mushrooms to stew in a sauce or blend into a soup because it feels like a waste of their beauty.

A note on shiitake mushrooms which have an excellent reputation as the most nutritious of all mushrooms. These are closer in shape to closed cup mushrooms, but with a skinny stalk and darker brown top. They're more robust than other wild mushrooms, so you might find them in ramen noodle soup. They will work in all cup mushroom recipes. I once ate a few raw ones while I was preparing them. Usually chef's perks but, on this occasion, a total disaster was brewing. Forty-eight hours later I ended up with a painful rash that looked like I'd done 9 rounds with a whip and subsequently discovered I'd had a toxic reaction called shiitake dermatitis. It took 3 weeks to go down, and so having experienced mother nature's warning, I now make sure all my non-closed cup mushrooms are properly cooked through before eating.

See Closed Cup Mushrooms (page 90) for flavour pairings.

RECIPE IDEA Enrich cooked wild mushrooms with a splash of cream, garlic, and tarragon or parsley, and serve on toast.

TOP TIP

If you're up for a mushroom adventure without the foraging, look for an oyster mushroom home growing kit. In the space of a couple of weeks, they will grow out of a box on your kitchen worktop, which is great fun to watch and will give you a fabulous mushroom harvest to enjoy.

Wild Mushroom Pizza with Ricotta and Mozzarella

Biancaneve is Snow White in Italian, and also the name of a pizza that has a white base rather than a tomato sauce. I remember when I had my first one on a family holiday in Italy. I love tomatoes, but I also loved that it was different. The mushrooms are the hero of this dish, with creamy ricotta and stringy mozzarella performing the Snow White role. Without a pizza oven, or space to build one, I cook my homemade pizzas in the oven on its highest setting. You can bake on a pizza stone, which helps char the base, or like I do, on a hot upturned baking tray. This recipe will make 4 bases. You can wrap the spare two in clingfilm and chill (or freeze) to use the next day, bring to room temperature before stretching out.

Other toppings that work well with a ricotta and mozzarella pizza base include ribbons of courgette or curly kale and sausage.

SERVES 2 (MAKES 4 BASES)
TIME TO PREPARE – 1 HOUR 30 MINUTES

FOR THE BASES
500g/1lb 2oz strong white bread flour
1 x 7g sachet of fast action dried yeast
½ tbsp caster sugar
½ tsp flaky salt, crumbled
325ml/11fl oz warm water
olive oil

FOR THE TOPPING
200g/7oz mixed wild mushrooms, sliced or torn
1 garlic clove, finely chopped
2 tsp finely chopped parsley
250g/9oz ricotta, drained
240g/8½oz ball of mozzarella cheese, torn
salt and pepper

TO SERVE (OPTIONAL)
truffle oil, shaved Parmesan cheese, rocket

First make the dough. In a large bowl, mix together the flour with the yeast, sugar and salt. Measure out 325ml/11fl oz warm water, add 2 tablespoons of olive oil. Make a well in the flour and pour around 90 per cent of the water-oil mix into the flour. Using your hands, loosely mix, then gradually work it into a raggy dough. Add the remaining water if it looks like it needs it. Turn out onto your kitchen worktop and knead for around 10 minutes, until the dough has gone from raggy to smooth and soft. Be patient with it if wet and sticky, it will eventually end up smooth! Pop the dough back in the large bowl, cover with a tea towel and leave to rise for 45 minutes or until it has doubled in size.

After 45 minutes, turn out the dough, punch down and divide into 4. Briefly knead each piece of dough into a ball and pop onto a tray, cover and rest for a further 15 minutes.

Preheat the oven to 220°C fan/240°C/475°F/gas mark 9. Place a pizza stone or large baking tray (or two smaller ones) upside down in the middle of the oven.

Warm 2 tablespoons of oil in a large frying pan on the hob over a medium-high heat. Add the torn mushrooms, and cook for 3–4 minutes until browned, toss the pan, rather than stir. Add the garlic and the parsley for a final 30 seconds, season the mushrooms, and slide off onto a plate.

Turn the ricotta out of its tub into a bowl, season with salt and lightly whisk to a smooth paste.

Roll or stretch out your pizza dough as thin as possible onto a piece of baking paper on top of a movable flat surface such as a chopping board. Brush the base and crusts with around ½ tablespoon of olive oil each. Add 3–4 small blobs of ricotta, and smooth down with the back of a spoon. Then add the torn mozzarella and cooked mushrooms. Season the top of the pizza with salt and pepper. Working quickly, slide the pizzas off your chopping board straight into the oven on top of the pizza stone or upturned baking trays. Bake for 8–10 minutes, until the crust and base are browned and crisp.

To serve, drizzle over some truffle oil, a few shavings of Parmesan, and a handful of fresh rocket.

Garlicky Wild Mushrooms and Burrata, with Sun-dried Tomato Bulgur Wheat

Simple ingredients that go very well together; the flavours of garlicky mushrooms, oozy burrata and sun-dried tomatoes would be just as happy on top of a pizza as they are in this bulgur-based vegetarian dish. I cook my bulgur wheat via the absorption method for dishes like this when I want the texture of chewy individual grains of bulgur rather than a soft porridge. Serve with a huge pile of rocket leaves on the side.

A wild mushroom mix such as oyster, shiitake, and maitake is perfect for this. Or, in fact, any mushrooms in this chapter.

SERVES 2
TIME TO PREPARE – 30 MINUTES, INCLUDING 20 MINUTES RESTING TIME

150g/5½oz medium-grind bulgur wheat, rinsed
250ml/9fl oz boiling hot vegetable stock
olive oil
200g/7oz wild mushrooms, brushed clean and large pieces torn or sliced
3 garlic cloves, finely chopped
2 tbsp finely chopped parsley
2 tbsp balsamic sun-dried tomato paste (or good quality sun-dried tomato paste plus
   1 tsp balsamic vinegar)
1 tbsp balsamic vinegar
150g/5½oz ball of burrata, room temperature, torn into bite-size pieces
salt and pepper

First prepare your bulgur wheat. Place in a heatproof bowl. For this amount of bulgur, submerge under a 3cm/1¼ inch layer of boiling hot vegetable stock (around 250ml/9fl oz), cover the bowl with a plate and leave for up to 20 minutes, by which time the grains will be tender, and all the water absorbed. Fluff up with a fork.

Next, heat 2 tablespoons of olive oil to a medium-high heat in a large frying pan big enough to take the bulgur. Fry the mushrooms for 3–4 minutes until browned – toss the pan (rather than stir) to avoid them going soggy. Add the garlic and half of the parsley for a final 30 seconds, season the mushrooms, and slide off onto a plate while you finish the dish.

Lower the heat of the pan and add another 1 tablespoon of olive oil plus the sun-dried tomato paste. Stir together into a thick red paste. Add the cooked bulgur, stir well to coat all the grains in the red paste, and continue to cook for a few minutes so that any excess moisture in the bulgur has evaporated. Splash in the balsamic vinegar, add the rest of the parsley and season to taste, adding more sun-dried tomato paste if needed.

Either plate up the tomatoey bulgur wheat on one sharing platter or divide between two plates. Tear the burrata, and strew across the bulgur, top with the wild mushrooms and a drizzle of olive oil.

LEAVES

Crunchy, soft, bitter, peppery, spicy, mild.
All words that can be used to describe the
range of leaves featured in this chapter;
chicory, lettuce, rainbow chard, spinach,
watercress, and wild garlic. If you were
expecting salads, there's more than that.
This chapter includes recipes for griddled,
wilted, blended, and dressed leaves.

Chicory

WINTER / AVAILABLE YEAR ROUND

You will be able to find bitter chicory all year round, but it is primarily a winter leaf, ideal for vibrant winter salads when there are little other leaves around. This section focuses on two types of chicory. Firstly, the tightly packed available everywhere candle light bulb shaped chicory (sometimes called Belgian endive). Secondly the family of Italian chicories, primarily the magenta and white veined leaves of the radicchio. Radicchio leaves are most commonly found in packets of supermarket mixed salad, but you can buy whole heads from retailers who aren't afraid of its bitter streak.

Chicory (Belgian endive) is produced with white or red-purple-pink tipped leaves. Like forced rhubarb, it's grown in darkness, which explains the absence of any green in its leaves. The leaves are whiter, crunchier and most bitter towards the root, then thin out towards the tips. There are a number of varieties of radicchio; the ball shaped Chioggia radicchio (often just labelled radicchio), Tardivo, and Trevisano which are twirly and oversized lookalikes of red chicory. There is also the milder-tasting Castelfranco radicchio, inexplicably beautiful with its pink and white speckled softer leaves.

Both types of chicory can be cooked. Cooking will mellow some of the bitterness, especially if roasted, grilled, or griddled in halves or wedges. You can also braise or sauté. Add the north Italian recipe for red wine radicchio risotto to your list of recipes to try. Chicory leaves are too bitter to eat on their own raw in a salad. Mix with sweeter green leaves, or slices of fruit such as oranges (*see* page 116), figs, or pear, and be sure to use a dressing that errs on the sweeter side of life.

If cutting endive into wedges, leave the core in place to hold it together. To use the leaves, simply pull apart from the base and use whole or shred.

Tasty flavour pairings for endive you'll find in my recipes are; balsamic vinegar, blue cheese, lemon, orange, parsley, and watercress. Others to try include; apples, butter, mushrooms, figs, pear, pomegranate, rocket, and walnuts.

RECIPE IDEA Pan fry halves of white chicory, in olive oil or butter with thyme and a little balsamic vinegar, until charred on both sides. Serve with crumbled feta and toasted walnuts.

TOP TIP
Chicory leaves can be utilized as a canapé base – top with whipped ricotta and olive tapenade or pea hummus and dill.

Griddled Radicchio Wedges with Lemony Gorgonzola Cannellini Beans

Split into wedges and charred on the griddle pan, radicchio's purple and white-veined leaves are giving main character energy in this dish. Gorgonzola is often paired with radicchio as the creaminess helps counteract the bitterness, as does the griddling process. I tried this dish so many times with gnocchi, but it just wasn't working for me, too stodgy, too claggy. Cannellini beans simmered in the same milky cheese sauce, with the added freshness of lemon zest are a much better partner for the radicchio. Serve with bread for a light supper, or for a more substantial dinner add some roasted chicken thighs on the side.

Try replacing the radicchio with a halved pink-purple endive.

SERVES 2 | TIME TO PREPARE – 20 MINUTES

FOR THE BEANS
2 tsp butter
1 garlic clove, finely chopped
100ml/3½fl oz whole milk
75g/2½oz gorgonzola, broken into small chunks
1 x 400g/14oz can cannellini beans, drained and rinsed
1 tbsp finely grated Parmesan cheese, plus extra to serve
zest and juice of 1 lemon
1 tbsp finely chopped parsley
1 tbsp toasted pine nuts (optional)
salt and pepper

FOR THE RADICCHIO
1 head radicchio, rusty end trimmed and sliced through the root into 4 or 6 wedges, depending on size
3 tbsp olive oil
1 tbsp balsamic vinegar
½ tsp caster sugar

Melt the butter in the large frying pan over a medium heat, and when frothy, sauté the garlic briefly to soften. Lower the heat, add the milk, and the gorgonzola chunks. Allow the cheese to slowly melt into the milk over a couple of minutes, give it a stir every now and again. Add the beans, slightly crushing some of them into the sauce with the back of your spoon. Continue to cook on a gentle heat for 4–5 minutes.

Meanwhile, heat up a griddle pan on the hob for the radicchio. Mix together the oil, balsamic, sugar and a little salt in a large bowl, and toss the radicchio wedges in the dressing. Sear on a hot griddle pan for around 3 minutes each side until soft and charred. Reserve any dressing left in the bowl.

When the beans have warmed through, add 1 tablespoon of grated Parmesan, the lemon zest, parsley, and season to taste – be liberal with the pepper. Add just enough lemon juice to give it some zing. Add a splash more milk for a looser consistency.

To serve, spoon the beans into pasta bowls, top with the radicchio wedges, drizzle over any remaining dressing, add a dusting of Parmesan, and scatter over the pine nuts (if using).

Red Chicory, Orange, and Stilton Salad with Toasted Coriander Seeds

Red chicory leaves and fresh segments of orange are exactly the ingredients you need for a bright winter salad. Sherry vinegar is sweeter than red wine vinegar so works well here to balance chicory's bitterness. It's expensive though, so if you don't want to shell out for a whole bottle just to use 1 tablespoon, substitute with red wine vinegar. Start with 1–2 teaspoons and taste the salad dressing as you go, or add a little sugar to balance. I'd have this for a light lunch, with some bread on the side, or serve as a side for supper.

You can replace the red chicory with white chicory leaves or any type of radicchio leaf.

SERVES 2 | TIME TO PREPARE – 10 MINUTES

FOR THE SALAD
1 tbsp coriander seeds
250g/9oz red chicory (approx. 3–4 heads), base trimmed and pulled apart into leaves
a handful of spicy green leaves such as watercress or rocket (approx. 25g/1oz)
60g/2¼oz Stilton or other firm blue cheese you can crumble
2 oranges, segmented (see page 13)

FOR THE DRESSING
1 tbsp orange juice (caught from the segmented orange)
1 tbsp sherry vinegar
3 tbsp olive oil
salt and pepper

Toast your coriander seeds in a dry, hot frying pan until fragrant, then set aside to cool.

Next, make up the dressing. In a small bowl, whisk together 1 tablespoon of the caught orange juice with the sherry vinegar, then whisk in the olive oil until combined. Season to taste, use a bitter leaf of chicory to dip in and taste rather than a spoon.

Place the chicory leaves, and the greens into a medium-sized mixing bowl and toss through just enough of the dressing so everything is lightly covered. Crumble in the Stilton cheese, followed by the toasted coriander seeds, and gently fold in the orange segments. Taste and adjust seasoning or add more dressing if required. Serve on individual plates or in one bowl to share.

Chicory leaves
are too bitter to
eat on their own
raw in a salad. Mix
with sweeter green
leaves, or slices
of fruit such as
oranges, figs, or
pear, and be sure to
use a dressing that
errs on the sweeter
side of life.

Lettuce

WILL DEPEND ON VARIETY – TYPICALLY SUMMER TO AUTUMN

I used to think that salad meant lettuce, and lettuce meant salad. It blew my mind to discover that lettuce has many other, possibly more delicious uses. Lettuce is a broad category, and there are many varieties. They might be loose leafed or 'hearted' where the leaves are clustered around a central heart.

Varieties of lettuce you might come across include the crunchy little gem, mild tasting round lettuce, curly and slightly bitter frisée, crimped lollo rosso, or red-tinged red oak leaf. The only lettuce that is not welcome in my kitchen is the iceberg, except perhaps when I'm feeling nostalgic for the taste of it smothered in mayo on top of a burger in its bun.

When eaten raw in a salad, a mix of leaves works best, giving some variety in taste and structure. I personally welcome the addition of some strong tasting non-lettuce leaves such as chicory or rocket to spice up mellow lettuce. You can braise, grill, or griddle lettuce, and this is best done with the hearted lettuces like gem and romaine. Lettuce doesn't withstand a long cooking time, so keep the braises and griddles fairly brief. Some lettuces can also be cooked and blended into summery soups.

To prepare lettuce, pull off the leaves and use whole if small. If the leaves are larger, I tear them in half with my hands instead of precisely chopping with a knife – the rustic look. To prepare a lettuce for griddling or braising very carefully, shave any rusty bits from the end of the stalk, then slice into halves or quarters though the core, leaving it intact to hold them together. If any of the outer leaves aren't secure, discard them. To avoid soggy salads, a salad spinner is immensely useful for drying lettuce leaves – if you don't have one, use a clean tea towel to pat dry.

Tasty flavour pairings you'll find in my recipes are; capers, Parmesan cheese, hard boiled eggs, lemon, Dijon mustard, pancetta, and peas. Others to try include; avocado, feta, cucumber, endive leaves, olives, tomatoes, and walnuts.

RECIPE IDEA You can't better a crisp, lettuce-based Caesar or Niçoise salad.

TOP TIP Salad dressings usually have a ratio of 2 or 3 : 1 fat to acid. You can use this ratio to come up with your own dressings, but you can't go wrong with extra-virgin olive oil and lemon juice. Added flavours like garlic, herbs, honey, and mustard can up the flavour ante.

Charred Romaine with Burnt Lemon Mayo

If you thought eating an entire lettuce in one go was only something your pet rabbit could achieve then perhaps you haven't tried it charred and served as the dish hero? The cut sides darken and caramelize, giving texture and flavour variations to this leafy vegetable usually reserved for the salad bowl. Once you've mastered the homemade mayo, flavoured with the incredible notes of the burnt lemon, it's very quick to put together, and can be topped with whatever you fancy. Sometimes that might be a soft boiled egg and capers, other times a few anchovies, or a can of tuna.

You can also try this recipe with gem lettuce.

SERVES 2 | TIME TO PREPARE – 20 MINUTES

FOR THE BURNT LEMON MAYO
1 lemon, cut in half through the middle
8 tbsp (120ml/4fl oz) light olive oil
1 egg yolk
1 tsp Dijon mustard
salt and pepper

FOR THE DISH
2 romaine lettuce, split in half lengthways
olive oil
Parmesan or other vegetarian style hard cheese
salt and pepper

TO SERVE
choice of; soft boiled eggs, canned tuna, anchovies, smattering of capers

First char your lemons. Heat a griddle pan over a medium-high heat. Dip the surface of each half of the cut lemon into your measured out olive oil. Char the lemons cut side down on the hot griddle pan for 2–3 minutes, until dark, almost burnt, tramlines appear. Turn off your griddle for now, and set the lemons aside to cool while you whisk your mayo.

Grab a medium-sized heavy bowl, and place it on top of a folded tea towel, which will keep it steady while you whisk. Use a balloon whisk to whisk together the egg yolk, Dijon mustard, and a pinch each of salt and pepper. Very slowly start dribbling in the oil with one hand while constantly whisking with the other, go slowly if uncertain and pause between dribbles to make sure each bit of oil has emulsified into the yolk before adding more oil. Once all the oil has been whisked in the mayo should be thick and luscious. Squeeze in the juice from your charred lemons, and scrape in the burnt flesh too. This will loosen the mayo into a drizzle-able sauce. Season to taste.

Now cook your romaine, unless your pan is huge you may need to do this in batches. Re-heat the griddle pan over a medium-high heat. Drizzle olive oil on the cut face of the lettuces and cook, cut-side down around 2–3 minutes until char marks appear. Using tongs, flip them over and cook for another 2–3 minutes or until the lettuce has softened and is almost floppy.

Plate up on individual plates or a sharing platter. Start with the lettuce, season with a little salt and pepper, and drizzle over as much burnt lemon mayo as you think is appropriate. Shower with a little finely grated Parmesan to finish. Add whatever else you fancy whether that be halves of gooey soft boiled egg seasoned with black pepper, canned tuna, anchovies, or capers.

Braised Baby Gem, Pancetta, and Peas

Cooked lettuce is best for days when the calendar says summer, but British weather is giving you damp autumn. A variation on a French-style recipe for braising lettuce with peas and sometimes bacon, which I once tried in a pub in, err, South East London. Just a little pancetta is used in this braise, most of the body comes from the lettuce, peas, and chickpeas. It's a really good example of how meat can be used in small quantities to add depth of flavour but doesn't distract from the vegetables. Serve with bread to mop up the juices, or with rib-sticking mashed potatoes for something more substantial.

You can try substituting the gem lettuce, for larger romaine, cos, or wedges of endive.

SERVES 2 AS A MAIN | TIME TO PREPARE – 20 MINUTES

100g/3½oz diced pancetta
2 little gem lettuce (approx. 100g/3½oz each), sliced into quarters through the core
2 spring onions, finely sliced
1 x 400g/14oz can chickpeas, drained and rinsed
160g/5¾oz frozen peas
200ml/7fl oz chicken stock
2 tbsp crème fraîche
1 tbsp finely chopped herbs (e.g. tarragon, mint, or parsley, or a combination)
salt and pepper

Warm a lidded, deep, wide frying pan over a medium-high heat (no oil required) and cook the pancetta cubes for around 5 minutes, until browned. Remove using a slotted spoon and leave the fat in the pan. Cook the gem lettuce wedges in the pancetta fat, cut-side down for around 90 seconds on each flat side, until just starting to char. Use tongs to lift out of the pan, and set aside.

Lower the heat, and the pancetta back into the pan, along with the spring onions and soften for a minute or so. Next add the chickpeas, frozen peas and chicken stock, then nestle the charred lettuce back in, cut side up. Bring to a bubble, cover the pan with a lid and simmer for around 10 minutes, or until a knife glides easily through the stalk of the thickest wedge of lettuce. Remove the lid, and if the stock needs reducing, cook uncovered for a few minutes more. Dollop in the crème fraîche, and gently shake the pan to dissolve it into the sauce. Add the chopped herbs and season to taste – it may already be salty enough because of the pancetta, but you can afford to be liberal with the pepper.

The only lettuce
that is not welcome
in my kitchen is
the iceberg, except
perhaps when I'm
feeling nostalgic
for the taste of it
smothered in mayo
on top of a burger in
its bun.

Rainbow Chard

SUMMER TO EARLY WINTER

This large-leafed green vegetable related to beetroot, is grown with stalks in a variety of rainbow colours, which are packaged together in bunches. The king of the allotment, farmers market, or veg box schemes, I only started cooking with rainbow chard on a regular basis, because it was constantly appearing in my veg box. It's now becoming more readily available in larger supermarkets, but you'll still have to know where to source it. I prefer it to spinach, it's less tinny on the teeth.

Alongside rainbow chard, regular chard or Swiss chard has thicker white stems and sometimes gigantic green leaves. Cook Swiss chard in the same way as rainbow chard, the stalks can be diced and eaten too, they're just not as colourful. Baby chard leaves are used in mixed bags of prepared salad.

Aside from baby chard leaves, chard should always be cooked for eating; sauté, stir fry, steam, or braise. Once cooked it can be served with pasta, served gratinée, or with cheese in a number of Mediterranean specialty pies. I generally treat it the same way as spinach, cooking gently rather than stewing for hours, and adding to the end of a dish for colour and nutrition.

To prepare chard, you will want to separate the stems and leaves. Simply slice out the stalk with a knife. If shredding the leaves, stack a number of leaves together, roll them up tightly, slice across your roll, then unravel into ribbons. Stalks should be diced.

The edible stalks are tougher than the leaves, so dice and add to your dish at the start to soften along with the onions. Two vegetables for the price of one.

Tasty flavour pairings for chard you'll find in my recipes are; butter, feta cheese, garlic, pasta, and saffron. Others to try include; cumin, chilli, chickpeas, eggs, leeks, mustard seeds, raisins, pine nuts, and potato.

RECIPE IDEA Shred chard, sauté with mustard seeds and chilli in olive oil or butter until wilted. Serve with scrambled eggs on toast.

TOP TIP If your chard leaves are big enough, they can be blanched, cooled and used as an alternative to vine leaves to wrap around a stuffing, dolmades-style.

Rainbow Chard and Saffron Orzotto with Prawns

I use rainbow chard's stalks and leaves in this no waste orzo take on risotto, which is topped with garlicky prawns. Orzo is a pasta-shaped like rice which can either be cooked like regular pasta, or fed with stock during cooking like risotto rice, which gives a creamier, more risotto-like result from the pasta starch. The saffron in the stock adds a subtle flavour and warm yellow glow.

Try replacing the chard with spinach or kale.

SERVES 2 | TIME TO PREPARE – 40 MINUTES

FOR THE ORZOTTO
1 tbsp olive oil
1 banana shallot, finely chopped
175g/6oz rainbow chard, leaves stripped and shredded, stalks finely diced
1 garlic clove, finely chopped
180g/6½oz orzo
approx. 850ml/1½ pints warm chicken stock or vegetable stock, with a pinch of saffron
2 tsp butter
2 tbsp finely grated Parmesan cheese, or more to taste
2 tbsp finely chopped dill, plus a few sprigs for garnish
1 lemon
salt and pepper

FOR THE PRAWNS
150g/5½ oz raw king prawns
1 tbsp olive oil
1 garlic clove, finely sliced
a pinch of saffron

In a small shallow bowl toss together the prawns with the olive oil, sliced garlic, saffron, and a pinch of salt. Leave to marinate while you make your orzotto.

In a wide, deep frying pan that you have a lid for, heat 1 tablespoon of olive oil over a low-medium heat. Sauté the shallot and rainbow chard stalks with a pinch of salt until soft, about 5 minutes. Add the garlic and cook briefly, then add all of the orzo and around one-third of the warm stock. Stir, then turn up the heat and bring to a simmer. Continue to add warm stock, a ladleful at a time until it is absorbed, and the orzo is al dente. This should take around 10–12 minutes. Stir regularly so the orzo doesn't stick to the pan.

When the orzo is ready, lower the heat, stir in the shredded chard leaves, then pop the butter and Parmesan into the pan. Cover with a lid and cook for another minute, or until the chard has wilted. Stir in the chopped dill and zest over the lemon. Taste and adjust seasoning. Turn off the heat but cover the pan to keep warm while you cook your prawns.

Heat a separate frying pan to medium-high, tip in the prawns with their olive oil marinade and fry for around 2 minutes until pink and cooked through.

To serve, split the orzotto between two pasta bowls, top with the prawns, and garnish with a sprig of dill. Chop the zested lemon into wedges and serve alongside to squeeze on top at the table.

Rainbow Chard and Feta Filo Triangles

A slice of spinach and feta pie from my local Greek deli is my weakness. I can't walk past without finding some excuse that I absolutely need to eat one. Making a whole pie is just too much work for a portion for two at home, so an easier way to bring the filo feta spirit is to bake individual triangles. I like using rainbow chard instead of spinach, as the stalks add flavour to the filling. Serve two per person with my Cherry Tomato and Lentil Salad on the side (*see* page 271).

A variety of sautéed greens will work for these triangles, if you opt for spinach instead of chard, add in a small chopped onion as well but bear in mind it will need a little longer to soften.

SERVES 2 (MAKES 4 MEDIUM-SIZED TRIANGLES)
TIME TO PREPARE – 45 MINUTES

olive oil
200g/7oz rainbow chard, leaves stripped and shredded, stalks finely diced
3 spring onions, finely sliced
125g/4½oz feta cheese
2 heaped tbsp finely chopped dill
1 tsp sumac
4 sheets filo pastry
a sprinkle of black or white sesame seeds
salt and pepper

You will need a pastry brush for this recipe

Preheat the oven to 180°C fan/200°C/400°F/gas mark 6.

Heat 1 tablespoon of olive oil, over a low-medium heat in a medium-sized frying pan. Sauté the diced rainbow chard stalks with the spring onions with a pinch of salt for around 5 minutes or until softened. Add the shredded chard leaves and cook until completely wilted. Scrape the mixture into a sieve over a bowl to cool and let any excess moisture drip out. When the chard is no longer steaming hot, transfer to a bowl, crumble in the feta cheese, add the dill and sumac and mix well to combine. Season to taste.

Open out the filo, take one sheet, and keep the remaining pile under a damp tea towel while you work. Lightly brush all over with olive oil, fold in half lengthways and brush the new top with olive oil. With the short edge facing you, visually mark out a square the width of the folded pastry at the bottom. Pile a quarter of the filling into the top right hand triangle of your imaginary square keeping a border around 1cm/½ inch to the right. Fold up the empty bottom-left-hand triangle over the filling and press down the edges to form an enclosed triangle. Keep folding your filled triangle up the sheet to trap in all the filling. Use a slick of oil to stick down the final loose edge. Place on a baking tray, brush the tops with oil, and sprinkle over the sesame seeds. Bake for 20–25 minutes until crisp and deep golden brown all over.

Cool for 5–10 minutes before eating to avoid burning your tongue on the molten feta.

Spinach

LATE SPRING TO SUMMER

Spinach performs the most intriguing magic trick. I don't think there is another example of a vegetable that will do such a convincing disappearing act once wilted. Serious question, where does all that volume go? Whether you add a handful of leaves just before finishing a dish or base a whole dish around it, you will always need more raw spinach than you think.

Loose leaf spinach, or the milder tasting and harvested young baby spinach leaves, are usually stored in air-packed bags as it wilts so quickly. It was only when I started getting a veg box I became more acquainted with perpetual spinach, it has much bigger leaves, and stems which you should remove before cooking. This spinach is hardy for year-round growing (hence the name perpetual) and doesn't bolt, so is popular with allotment growers.

Baby spinach needs no prep and can be cooked or eaten raw in salads. The larger spinach leaves are best cooked. Cooking methods include sauté, steam, stir fry, and braise. Wilt into a saag paneer/aloo, make a gratin, use with ricotta as a filling for cannelloni. Puréed spinach can be used to colour pasta or to go in a soup. You can blend spinach in a smoothie, but if you don't want to, it's fine with me.

To prepare loose leaf or perpetual spinach, wash well and remove the tougher stems. If the leaves are big, shred like chard (*see* page 124). Rather than boil spinach to then use in recipes, I often take the lazy route and pour a kettle of boiling water over it, let it sit for a minute or two until wilted, then drain and squeeze out the excess water using my hands – much less faff with a smaller amount.

Tasty flavour pairings for spinach you'll find in my recipes are; butter, chicken, cumin, garlic, and yoghurt. Others to try include; bacon, chickpeas, feta cheese, ricotta, cream, dill, eggs, fennel, mushrooms, pasta, potatoes, soy sauce, tomatoes, and thyme.

RECIPE IDEA Spinach and eggs go well together. On top of a pizza, on an English muffin with pools of hollandaise sauce, or more simply just scrambled eggs for breakfast.

TOP TIP Frozen pellets of cooked spinach, usually whole leaf, are really useful for when you need cooked spinach in larger quantities, or prefer the ease of throwing a handful straight into a soup, stew, or curry.

Yoghurt with Wilted Spinach and Olives

I'd read that spinach and yoghurt were a good pairing in one of my flavour books, but it wasn't until I tried it myself that I understood why – pairing spinach with yoghurt somehow manages to reduce spinach's metallic taste. There are many recipes for spinach and yoghurt together in Turkish and Iranian cuisines, and this is a riff using flavours that I think go nicely together. Great on toast or warm pitta, with a poached egg on top.

You can use perpetual or baby spinach in this recipe. I would weigh your spinach, after you have removed the large stalks, to make sure you have enough. Or, try with chard.

SERVES 2 | TIME TO PREPARE – 15 MINUTES

150g/5½oz spinach leaves (any variety), washed
1 tbsp butter
4 spring onions, finely sliced
1 garlic clove, finely chopped
½ tsp ground cumin
150g/5½oz Greek yoghurt
a handful of pitted black Kalamata olives, roughly chopped
1 tbsp finely chopped parsley
½ tsp pul biber
salt and pepper

Place the spinach leaves in a heatproof bowl, and submerge under freshly boiled water from the kettle for 1–2 minutes, move the spinach about using tongs to keep everything submerged and to make sure it is wilting. Drain and wring out. Roughly chop and set aside.

In a small frying pan, heat half of the butter over a low-medium heat. Add the spring onions and sauté for 2 minutes until softened. Add the garlic, cumin, a pinch of salt, and the chopped spinach. Stir so everything is combined and cook for another couple of minutes for the spinach to dry out and for the flavours to infuse. Scoop out into a bowl and leave to cool off for around 5 minutes. Stir in the yoghurt, chopped olives, and parsley. Season to taste.

Rinse out the frying pan, and put back on a medium heat. Melt the rest of the butter with the pul biber. Wait for it to start to sizzle, then take off the heat.

If serving as a side dish, plate up the spinach yoghurt into a serving bowl, then drizzle over the spiced butter. If serving on toast, spread the spinach yoghurt over the toast, top with an egg then drizzle over the spiced butter.

Chicken Tagliata with Baby Spinach, Rocket, and Strawberry Salad

Many years ago, my friends booked me an Italian cooking class for my birthday. One of the recipes we learnt was chicken tagliata – a pan-fried piece of flattened chicken, sliced, and dressed with a garlic, chilli, balsamic and olive oil dressing. I have long since lost the recipe from that day, so this is how it floats in my memory. The sweet balsamic dressing is a perfect match for the baby spinach, spicy rocket, and – don't knock it 'til you've tried it – strawberries.

Any salad leaves will work well with this dressing. If strawberries aren't in season, try wedges of figs.

SERVES 2 | TIME TO PREPARE – 15 MINUTES

2 chicken breasts (approx. 175g/6oz each)
olive oil
100g/3½oz mix of baby spinach and rocket leaves
175g/6oz strawberries, stalks removed, sliced in half or quarters depending on size
Parmesan cheese
salt and pepper

FOR THE DRESSING
1 garlic clove, finely chopped or grated
¼ tsp chilli flakes
1 tbsp balsamic vinegar
3 tbsp olive oil

Make your dressing so the flavours have time to mingle. In a small bowl (or jar with a lid) whisk (or shake) together the garlic, chilli flakes, balsamic vinegar, and 3 tablespoons of olive oil. Season with salt and pepper to taste.

Place the chicken breasts in between 2 pieces of clingfilm and use a rolling pin to bash out the chicken to an even thickness of around 1cm/½ inch. Rub each of the chicken breasts with 1 teaspoon of olive oil and season with salt and pepper. Heat up a heavy bottomed frying pan over a medium-high heat and cook the chicken breasts for around 4 minutes each side, flipping once, until browned and cooked through (slice open and check no pink flesh remains). Once cooked, transfer to a chopping board and slice into around 5 pieces on a 45-degree angle. Lightly coat the spinach, rocket, and strawberries with around 2 tablespoons of dressing. Pile up on serving plates and top with the cooked sliced chicken. Drizzle the remainder of the dressing over the top, and use a vegetable peeler to shave over as much Parmesan cheese as you fancy.

Watercress

Peppery watercress is from the mustard side of the brassica family. Perhaps, better described as a long-lost brassica cousin, since watercress couldn't be more different from the weighty cabbages and cauliflowers it's related to. Use as a peppery garnish, a herb substitute, a leaf mixed with others in a salad, or find some tips below for incorporating into a cooked dish. The stalks are juicy and hold a lot of flavour, so these are eaten along with the softer leaves.

Look out for land cress, a similar tasting related leaf.

Watercress can be eaten raw or cooked. If using raw in a salad, mix it with a sweet dressing or with sweet ingredients to balance the flavours. A pesto is a good way to use up a whole raw bag at once, and again just a touch of sweetness helps to calm some of that bitter tang (*see* Watercress Pesto on page 137). When cooked, watercress loses some of its pepperiness, it can be wilted down like spinach, but is better puréed into a soup along with potato.

If your watercress comes bunched rather than pre-washed in a bag, trim off any roots if still attached, and chop the stalks into a manageable size for fork wielding. Discard any yellow or wilting leaves.

Tasty flavour pairings for watercress you'll find in my recipes are; garlic, ginger, lemon, lime, shallots, and salmon. Others to try include; beetroot, blue cheese, chicken, cream, cucumber, endive, potatoes, peas, tomatoes, and walnuts.

RECIPE IDEA Whizz watercress in a food processor with mayonnaise and serve this as a sauce alongside roasted new potatoes, chicken, or fish.

TOP TIP Another mustard family leaf is rocket. Rocket is also peppery, but is far more bitter than watercress. It's a good substitute for watercress, but only when their slightly differing flavour profiles won't totally throw off the balance of a dish, such as in a mixed salad.

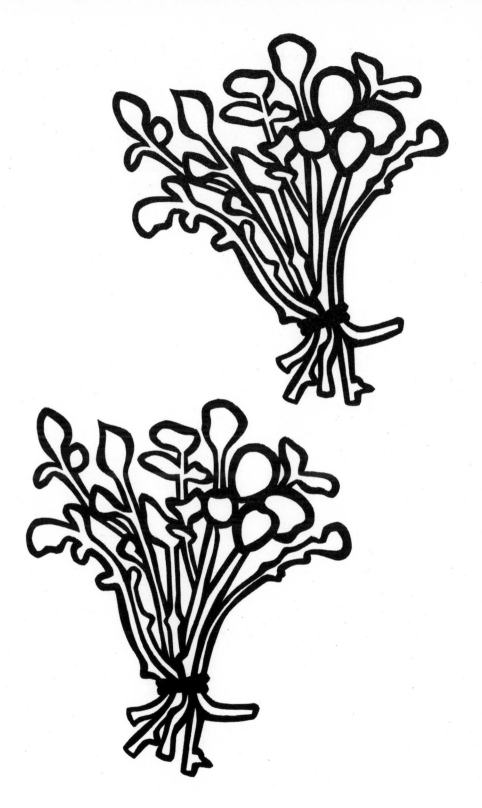

Poached Salmon with Watercress and Coconut Milk Sauce

Creamy watercress sauce is a classic accompaniment to fish. I use coconut milk for the base of my creamy sauce and spike it with ginger and lime for something a bit unexpected. Blitzed watercress is stirred in at the last minute to help keep its vibrant green colour. Keep the skin on the salmon while it's poaching in the coconut milk, as it helps hold the shape of the fish. Serve the salmon and sauce with the traditional spring accompaniment of boiled new potatoes, or steamed basmati rice, plus some vibrant al dente green beans or asparagus on the side.

Instead of watercress, a handful of wild garlic, or herby coriander could be blitzed into the sauce.

SERVES 2 | TIME TO PREPARE – 20 MINUTES

85g/3oz watercress
1 tbsp rapeseed oil
1 banana shallot, finely chopped
2 garlic cloves, finely chopped
a thumb-tip sized piece of ginger (approx. 5g/⅛oz), peeled and finely chopped
1 x 200ml/7fl oz can coconut milk
2 x 125g/4½oz salmon tail fillets
juice of 1 lime
a pinch of sugar
salt and pepper

Keep a few sprigs of watercress back for garnish and blitz the rest in a food processor until finely chopped. You may need to scrape down the sides. Set aside.

Heat the rapeseed oil in a medium-sized deep frying pan you have a lid for over a medium heat. Sauté the chopped shallots with a pinch of salt for 3–4 minutes until starting to soften, add the garlic and ginger and cook for one minute more. Pour in the coconut milk and bring to a bubble.

Pat dry the salmon with kitchen paper, then season the flesh with salt and pepper. Lower skin-side down into the coconut milk sauce, then turn down the heat to a gentle simmer. Cover the pan with a lid, and cook for around 8 minutes, or until the salmon is opaque and will easily flake at the thickest part. Lift the poached salmon out of the coconut sauce and stir in the chopped watercress. Squeeze in the lime juice and a pinch of sugar, and season to taste. Pop the salmon back into the sauce and serve straight away.

Watercress Pesto

Pesto isn't just a recipe for basil – many other leaves can be spun into pesto and this is a great way to use them up if they're just past their best for a fresh salad. I make this watercress pesto without cheese, as I find it has more versatility. One can think of a thousand ways to utilize pesto; spread on crostini, stirred through hot or cold pasta. There are many other ideas in this book because I just can't get enough of it.

This watercress pesto recipe also works with rocket. Although, since rocket isn't as juicy as watercress, use a smaller amount (50g/1¾oz) for the same amount of oil. You may need to add more sugar than for watercress, as rocket is way more bitter.

MAKES APPROX. 200ML/7FL OZ OF PESTO
TIME TO PREPARE – 10 MINUTES

50g/1¾oz almonds
1 garlic clove, finely chopped
85g/3oz watercress
8 tbsp (120ml/4fl oz) olive oil
zest and juice of 1 lemon
caster sugar or honey, to taste
salt

Toast the nuts in a medium-hot dry frying pan, for 1–2 minutes, tossing frequently, until golden brown. Remove from the pan immediately to prevent them from cooking in the residual heat of the pan.

Blitz your toasted nuts and garlic together in a food processor until broken down into crumbs. Add your watercress and blitz briefly to break down, then steadily pour in the oil with the motor running. Add the lemon zest, juice and blitz again. Season to taste with salt and a little sugar to balance any bitterness of the leaves.

If not using straight away, transfer to a jar and top with olive oil to keep any green submerged. It will keep for around 1 week in the fridge. You can also freeze into small portions in ice cube trays.

Wild Garlic

SPRING

In early spring, British woodlands are carpeted with this wild green leafy allium that honks like garlic. Its garlic flavour is less pungent than the cloves, so you can safely stir a large handful into a dish without losing all your friends. Wild garlic is abundant in the countryside, but only forage if you're sure what you're picking, and never take more than you need. I'm rather sceptical about foraging from patches in city parks, where the risk of it being contaminated by passing dogs is high. Due to its popularity, many farmers' market or veg box suppliers now source dog contamination free wild garlic en masse for sale.

To cook wild garlic, you can gently wilt into the final moments of a dish, use it to infuse an olive oil, or add a handful into a blended soup or purée. It makes an excellent herb substitute offering both colour and flavour to a variety of raw chopped or blended sauces – what about a wild garlic butter, Chimichurri (*see* page 141), chermoula, pesto, or salsa verde?

To prepare wild garlic, rinse and dry the leaves. Leave the leaves whole, roughly chop in chunks or finely shred.

Wild garlic flowers appear towards the end of its season – these can be eaten too.

Tasty flavour pairings for wild garlic you'll find in my recipes are; butter, chicken, and mushrooms. Others to try include; asparagus, carrots, cream, fish, new potatoes, and pasta.

RECIPE IDEA Add a handful of wild garlic leaves to a pea purée, blitz, then stir through cooked risotto for a vibrant green springtime dish.

TOP TIP Three-cornered leek is a similar tasting wild plant and can be used as a substitute for wild garlic.

Wild Garlic and Leek Butter Beans with Sumac Roasted Chicken Legs

In this dish the wild garlic is treated like a big bunch of herbs, shredded and folded through the buttery creamy beans in their last minutes of cooking to add a strong spring allium hit. Vegetarians, don't skip past this recipe! The chicken and beans are cooked separately, so the wild garlic and leek butter beans are also brilliant on their own or with a vegetable 'steak'.

Try replacing the leek with onions, or the wild garlic with other soft herbs, baby spinach or chard. For the same garlic intensity, increase the quantity of garlic in the bean base.

SERVES 2 | TIME TO PREPARE – 45 MINUTES

2 skin-on chicken legs
olive oil
2 tsp sumac

FOR THE BEANS
1 tbsp butter
1 leek, finely sliced
1 garlic clove, finely chopped
1 x 400g/14oz can butter beans, rinsed and drained
125ml/4fl oz chicken or vegetable stock
25g/1oz wild garlic leaves, stalks removed and shredded
1 tbsp crème fraîche
lemon juice
salt and pepper

Preheat the oven to 200°C fan/220°C/425°F/gas mark 7. Rub the chicken legs all over with olive oil, then place in a baking dish. Season with salt and pepper and sprinkle 1 teaspoon of sumac over each leg. Roast for 40 minutes, until the chicken juices run clear and the flesh is cooked through at the deepest part of the thigh. When the chicken has 15 minutes left, start on the beans.

Melt the butter over a low-medium heat in a wide, deep, medium-sized frying pan. Sauté the leeks with a pinch of salt for around 10 minutes, until completely softened but not browned. Stir in the garlic and beans, and cook briefly, then pour in the stock. Turn up the heat and simmer for 5 minutes, until the beans have warmed through and the starch from the beans has thickened the stock so it's nice and creamy. Stir in the wild garlic to wilt, then add crème fraîche. Season to taste with salt, pepper, and a little lemon juice to lift. Serve the beans in wide bowls with the chicken legs sitting on top.

Wild Garlic Chimichurri with Portobello Mushroom 'Steaks'

As a lover of all things herbs, and herb sauces, chimichurri is up there with the best. It's an Argentinian condiment for steak, characteristically made with parsley and the strong tang of red wine vinegar. For average weeknight cooking I'm much more likely to be found cooking a mushroom than a steak, so here's my method for cooking them on a grill pan to give a steak-like quality. The wild garlic chimichurri is the perfect companion. Serve with oven chips as a treat or with steamed green beans.

For other times of the year, replace the wild garlic with extra parsley.

SERVES 2 | TIME TO PREPARE – 15 MINUTES

10g/¼oz (approx. 5 leaves) wild garlic, stalks removed
1 heaped tbsp finely chopped parsley
½ tsp dried oregano
a pinch of chilli flakes
1 tbsp red wine vinegar
2½ tbsp olive oil

FOR THE MUSHROOM 'STEAKS'
olive oil
2 tbsp balsamic vinegar
4 large Portobello or large flat mushrooms (approx. 85g/3oz per mushroom), stalks popped out
salt and pepper

Finely chop the wild garlic and parsley together on a chopping board. Transfer to a small bowl, add the dried oregano and chilli, vinegar, and olive oil, and stir to combine. The texture should be chunky, with the herbs swimming in the oil. Season to taste with salt and pepper.

Heat a griddle pan to a medium-high heat. On a large plate, pour 2 tablespoons of olive oil and 2 tablespoons of balsamic vinegar. Swish the mushroom caps into the mix, then flip over and swish again. When the griddle pan is hot, cook the mushrooms cap-side down for a couple of minutes, then flip over. Cook for around 6–8 minutes total, flipping again as necessary, until deep golden brown, and the mushrooms have stopped releasing any excess water. Remove from the pan and rest on kitchen paper for a few moments to collect any remaining moisture. Season with salt and pepper, and then plate up with the chimichurri drizzled over the top.

PODS

A chapter of green legume pods and their seeds. Some pods are eaten whole, whilst others require the services of a pod shelling team. Take your pick from blankety broad beans, crisp green beans, or the popular, yet humble, sweet garden peas often found in the freezer section.

Broad Beans
144 – 149

Green Beans
150 – 155

Peas
156 – 161

Broad Beans

SUMMER TO EARLY AUTUMN, FROZEN AVAILABLE YEAR ROUND

"Broad beans sleeping in their blankety beds" is a line taken from a song about vegetables I learnt at school and it comes back as an annoying earworm that I just can't shake every broad bean season. Although I do agree that a blankety bed is the perfect way to describe a broad bean pod, with its soft velvety lining. Once you've opened up a broad bean pod, you'll find the pale green beans cozying inside. All of these beans have a skin which protects the vibrant green bean underneath. Taking the beans out of their jackets, then removing this skin for eating is called double-podding. I deem it a necessity.

Broad beans are also called fava beans, and when dried look much like a butter bean. Dried fava beans are the main ingredient in Egyptian falafel. At the start of the season younger broad beans are small and tender, and can be eaten raw. As the bean season develops the beans get larger, and with it thicker skins – these need to be cooked and double-podded. Once you've blanched and double-podded, broad beans can be added to salads, smashed and served on toast, or stirred through rice dishes, such as risotto or my Broad Bean, Chorizo and Pepper Rice (*see* page 146). They can also be blended into a hummus substitute, but you'd need a double-podding team to help you prepare enough beans to blend first.

Preparing broad beans is a fiddly task, best done when not in a rush so it can be a mindful experience. Unzip a broad bean pod by pulling apart along its side seam, then run a thumb along the furry inside, to pop out the beans. If you want to double-pod you'll need to blanch the beans first. Blanch for 2–3 minutes, cool, then gently pull apart the skin along the seam, and pop the vibrant green bean out. It might split into two halves, which is absolutely fine. Zero waste heroes will get you battering, deep frying and eating the pods too. I'm yet to be convinced.

Tasty flavour pairings for broad beans you'll find in my recipes are; goat's cheese, garlic, peas, and prosciutto. Others to try include; ricotta cheese, fish, lamb, mint, parsley, pasta, sage, tomatoes, and yoghurt.

RECIPE IDEA Make a salsa from mixing double-podded broad beans with finely chopped mint, olive oil, and lemon juice. Serve with lamb or salmon.

TOP TIP Whilst in Italy over Easter, I discovered that in springtime young broad bean pods are served straight to the table to eat raw alongside a plate of salami as a pre-dinner snack. Guests are invited to do their own podding.

Broad Bean, Chorizo, and Pepper Rice

Paella, Pilaf, Jollof, and Jambalaya are all great examples of centrepiece rice dishes. For all of these, raw rice is added to an aromatic base, then cooked by absorption in just the right amount of liquid. I use this method for my broad bean rice dish, and with the inclusion of chorizo, smoked paprika, and peppers, is loosely inspired by Spanish flavours. Serve as is, or with a few leaves on the side.

For a vegetarian version, skip the chorizo and use 1 tablespoon of olive oil to soften the sofrito (onion, celery, pepper). You may want to increase the beans. Broad beans can be substituted for cooked garden peas or other trimmed -down-to-size green beans.

SERVES 2 | TIME TO PREPARE – 25 MINUTES

500g/1lb 2oz broad beans (weight in the pod) or 125g/4½oz frozen broad beans
90g/3¼oz cooking chorizo, diced
1 red onion, finely diced
1 celery stick, finely diced
1 red pepper, finely diced
1 garlic clove, finely chopped
1 tsp dried oregano
½ tsp hot smoked paprika, or ½ tsp smoked paprika plus a pinch of cayenne pepper
150g/5½oz basmati or long grain rice, rinsed
4 tbsp white wine
300ml/10fl oz hot chicken or vegetable stock
2 tbsp finely chopped parsley
juice of 1 lemon, to taste
salt and pepper

If using fresh broad beans, pod them from their velvety jackets, you should end up with around 125g/4½oz beans. Frozen broad beans can be cooked straight from the freezer. Bring a small saucepan of salted water to boil and blanch the broad beans for 2–3 minutes or until tender enough for their skins to be slipped off. Drain and refresh under a cold tap until cool to the touch and set aside.

Heat a medium-large wide frying pan that you have a lid for over a medium heat and add the diced chorizo. Cook for around 4 minutes until plenty of red oil has released and the chorizo is starting to brown. Scoop out the chorizo leaving the oil in the pan (around 1 tablespoon) and put back on to a low-medium heat. Add the chopped red onion, celery, and pepper with a pinch of salt, and sauté for 8–10 minutes until completely softened. Add the garlic, oregano, smoked paprika, and pop the chorizo back in. Stir well, then add the rice and splash in the wine. Wait until the wine has almost evaporated then pour in the hot stock. Bring to the boil, turn to a very low simmer, cover, and cook for 10–12 minutes or until the rice is tender and cooked through. Check on it occasionally to make sure it hasn't dried out. Add more water if necessary – if on a low enough heat you shouldn't need to.

While the rice cooks, use the time to slip the broad beans from their skins.

When the rice is tender, stir in the double-podded broad beans and the parsley. Season to taste with salt, pepper, and add lemon juice to lift, then serve straight away.

Broad Bean, Goat's Cheese, and Prosciutto 'Quesadilla'

Cooked in a tortilla wrap like a Mexican quesadilla but with a stuffing that is more suited to an Italian piadina – is it just a cheese toastie with another name? Sprinkle pops of double-podded broad beans and sliced spring onions, with soft goat's cheese, prosciutto, and rocket inside a tortilla and cook for a tasty, but quick-to-prepare, bite. Quesadillas are always a popular thing to make in my kids' cooking classes, although as you'll find out, they're great fun for adults too. Serve with some dressed salad leaves on the side for a light meal.

As an alternative, you can swap the broad beans for cooked peas.

SERVES 2 | TIME TO PREPARE – 15 MINUTES

400g/14oz broad beans (weight in the pod) or 100g/3½oz frozen broad beans
2 large flour tortillas
85g/3oz soft spreadable goat's cheese
4 spring onions, thinly sliced
4 slices of prosciutto crudo
a handful of rocket
olive oil
salt and pepper

Bring a small saucepan of salted water to the boil and blanch the broad beans for 2–3 minutes until soft enough for their skins to be slipped off. Drain and refresh under a cold tap until cool to the touch. Slip the broad beans from their skins.

Place a tortilla on your chopping board and spread half of the goat's cheese all over the top. Using half of each ingredient over one half of the tortilla, scatter the double-podded broad beans, sliced spring onions, prosciutto, and rocket. Season with salt and black pepper and drizzle over a little olive oil. Fold the tortilla in half to enclose the filling and form a semicircle. Repeat with the second tortilla.

Heat an appropriately sized frying pan over a medium-high heat (no oil required). Carefully place the quesadilla in the hot pan and cook for around 60–90 seconds, until the underside has started to brown. Using a spatula, flip the quesadilla over and cook for another 60–90 seconds on the other side. Slide out of the pan onto a chopping board and slice into thirds. Cook the second quesadilla in the same way and serve straight away.

Taking the beans out of their jackets, then removing this skin for eating is called double-podding. I deem it a necessity... Preparing broad beans is a fiddly task, best done when not in a rush so it can be a mindful experience.

Green Beans

SUMMER TO EARLY AUTUMN

No podding required this time because the pod is the vegetable. I've popped a couple of crisp and crunchy beans together here, because even though they have varying shapes, sizes, and surface areas for sauces to cling to, in the recipes that follow, they can be swapped around.

French, bobby, and fine are all types of skinny finger-sized green beans (sometimes for ease just called green beans). Flat beans, also called stringless or Helda beans, are the stringless varieties of the longer runner bean. If you're adverse to stringy bits, as I am, then choose these.

Green beans need cooking and turn out best when blanched in salted water until just al dente. I usually shock them in cold water once cooked to lock in their colour, especially if they are destined for a cold salad. All these beans can be blistered in a hot griddle pan or roasted in the oven. You'll also find recipes to braise them in a slow cooked Mediterranean-style tomato stew, totally delicious of course, but don't expect them to stay vibrantly green.

All types of green beans need to be topped and tailed before cooking. Line a small number up in a row and cut together to save time. Whether the beans are cooked whole or cut down to size is up to you (and the recipe). The only other knife skill you'll be judged on is your ability to slice flat beans on an angle and into even-sized pieces. That rhombus shape you learnt about in primary school has finally landed a use! The angles are purely for aesthetic reasons, but the regular sizes ensure the beans will cook evenly.

Tasty flavour pairings for green beans you'll find in my recipes include; basil, Parmesan, chilli, coriander, garlic, ginger, lemon, and mint. Others to try include; almonds, cumin, dill, tarragon, and tomatoes.

RECIPE IDEA Blanch green beans, and toss with olive oil, pine nuts, and a few chopped tomatoes for an easy side dish.

TOP TIP Frozen green beans can be eaten out of season. They are useful for stews or to serve with pasta but will never have the crispness of fresh.

Gnocchi with Green Beans, Fresh Basil Pesto, and Lemon Breadcrumbs

Pesto with trofie pasta, green beans, and potatoes is one of the regional dishes of Italy's Liguria region. It's a delicious way to enjoy green beans so, keen to include it, I asked my Ligurian-residing Welsh uncle, Wyn, for his pesto recipe. He wasn't very precise with the quantities, but very particular on the ingredients – Ligurian basil, half pecorino, half Parmesan, garlic, pine nuts, salt, and olive oil. No lemon. For authenticity, it should be made in a pestle and mortar, and it should be creamy in texture. His preference is to make large batches in a blender. What you are able to do in your home kitchen is up to you. I'm a recent convert to gnocchi, which I use instead of potatoes and hard to find trofie. Alone, I find gnocchi a bit claggy, so crispy breadcrumbs help give it texture.

Instead of the green beans, you can try flat beans, peas, or asparagus.

SERVES 2 | TIME TO PREPARE – 30 MINUTES

FOR THE PESTO
1 tbsp toasted pine nuts
1 large garlic clove, finely chopped
30g/1oz basil, stalks removed
6 tbsp olive oil
2 tbsp finely grated pecorino cheese
2 tbsp finely grated Parmesan cheese
salt

FOR THE LEMONY BREADCRUMBS
2 tbsp olive oil
50g/1¾oz coarse breadcrumbs or day-old bread, blitzed into breadcrumbs using a food processor
zest of 1 lemon

FOR THE DISH
400g/14oz fresh gnocchi
175g/6oz green beans, topped and tailed, and sliced into 2 shorter pieces

First make the pesto. In a pestle and mortar, break down the toasted pine nuts and garlic, with a pinch of salt, into a paste. Add in the basil and break that down, then keep bashing it towards a paste while you pour in the oil and add the cheese. If using a blender or food processor, blitz everything together in stages as you would do by hand. Season to taste and set aside.

Put a saucepan of salted water on to boil, in preparation for the gnocchi and green beans.

Move on to your lemony breadcrumbs. Heat 2 tablespoons of olive oil in a frying pan over a medium-high heat. Cook the breadcrumbs for 5–6 minutes, until starting to go golden, stirring intermittently so they don't stick (if you stir too much they won't crisp up) – adjust the heat as necessary. Zest over the entire skin of the lemon. Tip out the crumbs onto a piece of kitchen paper and set aside.

Add both the gnocchi and green beans to the boiling water and cook for 2–3 minutes, until the beans are al dente and the gnocchi floats. When ready, drain the gnocchi and beans, keeping back half a cup of the pasta water. Add the gnocchi and beans back into the empty saucepan with 2 large dollops of pesto and just enough pasta water to create a sauce to surround the ingredients. Toss well and serve immediately with the lemony breadcrumbs scattered over the top.

There may be a little pesto left – transfer to a jar, top with oil to keep the basil covered, and store in the fridge for about a week.

Green Bean, Aubergine, and Halloumi Sweet Chilli Tray Bake

Roasting green beans, as an alternative to blanching, produces a tasty blistered skin. I combine them with quarters of aubergine and slices of halloumi, tossed with sweet chilli sauce for a quick-to-put-together one-tray supper. Nigella seeds give an oniony tang. Serve with steamed bulgur wheat, rice, or flatbreads on the side.

You can use any green beans in this recipe, larger flat beans will need to be cut down to bite-sized pieces. Leave French green beans whole.

SERVES 2 | TIME TO PREPARE – 45 MINUTES

1 aubergine, sliced through the root into quarters
light olive oil
3 tbsp sweet chilli sauce
juice of 1 lime
250g/9oz green beans, top and tailed
225g/8oz block of halloumi cheese, sliced widthways into 6 rectangles
1 tsp nigella seeds
salt

Preheat the oven to 200°C fan/220°C/425°F/gas mark 7.

Use a baking dish big enough to take the beans and aubergine quarters snuggly in one layer, but start with just the aubergine quarters in the dish. Toss with 1 tablespoon of oil, season with salt, and roast for 20 minutes.

Meanwhile, in a medium-sized bowl, mix together the sweet chilli sauce, 1 tablespoon of oil, the lime juice, and season with a pinch of salt. Toss the green beans and halloumi into the sauce until well coated.

When the aubergine has had 20 minutes, pull the baking dish out of the oven and reduce the oven temperature to 180°C fan/200°C/400°F/gas mark 6. Top the aubergines with the marinated green beans, halloumi, and any remaining marinade. Pop back into the oven for 15–18 minutes, until the beans and halloumi have both charred a little. Garnish with the nigella seeds and serve.

Flat Bean, Radish, and Cannellini Salad with Miso Dressing

Blanched and shocked flat beans and peas combine with raw crunchy radishes, canned soft cannellini beans, and a gingery sweet miso dressing in this quick summer salad. I specifically use light olive oil in my dressing, as I don't want extra-virgin olive oil's strong flavour fighting with the miso paste. Serve as a side dish; I really enjoy this salad with tinned tuna and some salad leaves.

A versatile salad that will work with all varieties of peas and green beans.

SERVES 2 AS A GENEROUS SIDE | TIME TO PREPARE – 10 MINUTES

200g/7oz flat beans, topped and tailed and sliced into 2–3cm/¾–1 inch pieces
85g/3oz frozen peas or petit pois
1 x 400g/14oz can cannellini beans, drained and rinsed
85g/3oz radishes, topped and tailed and thinly sliced
1 tbsp finely chopped coriander, plus a few extra sprigs for garnish
½ tbsp finely chopped mint
salt and pepper

FOR THE DRESSING
½ tbsp white miso paste
1 tsp honey or maple syrup
½ tsp finely grated fresh ginger
1 tbsp rice vinegar
2 tbsp light olive oil

Blanch the flat beans in salted boiling water for 2–3 minutes until just al dente, adding the peas for the final minute. Drain and refresh under cold water, then shake dry.

Place the white miso, honey, ginger, and rice vinegar in a small bowl, and stir together until smooth. Whisk in the oil until the dressing is creamy and emulsified. Don't season yet, as miso pastes are varyingly salty, it's better to adjust seasoning when the whole salad has been tossed together.

In a medium-sized bowl, mix together the peas, flat beans, and cannellini beans with the chopped radishes. Pour over the dressing and stir through the chopped herbs. Season to taste with salt and pepper. Transfer to a serving dish and garnish with a few coriander sprigs.

Peas

SUMMER

Plump green pods of peas are available in just a small window each summer, but the pea is a year-round constant in our lives because it freezes so well. Tell me someone who doesn't have a bag of peas in the freezer as a backup vegetable? Available for those times when the veg drawer is bare, or to use as an emergency ice-pack for a sprained ankle. Peas' natural sugars turn to starch after picking, so the turnaround from harvesting through podding to freezing is lightning quick. This ensures that the peas that end up on our plates are as fresh, sweet, and green as they can be.

French for small peas, petit pois are picked when younger and have a sweeter flavour, you'll also find these in the freezer section. Snow peas, mange tout, and sugar snap peas are a little different in that you cook and eat the pod as the vegetable.

Young, tender, fresh peas can be eaten raw, but peas are usually cooked before eating. Blanch until just tender then shock to keep the vibrant green colour. Shocking is particularly important if going into a cold dish. Fresh peas will take a little longer to blanch than frozen. Peas can be blended smoothly for soups and purées, or blitzed, keeping a little texture for a hummus-style dip you can also spread on toast. Peas can be added to frittatas, salads, or curries, served with pasta or risotto, or just with fish fingers like it's the 1990s.

If using fresh peas, you'll first need to pop them out of their pods. Use your fingers to press the pods open down the seam, and your thumb to slide the peas out. Leafy green tendrils of pea shoots are the first edible leaves from a germinated pea. You can often find these in the chiller cabinet alongside other bagged salads, but it's really easy and satisfying to grow your own. To do this, find two old plastic mushroom trays. Poke some drainage holes in one and stack inside the other. Soak a handful of marrowfat peas overnight, drain and densely sow in one inch of compost, then cover with another thin layer. Place on a warm windowsill and water regularly to keep the soil moist. In two weeks you'll have enough shoots to use as a garnish or toss into a salad.

Tasty flavour pairings for peas you'll find in my recipes are; asparagus, butter, broad beans, garlic, chilli, lemon, mint, parsley, and pancetta. Others to try include; basil, dill, cream, fish, leeks, mustard, pasta, and spinach.

RECIPE IDEA A simple dip – blend 400g/14oz defrosted peas with 120ml/4fl oz olive oil and a clove of garlic until smooth. Season with Dijon mustard, salt, and lemon juice.

TOP TIP
If using small quantities of frozen peas, to avoid over
cooking, defrost in freshly boiled water, then drain and
add straight into a recipe instead of blanching.

Pea Purée with Poached Eggs, Sizzling Pul Biber Butter, and Pea Shoots

I usually serve this pea purée with fish, but while staring into a fridge of leftovers I had an inspired idea to use it as a substitute for the creamy yoghurt element of Turkish eggs (or eggs Çilbir). Turkish eggs is a dish of poached eggs served on top of a creamy garlic yoghurt base, finished with sizzling warming pul biber butter. I love it with yoghurt, but think it works so well with the sweet creamy pea purée. If making four poached eggs at once is too tricky, go for Six-Minute Eggs instead (*see* page 40). Serve with flatbreads or sourdough toast for dunking.

Double-podded broad beans also make a tasty purée, although that's a lot of work for just 250g/9oz, so probably best to stick with frozen peas.

SERVES 2 | TIME TO PREPARE – 30 MINUTES

FOR THE PURÉE
1 tbsp olive oil
1 banana shallot, finely chopped
1 celery stick, finely chopped
2 garlic cloves, finely chopped
250g/9oz frozen peas
100ml/3½fl oz whole milk
butter, to taste
salt and pepper

FOR THE PUL BIBER BUTTER
2 tbsp butter
½ tsp pul biber (or substitute with ¼ tsp chilli flakes)

TO SERVE
1 tbsp white wine or cider vinegar
4 eggs
a handful of pea shoots

First make your purée. Add 1 tablespoon of olive oil to a medium-sized saucepan over a low-medium heat. Sauté the shallot and celery with a pinch of salt for around 5 minutes until starting to soften. Add the garlic and cook briefly, then add the frozen peas and milk. Turn up the heat, cover, and cook for 4–5 minutes until the peas are completely soft. Blend into a silky smooth purée using a handheld or high-speed blender. Return the purée to the saucepan, season to taste with salt, pepper, and a little knob of butter for richness. Keep on a very low heat while you finish the dish.

Put on a saucepan of water to simmer for the eggs, and while you wait, make the pul biber butter. Melt the butter and pul biber together in a small pan over medium heat. Wait for it to start to sizzle, then take off the heat and set aside.

Now it's time to poach the eggs. Unless your pan is large and your skills top notch, cook two at a time. Add 1 tablespoon of vinegar to the saucepan of simmering water. Turn the heat down to barely a bubble. Crack an egg into a ramekin, then bring the ramekin to the surface of the water and gently tip in. Wait for the whites to start to coagulate around the yolk, then add the second egg into the water. Leave to poach for 3–4 minutes until the whites have set. Use a slotted spoon to lift the egg out of the water and to check if it is done lightly press down on the yolk. It should feel like the fattiest part of your cheek. If so, drain on a piece of kitchen paper. Repeat with your remaining two eggs.

To plate up, divide the purée between two pasta bowls. Top each with two eggs, pour over the flavoured butter, and season the top of the eggs. Garnish with the pea shoots.

Peas, Beans, or other Greens
with Mint and Chilli Dressing

Only greens allowed for this platter of crisp blanched pods with a
refreshing mint and chilli dressing. A recipe for summer days when you're
too hot and bothered to do anything else. Serve as a simple summer side
for anything rich, or on its own with a torn ball of mozzarella or burrata,
and some really good bread – that'll do nicely thank you very much.

This recipe gives you flexibility to use the whole family of pods, as well as
asparagus when their seasons collide.

SERVES 2–3 AS A SIDE | TIME TO PREPARE – 15 MINUTES

250g/9oz total of at least 2 green vegetables from the pod family (e.g. green beans,
    flat beans, broad beans, sugar snap peas, mange tout, or asparagus)
200g/7oz frozen peas or petit pois
salt and pepper

FOR THE DRESSING
1 lemon
5 tbsp olive oil plus extra for drizzling
1 small garlic clove, finely chopped
¼ tsp chilli flakes
1 tbsp finely chopped mint, plus a handful of extra leaves left whole, to garnish

Prepare your beans or other greens. Top and tail as required, up to you
whether to keep them whole or chop into smaller bite-sized pieces.

Bring a large saucepan of salted water to the boil. Blanch the greens for
around 3 minutes until just al dente, add the peas for the final minute.
Drain and refresh under cold water until completely cool to the touch, shake
off any water still clinging to them, or spread out on a clean tea towel to dry.

Zest the lemon and keep to one side, then juice. Place the olive oil, lemon
juice, chopped garlic, chilli flakes, and finely chopped mint into a small bowl
or jam jar and whisk or shake everything together until combined. Season
with salt and pepper. The best way to check the flavour and seasoning is by
dipping in one of your cooked green vegetables and tasting that. It will taste
quite lemony on its own but the vegetables will mute that.

Spread the cooled vegetables across a serving platter, season the top with a
little salt (tear over the burrata or mozzarella now, if using), and drizzle over as
much of the dressing as you think the veggies require. Finish with the reserved
lemon zest, a drizzle of olive oil, and the remaining whole mint leaves.

Peas' natural sugars turn to starch after picking, so the turnaround from harvesting through podding to freezing is lightning quick. This ensures that the peas that end up on our plates are as fresh, sweet and green as they can be.

ROOTS

The underground gang; beetroot, carrot,
celeriac, Jerusalem artichoke, potatoes,
swede, and sweet potato. Whether roasted
or puréed for soups, the oranges, pinks,
reds, and creamy white roots of this
chapter are here to brighten up your
plates, from the depths of winter to
lighter summer days.

Beetroot

SUMMER TO EARLY WINTER

Beetroot is often described as 'earthy' which is not the word I'd choose for its PR campaign, instead I'd opt for 'sweet' or highlight its incredible pink colour which will liven up any dull looking plate. I think some are put off beetroot because they have only ever eaten it pre-boiled from a vacuum pack or from an overly astringent jar of pickles. However, I promise there is a way to convert the beetroot sceptics and that's by careful consideration of selection and preparation.

Beyond the round, deep-maroon skinned bulbs, there are also yellow and orange varieties, and the brilliantly named candy striped beetroot, which has a pale pink outer skin and a white flesh with circular pale pink candy stripes inside – its official name is Chioggia. The yellow and candy beetroots are less earthy than the darker bulbs, so if you are new to beetroot, I suggest you start your beetroot journey here.

Beetroot can be boiled or steamed but I think that roasting brings out the best flavour. Roast as you would any other root veg. For a more refined affair, I like to steam roast (*see* Glazed Beetroot on page 168 for instructions). Once cooked, beetroot can be blended. Try blitzing a few chunks into a basic chickpea hummus, or blending with tahini and water into a vibrant fuchsia-pink smooth dressing for a cooked grain-based salad. Beetroot can also be grated and eaten raw. Add to coleslaw or mix with grated carrot for a salad.

Beetroot peel can be eaten but the bulbs will need a good scrub first. Leave the peel on if roasting in chunks or cubes. If steam roasting or steaming, beetroot can be peeled after cooking, you should be able to just rub it off. Gloves are a good idea unless you want pink hands for the next few days.

Beetroot leaves and their stems are edible. Stems can be cooked or pickled. If in good enough nick, treat the leaves like a leafy green or chard. You'll find some recipes for these in the Leaves chapter (*see* page 110).

Tasty flavour pairings for beetroot you'll find in my recipes are; butter, goat's cheese, ricotta, endive, orange, parsley, and honey. Others to try include; apple, dill, carrots, blue cheese, cumin, fennel, radish, rocket, tarragon, walnut, watercress, and yoghurt.

RECIPE IDEA Steam roast beetroot whole in foil, peel and slice thinly into rounds, and dress with olive oil and lemon juice in a 2:1 ratio. Serve 'carpaccio' style with segments of orange or grapefruit and sprigs of watercress.

Beetroot, Onion, and Goat's Cheese Galette

If you find the idea of perfecting the pastry on a quiche too overwhelming, then you'll be much happier, as I am, to get to know the free-form galette instead. The filling is made from grated raw beetroot which not only cooks quicker than you might expect, but also turns the onions pink. Serve with a simple leafy side salad.

This recipe will also work with grated carrot. Replace the goat's cheese with feta and add coriander seeds instead of mustard and cumin to change the flavour profile.

SERVES 2
TIME TO PREPARE – 1 HOUR, PLUS COOLING

FOR THE SHORTCRUST PASTRY
120g/4½oz plain flour
½ tsp salt
60g/2¼oz fridge cold butter, diced into cubes
1–2 tbsp ice cold water
1 egg, lightly whisked

FOR THE FILLING
1 tbsp olive oil
1 large onion, finely sliced
1 garlic clove, finely chopped
1 tsp black mustard seeds
½ tsp cumin seeds
3 sprigs of thyme, leaves stripped
250g/9oz beetroot, peeled and grated
2 tsp butter
60g/1¾oz goat's cheese with rind, cut into 5–6 rounds
a drizzle of honey
salt and pepper

First make the pastry. Place the flour and salt into a bowl and add the diced butter. Cut the fat into the flour with a knife and then use your fingertips to gently rub the butter into the flour until crumb-like. Add the ice cold water a little at a time as needed to gently bring the mix together into a smooth dough. Wrap the pastry in clingfilm and chill in the fridge for at least 20 minutes.

While the pastry is chilling, make the filling. Heat 1 tablespoon of olive oil in a medium-sized frying pan over a low-medium heat. Sauté the onions with a pinch of salt for 10 minutes, until softened but not crispy. Stir in the garlic, mustard and cumin seeds, thyme leaves, and grated beetroot. Cook for another 10 minutes, until the beetroot has softened, most of the water has evaporated and everything is pink. Stir regularly to avoid sticking. Add the butter, stir to melt, and season to taste. Set aside to cool.

Preheat the oven to 180°C fan/200°C/400°F/gas mark 6.

Roll out the pastry on top of a piece of parchment paper in an oval shape to 3mm/⅛ inch thickness. Pile in the beetroot filling leaving a 3cm/1¼ inch gap around the edge. Layer the goat's cheese rounds over the beetroot mix, then using the parchment to help you, fold the exposed pastry edges inwards and slightly over the beetroot filling to form the rustic crust. Glaze the exposed pastry with whisked egg. Transfer the galette, along with the parchment paper to a suitably sized baking tray. Bake for 25–30 minutes until the pastry and the goat's cheese are golden brown. Once baked, drizzle over honey and cool on the tray for 10 or so minutes before serving.

Glazed Beetroot with Whipped Ricotta, Pink Leaves, and Orange

Slow roasted beetroot, glazed with a sweet and sour dressing, sits on top of a creamy whipped ricotta, crisp pink salad leaves, and sweet orange for a vibrant sharing plate. The roasting and glazing method will work with all colour varieties of beetroot, but if mixing, it's a good idea to both roast and glaze them separately to avoid the deep maroon of the regular beetroot bleeding out on the others.

Swap beetroot with roasted carrots – give them 30–40 minutes in the oven.

SERVES 2 AS A MAIN | TIME TO PREPARE – 1 HOUR 45 MINUTES

500g/1lb 2oz beetroot – any variety, scrubbed clean, stalks removed
olive oil
3 tbsp apple cider vinegar
1 tbsp maple or golden syrup
1 pink chicory, leaves separated (or a handful of radicchio leaves)
2 oranges or blood oranges, peeled and sliced into rounds or segmented (*see* page 13)
1 heaped tbsp finely chopped parsley
salt and pepper

FOR THE WHIPPED RICOTTA
250g/9oz ricotta cheese
2 tbsp finely grated Parmesan cheese
zest of 1 lemon
1 heaped tbsp finely chopped parsley

Preheat the oven to 200°C fan/220°C/425°F/gas mark 7. Place the whole beetroot (or cut in half if it's huge) in a foil parcel with 2 tablespoons of olive oil and 4 tablespoons water. Season. Scrunch up the foil to close the parcel and bake in the oven on a baking tray for 1 hour – 1 hour 30 minutes, until a knife glides easily through the centre of the beetroot. Set aside until it's cool enough to handle, then peel off the skins (wear gloves if you don't want pink-stained hands). Chop the beetroot into wedges and transfer to a bowl. While the beetroot cooks, use a hand whisk to lightly whip together your ingredients for the ricotta. Season to taste with salt and pepper, and refrigerate until ready to use.

Make the glaze just before serving. Pour the vinegar and maple syrup in a small saucepan, simmer over a medium-high heat until reduced by half. Pour over the warm beetroot wedges and season to taste. To serve, spread the ricotta across a serving platter, top with the pink leaves, then the beetroot and orange segments. Drizzle over any spare glaze and chopped parsley.

Beetroot leaves and their stems are edible. The stems can be cooked or pickled. If in good enough nick, treat the leaves like a leafy green or chard.

Carrot

**NEW SEASON IN SUMMER, BUT AVAILABLE MOST OF THE
YEAR DUE TO SECONDARY HARVESTS AND STORAGE**

From its vital role as a member of the *mirepoix* trio, to its supporting role in
salads and side dishes, we are not short of ways to use the humble sweet root
carrot – it even does a convincing job in cake. Carrots were actually purple
before they were orange. Orange carrots now form the bulk of those sold
and eaten but you will find heritage varieties sometimes sold as 'rainbow
carrots', which are yellow, white, red, or purple like old times, each with a
slightly different flavour. Chantenay carrots are a short, thick variety that are
usually cooked whole. The biggest differentiator of taste in the carrot world
is whether they're organic or not. Organic carrots may be sweeter, juicier and,
well, more 'carroty'.

Carrots can be eaten raw or cooked. To enjoy raw, grate or peel into ribbons
and toss into salads. If cooking, you can roast, boil, steam, braise, stir fry, mash,
or purée into a soup – most classical with coriander. Roasting intensifies
the sweetness, and as per all other root vegetables, is my go-to method.
Carrot peel is edible – it's up to you whether you choose to remove it or not.
If roasting or boiling and then blending with a high-speed blender, I may
be tempted to just leave it. If grating, I will peel. I use the roll cut technique
for even cooking and stylish preparation of large chunky carrots. Slice off
the root, then make a diagonal cut from one side to the other, roll over the
carrot 180 degrees and make another diagonal cut, leaving you with a triangle
chunk, roughly 3–5cm/1¼–2 inches on the longest edge. Keep flipping over
the carrot after each cut and you'll work your way down the carrot in no time.

Carrot tops can be eaten. You won't always find them attached to carrots, due
to the practicalities of storage, and because after harvesting the tops continue
to feed moisture from the carrot root which dries it out. If you do get a bunch
with tops, detach them immediately and store them separately wrapped in
damp kitchen paper in the fridge. You may find that the tops have a bitterness
that makes them unpleasant to eat in large quantities, but a little blitzed into
a herby pesto or dressing (*see* page 174) is good.

Tasty flavour pairings in my recipes are; butter, cumin, coriander, lemon,
pistachio, tahini, and tarragon. Others to try include; chickpeas, dill, ginger,
honey, lime, orange, parsnip, raisins, rosemary, thyme, and yoghurt.

RECIPE IDEA Grate carrots and toss with a dressing of orange juice and olive oil.
Season, then fold through nigella seeds and chopped coriander for a simple,
tasty salad.

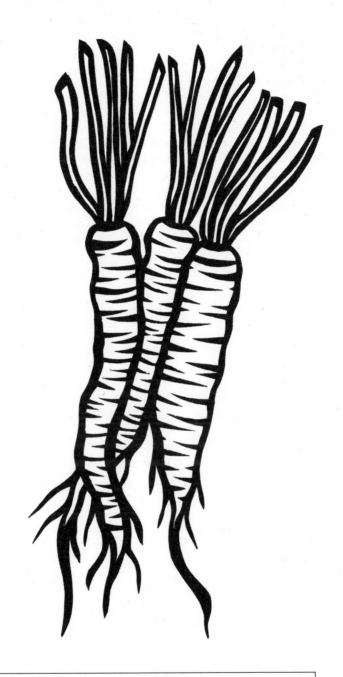

TOP TIP
Carrot is botanically classified as an umbellifer along with dill, parsnip, coriander, celery, celeriac, and fennel. It's a good flavour match for all of these.

Roll Cut Roasted Carrots with Freekeh, Tarragon Butter, and Pistachio

I learnt how to roll cut carrots at chef school in California, and have never understood why I rarely see them cut this way in the UK. Once roasted, they provide sweetness alongside smoky chewy freekeh, aniseed-y tarragon butter dressing, piquant quick pickled onions and crunchy chopped pistachios.

Freekeh is a young green cracked wheat and should be available in most larger supermarkets. If you can't find any, use bulgur wheat instead. A platter that's just as good warm as it is cold in tomorrow's lunch box.

Try replacing the carrots with wedges of roasted beetroot, fennel or a mixture of all three.

SERVES 2 | TIME TO PREPARE – 45 MINUTES

500g/1lb 2oz carrots, peeled and roll cut (*see* instructions on page 170)
olive oil
150g/5½oz freekeh, rinsed
2 tbsp (25g/1oz) toasted pistachios, roughly chopped
salt and pepper

FOR THE QUICK PICKLED ONIONS
1 red onion, thinly sliced
4 tbsp cider, white or red wine vinegar
1 tsp caster sugar

FOR THE TARRAGON BUTTER
4 tbsp butter
1 garlic clove, finely chopped
1 heaped tbsp finely chopped tarragon leaves

Preheat the oven to 180°C fan/200°C/400°F/gas mark 6.

Toss the roll cut carrots on a baking tray with 1 tablespoon of olive oil and season with salt. Roast in the oven for 30–40 minutes until the carrots are tender, browned, and just starting to caramelize on their edges.

In a small bowl, toss the thinly sliced red onion with the vinegar and sugar. Leave to pickle while everything else finishes cooking, giving them a toss every now and again.

Place the freekeh in a medium saucepan, cover with 450ml/15fl oz cold water, 1 tablespoon olive oil and season with salt. Bring to the boil and simmer for 15–20 minutes until the freekeh is cooked but still retaining a little bite. Drain and shake off as much excess water as possible.

Close to serving time make the tarragon butter. Melt the butter over a medium-high heat in a small frying or saucepan until bubbly and frothy. Take off the heat, drop in the garlic and chopped tarragon, and swirl.

To serve, spread out the freekeh across a serving platter, top with the carrots, drizzle the tarragon butter over the whole dish, then finish with as many pickled onions as you like, and the toasted chopped pistachios.

Roasted Carrot Pâté with Carrot Top Sauce

A creamy hummus-like pâté superb for spreading on toast. A simple recipe that is just as useful for a mound of forgotten bendy carrots or a bunch you have bought especially. The relatively small amounts of these ingredients in the pâté and sauce won't blend in a tall blender, so use a small hand blender and beaker. If this is all you have I recommend doubling the recipe. Serve the pâté spread on toast with the carrot top sauce drizzled on top.

If you don't have carrot tops, you can make the sauce from parsley instead. You'll likely not need the honey though as parsley is sweeter than bitter carrot tops. This pâté recipe will also work with roasted butternut squash.

SERVES 2, WITH LEFTOVERS | TIME TO PREPARE – 50 MINUTES

FOR THE PÂTÉ
400g/14oz carrots, topped and tailed, skin on and chopped into chunks,
    about 2cm/¾ inch
1 tbsp olive oil
1 tbsp tahini
zest and juice of 1 lemon
1 garlic clove, finely chopped
½ tsp ground cumin
½ tsp ground coriander
salt

FOR THE CARROT TOP SAUCE
20g/¾oz carrot tops
1 small garlic clove, finely chopped
3 tbsp olive oil
1½ tbsp red wine vinegar
1 tsp honey
salt and pepper

TO SERVE
2 slices of toast

Preheat the oven to 180°C fan/200°C/400°F/gas mark 6.

Toss the carrots onto a baking tray with 1 tablespoon of olive oil and season with salt. Roast in the oven for around 40 minutes until tender and starting to char but not burnt. Leave to cool until no longer steaming hot.

While the carrots cool, make the sauce. Blitz everything together with a hand blender until the carrot tops have broken down into a smooth paste. Season with salt and pepper to taste. Wash the blender.

Make the pâté. Blend together the carrots with 1 tablespoon of water, the tahini, zest and juice of a lemon, garlic, and the ground cumin and coriander until really smooth. Add more water 1 tablespoon at a time if necessary to get the pâté silky smooth. Season to taste. Scoop the pâté out into a bowl to chill completely, or serve slightly warm.

To serve, thickly spread the pâté over a slice of toast and drizzle over some carrot top sauce. If you don't use all the pâté and sauce, keep in separate sealed containers in the fridge for up to 3 days for the pâté, and a week for the sauce.

Celeriac

AUTUMN TO EARLY SPRING

Gnarly and knobbly, celeriac is not a beautiful looking vegetable, on the outside at least. Beneath those gnarly twists and brown lumps hides a creamy white root vegetable. I've never understood why celeriac isn't as popular as other root vegetables. I once tried to give away some spare celeriac at the end of a retreat after a mishap with an order. Most people wouldn't take them with the reason that they didn't know what to do with it. Yes, it looks more intimidating than a parsnip or potato, but I think it tastes just as good, if not better. A versatile veg that is delicious puréed into a silky soup, or have you tried it roasted with honey?

Celeriac is a type of celery grown for its root, rather than its stems. It does have a flavour of celery, although one that is mild.

Celeriac is good cooked or eaten raw. Roasting brings out its sweetness, but simmering then puréeing into soup shows a completely different side to celeriac. It will soften for blending in 12–15 minutes. Perhaps you've heard of a celeriac remoulade? This is how celeriac is best eaten raw, cut into matchsticks and marinated with mayonnaise or a lighter dressing as it is in my Curly Kale, Celeriac, and Apple Salad (*see* page 39).

The peel of a celeriac is not thick, but because of the gnarly roots using a hand peeler isn't always the most efficient way to peel. Cut the celeriac in half, then into quarters – now it's much more manageable. Rather than a vegetable peeler I use a sharp knife to slice off the skin, trying to take off as little flesh with it as possible. Once peeled, celeriac can be easily chopped. Dice into cubes for roasting or into matchsticks (julienne) for salads.

Tasty flavour pairings for celeriac you'll find in my recipes are; apple, butter, celery, cream, dill, fish and seafood, honey, lemon, and parsley. Others to try include; capers, hazelnuts, paprika, puy lentils, and potatoes.

RECIPE IDEA For an easy celeriac remoulade, mix matchsticks of celeriac and apple with a dressing made from equal parts mayonnaise and Greek yoghurt, a little lemon juice and zest, and a few flecks of parsley.

TOP TIP Let me introduce you to the new vegetable 'steak'. Cut the celeriac into thick discs, then glide a peeler round the edges to remove the peel. Marinate with a mix of smoked paprika, maple, and soy sauce. Bake or griddle until tender.

Honey Roasted Celeriac, Grapes, Orzo, and Tahini Drizzle

Honey enhances the flavour of celeriac in this salad dish that is perfect for a sharing platter or packing up in a lunch box. I've chosen orzo pasta as an accompaniment for celeriac in this recipe, but any other cooked grains or particularly puy lentils (*see* Cherry Tomato Salad on page 271 for method) would work well.

Other sweet root vegetables such as carrot, parsnip, or beetroot would also taste good with the flavours in this recipe.

SERVES 2 | TIME TO PREPARE – 35 MINUTES

500g/1lb 2oz celeriac, peeled and chopped into 2cm/¾ inch cubes
olive oil
2 plump garlic cloves, skin left on
1 tbsp honey, plus extra for drizzling
125g/4½oz red seedless grapes
150g/5½oz orzo
juice of ½ lemon
2 heaped tbsp of finely chopped parsley
1 tbsp toasted pine nuts
salt and pepper

FOR THE TAHINI DRIZZLE
2 tbsp tahini
juice of ½ lemon

Preheat the oven to 180°C fan/200°C/400°F/gas mark 6.

Toss the celeriac cubes onto a baking tray with 1 tablespoon of olive oil and season with salt. Roast in the oven for 25 minutes, until tender and the edges are starting to crisp up. With 10 minutes left on the clock, throw in the garlic cloves. When the timer is up, remove the tray from the oven, drizzle over the honey, and give a good shake. Scatter over the grapes and put back in the oven for 5–7 minutes, or until the grapes begin to burst. Remove from the oven to cool a little. Peel and mash the garlic cloves into a paste and set aside.

Meanwhile, cook the orzo according to packet instructions in salted boiling water. Drain and rinse under a cold tap to cool and stop the orzo from becoming sticky. Shake off as much excess water as possible.

Next, make the tahini drizzle. In a small bowl whisk together the tahini with the lemon juice and 1–2 tablespoons of water as required until completely smooth. Stir in half the roasted garlic paste and season the dressing with salt and pepper to taste.

In another small bowl, whisk together the remaining garlic paste with 2 tablespoons of olive oil and the other half of lemon juice, you'll use this to dress the orzo. Put the cooked orzo in a large mixing bowl and stir through this dressing and the chopped parsley. Toss through the cooked celeriac and grapes (still warm is fine), taste, and adjust seasoning. Spread the salad across a serving platter, drizzle over the tahini sauce, and garnish with the toasted pine nuts and a drizzle of honey.

Celeriac, Haddock, and Prawn Chowder

A creamy seafood soup that reminds me of the flavours of a good fish pie. A chowder is usually made with potato, but mine only has eyes for celeriac. Half of the celeriac is blended to create a silky base for the seafood, so only a small amount of cream is required to finish it off. A cunning move, as it tastes like there's so much more. The secret to this chowder is a really good fish or shellfish stock.

For an alternative substitute, replace some or all of the celeriac with white potato or parsnip. You could also use finely chopped fennel instead of onion and celery in the base.

SERVES 2 | TIME TO PREPARE – 35 MINUTES

olive oil
1 tsp butter
1 white onion, finely chopped
2 celery sticks, finely chopped
1 celeriac (approx. 450g/1lb), peeled and diced into 1.5cm/⅝ inch cubes
1 garlic clove, finely chopped
300ml/10fl oz fish or shellfish stock
1 skinless, boneless haddock fillet (approx. 125g/4½oz)
85g/3oz raw peeled king prawns
2 tbsp double cream
1 tbsp finely chopped dill, plus a few fronds for garnish
juice of 1 lemon, to taste
1 Braeburn or Gala apple
salt and pepper

Warm 1 tablespoon olive oil and the butter in a large saucepan over a low-medium heat. Sauté the chopped onions and celery, with a good pinch of salt for around 5 minutes until starting to soften. Add the celeriac cubes, cover the pan with a lid and sweat for another 5 or so minutes. Stir in the garlic to cook briefly, then add the stock. Bring to a simmer, cover, and cook until the celeriac has completely softened (around 10–15 minutes more).

Drain the cooked celeriac and vegetable mix, reserving the stock. Transfer the stock into the blender along with half of the celeriac and vegetable mix and blitz until it forms a silky smooth purée (or use a hand blender). Put the purée and unblended vegetables back into the saucepan. If the chowder is too thick, add 1 tablespoon of water at a time until you have the desired loose soup-like texture surrounding your unblended chunks of celeriac. Put the saucepan back onto the heat and bring to a gentle simmer.

Place the raw haddock on top of the chowder, cover the pan, and cook for 5–6 minutes, or until the haddock just starts to flake when nudged with two forks. Add in the raw prawns for the final 3 minutes of the fish cooking time, they will be ready when totally pink. Use two forks to flake the fish, then pour in the cream, and add the dill. Stir gently to combine. Season to taste and add just enough lemon juice to lift the flavours.

Plate up in two deep pasta bowls, evenly distributing the fish and prawns. Chop the apple into matchsticks and use a handful as a garnish with a few fronds of dill and a drizzle of olive oil.

Jerusalem Artichoke

WINTER TO SPRING

Smaller and more knobby than other root veg, Jerusalem artichokes have a distinct and instantly recognizable sweet nutty flavour. Veg enthusiasts may already know the hilarity that Jerusalem artichokes are neither from Jerusalem, nor an artichoke. If you're not familiar with this vegetable, then welcome to the madness of etymology. They're a member of the sunflower family, and the link to Jerusalem is due to its phonetic similarity to 'girasole' – the Italian word for sunflower. They have a mild resemblance in flavour to a globe artichoke heart, hence the use of artichoke. In the USA, they're known as sunchokes, which is less confusing.

Jerusalem artichokes vary in skin colour, depending on the variety from purple to light brown. The flesh inside is always creamy white.

Jerusalem artichokes must be cooked. Either roast in their skins, or boil/steam and purée. When roasted, their skins ooze with the caramelization of the natural sugars and go almost chewy. Add to salads, risotto, or eat as a side dish. They make an incredibly smooth purée when blended with cream, and this can be used as the base for soup, served as a purée with fish, or as a pasta sauce (*see* pasta recipe, page 184). Thin slices can be fried into chips and used as a garnish.

There's no need to peel Jerusalem artichokes before roasting, but you'll need to give them a really good scrub to avoid any grittiness. A veg scrubbing brush is a fantastically useful piece of kit. If boiling to purée, peel first, if you can. Of course, it helps if the Jerusalem artichokes you select are less knobbly to start with.

Tasty flavour pairings for Jerusalem artichoke you'll find in my recipes are; goat's cheese, cream, pancetta, and sage. Others to try include; butter, cumin, dill, hazelnuts, parsley, and thyme.

RECIPE IDEA Make a Jerusalem artichoke soup by simmering artichokes with potatoes in stock with a base of softened onions, then puréeing with a touch of cream. Garnish with toasted hazelnuts.

TOP TIP Thanks to their high quantity of non-digestible carbohydrate inulin, they have unfortunate wind inducing side effects. Add lemon juice to the water if simmering Jerusalem artichokes for a purée or soup. It helps reduce the symptoms! Or, just keep the portion small.

Creamed Jerusalem Artichoke Pasta with Pancetta, Sage, and Jerusalem Artichoke Crisps

Jerusalem artichokes simmered until soft, then blended with cream and a little starchy pasta water make a gorgeously silky sauce for pasta. Salty crisp pancetta, crispy sage leaves, and thinly sliced Jerusalem artichoke crisps give it more flavour and texture. There are quite a lot of elements to this dish as while the Jerusalem artichoke simmers you'll need to make the garnish, boil the pasta, and crisp up the pancetta. Read the recipe thoroughly before you start. Choose a pasta that works best with creamy sauces; I like farfalle, spaghetti, linguine, or conchiglie. For a vegetarian version, simply leave out the pancetta.

Try making a cream with celeriac or parsnip instead of the Jerusalem artichokes, both are also good with sage.

SERVES 2 | TIME TO PREPARE – 40 MINUTES

300g/10½oz Jerusalem artichokes, peeled and sliced into 5mm/¼ inch pieces
juice of 1 lemon
180g/6½oz pasta
100g/3½oz diced pancetta
1 tbsp white wine (optional)
4 tbsp double cream
25g/1oz Parmesan cheese, finely grated
salt and pepper

FOR THE GARNISH
olive oil
10 fresh sage leaves
1 small Jerusalem artichoke, skin on and sliced into thin coins

Place the peeled Jerusalem artichoke pieces into a medium-sized pan, cover with cold water, and add the lemon juice. Bring to the boil and simmer for 25 minutes, until the Jerusalem artichokes are soft enough to blend. Drain.

Make the garnish. Add just enough olive oil to a small frying pan so that the base is covered. Heat the oil over a high heat, and once shimmering add the sage leaves and fry until crispy, about 30 seconds. Remove with a fork/slotted spoon and drain on kitchen paper. Add the Jerusalem artichoke slices to the pan and fry until browned and crispy, about 3–4 minutes. Remove and drain on kitchen paper with the sage leaves. Set aside for now.

Next, cook the pasta in a large saucepan of salted boiling water for 11–12 minutes (or according to packet instructions) until just al dente. Drain, reserving the cooking water as you'll need it for the sauce.

Meanwhile, in a frying pan large enough to hold the pasta and sauce, fry the pancetta over a medium-high heat (no oil required) for around 5 minutes, until crispy. Drain any excess oil and add the wine if using to help scrape off any bits of pancetta back into the pan. Turn off the heat.

Make the Jerusalem artichoke cream. Blitz the cooked peeled Jerusalem artichokes in a high-speed blender with 4 tablespoons of double cream and 4 tablespoons of the pasta cooking water until completely smooth. Add three-quarters of the Parmesan cheese.

To bring the dish together, put the frying pan with the pancetta back onto a low heat, and add the Jerusalem artichoke cream and cooked pasta. Toss everything together, adding an extra splash of reserved pasta water or double cream to get the consistency you prefer. Season to taste. Plate up the pasta and sprinkle over the crispy sage, Jerusalem artichoke crisps, and the remaining Parmesan cheese.

Roasted Jerusalem Artichoke Salad with Honey Baked Goat's Cheese

The caramelized skins and soft centres of the roasted Jerusalem artichokes are a good flavour pairing for warm honey baked goat's cheese, a pile of green leaves, a gooey egg and a shower of Parmesan cheese. I use my reliable honey and mustard vinaigrette for the important job of dressing the salad leaves, but other dressings can apply. Serve with a few slices of crusty French baguette.

For an alternative to the Jerusalem artichokes, this same salad would work with roasted beetroot or carrots – adjust the cooking time accordingly.

SERVES 2 | TIME TO PREPARE – 40 MINUTES

4 medium-sized Jerusalem artichokes (approx. 200g/7oz), scrubbed clean, split in half lengthways
2 tsp olive oil
2 eggs
2 individual soft goat's cheese rounds (chèvre), 100g/3½oz each, brought to room temperature
2 tsp honey
60g/2¼oz mixed salad leaves
Parmesan cheese, to serve
salt and pepper

FOR THE HONEY MUSTARD VINAIGRETTE
½ tsp Dijon mustard
½ tsp honey
1 tbsp red wine vinegar
3 tbsp olive oil

Preheat the oven to 180°C fan/200°C/400°F/gas mark 6.

Toss the prepared Jerusalem artichokes onto a baking tray with 2 teaspoons of olive oil and season. Bake in the oven for 30–35 minutes, until the edges are crispy and the centres soft. Halfway through, give the baking tray a little shuffle to prevent sticking.

Meanwhile, make the vinaigrette. In a small bowl or jar, stir together the mustard, honey, and red wine vinegar until combined. Add the olive oil, then whisk (or add the jar lid and shake) together to emulsify. Season to taste. Set aside for the flavours to mingle.

Next, cook the eggs. Bring a small saucepan of water to the boil, and cook the eggs for 8 minutes for a slightly gooey yolk. Cool under the cold tap, peel, and slice in half.

Make a couple of slits on the top of each goat's cheese round, drizzle over the honey, and season with salt and pepper. When there are about 8 minutes to go for the Jerusalem artichokes, pop the goat's cheese rounds into the oven (onto the same baking tray if there is space), to soften and brown but not completely melt.

When ready to serve, toss the salad leaves with 1 tablespoon of the dressing, to very lightly coat and then split between 2 plates. Top the leaves with the roasted Jerusalem artichokes, the halved eggs, and the warm goat's cheese. Drizzle a little more dressing over the whole dish and finish with a shower of finely grated Parmesan.

Parsnip

AUTUMN TO WINTER

Creamy-fleshed sweet roots that are woefully overlooked. Best saved for wintry dishes, these sweet roots are the underdog of the British Sunday roast, because doesn't everyone prefer the potato? As a champion of the underdog, I always want parsnips with my Sunday roast, especially if roasted with thyme and honey.

Parsnips will vary a little in shape depending on their variety, but always have the same off-white coloured skins. Baby parsnips, along with baby carrots, are just harvested at a young stage of growth. These are cooked whole and look good on a plate, so you're more likely to find them on a restaurant menu.

Parsnips are generally best cooked, they can be roasted, braised in stock or into risottos, tagines, or curries. Use roasted parsnip wedges for a warm winter salad or side dish alongside other roots. Boil then purée for a smooth creamy soup – this is my favourite way to use up a glut – you don't even need to add cream. Grated parsnips can be cooked into a fritter or a parsnip and apple sweet baked cake.

Parsnips are not too firm or difficult to chop up as long as you have a sharp knife. A vegetable peeler will also come in handy for removing the peel, or for spinning the flesh into ribbons which, when baked with olive oil and salt into crisps, makes a crunchy garnish. The core of a parsnip can be woody and tough, and takes longer to cook. For most recipes I wouldn't bother to remove it, but doing so does add finesse (*see* Parsnip Speltotto, page 190). To remove, split the parsnip through the root into half, then quarters, then you'll easily be able to slice out the darker bit in the centre – this is the core.

Tasty flavour pairings for parsnips you'll find in my recipes are; butter, curry powder and garam masala, garlic, and parsley. Others to try include; apples, carrots, cream, ground ginger, honey, puy lentils, sage, and thyme.

RECIPE IDEA Roast parsnips with thyme and honey and serve over a base of puy lentils. Top with sliced clementines, crumbled feta, and toasted hazelnuts.

TOP TIP If your parsnips have been neglected and have gone bendy, then they're just a bit dehydrated. Likely not good enough for roasting, but may still be fine for soup after a simmer in stock.

Parsnip 'Speltotto' with Prosciutto Wrapped Haddock

Rice puts the 'ris' in risotto, but you can apply a similar cooking technique to other grains. For this speltotto, spelt, an ancient type of wheat, provides a chewy contrast to the soft buttery parsnips. Look for pearled spelt, which has had its outer husk removed and will cook in around 20 minutes. Paired with haddock wrapped in salty prosciutto crudo, this speltotto makes a comforting winter supper. This dish doesn't need a side, but a few salad leaves mixed with matchsticks of apple are a good complement.

For a variation, try this recipe with celeriac, but skip the crisp step.

SERVES 2 | TIME TO PREPARE – 35 MINUTES

FOR THE SPELTOTTO
2 medium-sized parsnips (approx. 250g/9oz), peeled
olive oil
1 tsp butter
1 banana shallot, finely chopped
1 garlic clove, finely chopped
3 sprigs of thyme, leaves stripped
125g/4½oz pearled spelt, rinsed
4 tbsp white wine
approx. 500ml/17fl oz warm chicken or vegetable stock
2 tbsp finely grated Parmesan cheese, or more to taste
salt and pepper

FOR THE PROSCIUTTO WRAPPED HADDOCK
4 slices of prosciutto crudo
2 skinless haddock fillets (approx. 125g/4½oz each)
2 sprigs of thyme, leaves stripped

Preheat the oven to 180°C fan/200°C/400°F/gas mark 6.

Use a vegetable peeler to peel off around 20 ribbons of parsnip for your crisps, toss these into a small bowl with ½ tablespoon of olive oil and season with salt. Set aside. Split the parsnips in half through the root, then quarter, remove the core, and dice into 1cm/½ inch pieces.

Over a low-medium heat, warm 1 tablespoon of olive oil and the butter in a medium-sized saucepan that you have a lid for. Add the chopped shallots and parsnip cubes, cook uncovered for a minute or so, then add a lid and cook for a further 4–5 minutes, stirring at regular intervals to avoid sticking (the lid helps the parsnips soften quicker). Remove the lid and cook uncovered from now on. Add the garlic, thyme, season with salt and pepper, then stir in the spelt. Splash in the wine and, once it has almost evaporated, start to add the warm stock a ladleful at a time. Keep on a moderate bubble and continue to feed the dish stock over the next 20 minutes, until the spelt has plumped up, is tender, and you have a loose 'risotto' consistency. Stir occasionally – it needs far less attention than a regular rice risotto.

While the speltotto is cooking, prepare and cook your haddock. Lay the prosciutto out on your board and overlap 2 slices for each haddock fillet to a width to match the longer edge of your pieces of haddock. Lay the haddock pieces on top of the prosciutto, top with the thyme leaves, a pinch of salt and pepper. Wrap the haddock tightly in the prosciutto and turn over so the join is hidden underneath. Transfer to a baking tray, lightly drizzle with olive oil and bake in the oven for around 12 minutes, until the fish is opaque, and the prosciutto lightly crisped.

Spread the oiled parsnip ribbons onto a baking tray and cook for 5 minutes (at the same time as the fish is fine) until crispy.

When the spelt is cooked, turn off the heat, add the Parmesan, and cover the pan. Let it sit for a minute for the cheese to melt in. Stir and season to taste.

To serve, plate up pools of the speltotto into individual pasta bowls and top with the baked fish and parsnip crisps.

Lightly Spiced Parsnip Soup with Parsley Croutons

A warming, lightly sweet, and creamy soup perfect for the winter months. I make this with almond milk as I like the flavour with parsnips, but it also has the bonus of making it entirely plant based. I don't use any stock here, as it will detract from the parsnip flavour. It's for this same reason I only use a little garam masala – just enough to enhance the parsnips, but not to overpower.

This same soup method will work with celeriac or carrots. Or, try mixing up the ingredients in your sauté base to include leek or finely chopped fennel. Avoid using carrots in the base if you want to maintain a purely cream-coloured soup.

SERVES 2 | TIME TO PREPARE – 25 MINUTES

FOR THE SOUP
olive oil
1 onion, finely chopped
1 celery stick, finely chopped
500g/1lb 2oz parsnips, peeled, and sliced into 2mm/⅛inch coins
1 tsp garam masala
1 garlic clove, finely chopped
500ml/17fl oz unsweetened almond milk
salt and pepper
a pinch of chilli flakes (optional), to serve

FOR THE CROUTONS
¼ tsp garam masala
1 slice sourdough bread, chopped into 2cm/¾ inch cubes
1 tbsp finely chopped parsley

Heat 1 tablespoon of olive oil in a large saucepan over a medium heat. Sauté the chopped onions and celery with a good pinch of salt for around 5 minutes until starting to soften. Add the parsnip coins, cover the pan with a lid, and sweat for another 10 minutes until the parsnip is starting to soften. Stir frequently so that the parsnips don't stick. Add the garam masala and the garlic and cook briefly until fragrant.

Pour in the almond milk and simmer gently uncovered for a further 8–10 minutes, or until the parsnip is completely soft. Turn off the heat and cool for a few minutes (for safety) and then blend in a high speed blender or with a hand blender until silky smooth. If the soup is too thick, add a splash of water, to get the consistency you prefer. Season to taste. Keep warm on the hob while you make your croutons.

Heat 1 tablespoon of oil in a frying pan over a medium heat, add more if your slice of bread is big. Sprinkle in the garam masala and, when fragrant, add your bread, toss around in the pan, and cook until the bread has absorbed the spiced oil and is toasty all over. Sprinkle over the parsley.

Serve the soup in deep bowls with the herby spiced croutons on top and finish with a drizzle of olive oil. If you find parsnips too sweet, a pinch of chilli to serve is welcome.

Potato

**HARVESTED LATE SPRING THROUGH TO AUTUMN,
THOUGH AVAILABLE YEAR ROUND
NEW POTATOES HAVE A SHORTER SEASON IN LATE SPRING**

The ever-dependable root vegetable, always there in times of comfort. From rösti to gnocchi, potato farls to vichyssoise, and of course crisps and chips, many cuisines celebrate potatoes. Since entire recipe books have been written just about this king of the carbs, here I decided to concentrate on the three ways I am most likely to prepare potatoes.

There are many varieties of potatoes and the best way to differentiate them is by the consistency of their flesh – this will determine where they are best suited in the kitchen. Potatoes are either floury/fluffy or waxy. To massively over-simplify, floury potatoes are best for roasting, baking, or mashing, whilst waxy new potatoes such as Jersey Royals are best for boiling and served with knobs of butter or in a potato salad.

Potatoes need to be cooked and are good nearly every which way; roasted, baked, deep fried, steamed or boiled and mashed, simmered into a stew, blitzed into a soup, or used as a topping for a pie. They can also be grated and formed into potato cakes and röstis. Despite being one of the most popular vegetables, potatoes are not actually very tasty on their own, they need fat and seasoning. Ever tried a baked potato fresh out the oven without butter and salt? Disappointing.

Potato peel can be eaten, and it's up to you whether you leave it on for roasting. Obviously you'll want to remove before boiling or mashing. If peeling your potatoes specifically for a dish, save up the peels, toss with olive oil and salt, and bake in a hot oven until crispy for a zero waste hack snack.

Potato leaves and stems are poisonous, don't eat them, or any bits sprouting out of a potato that's been in your cupboard too long. You can usually chop sprouting bits off if they do appear and if the potato looks otherwise healthy.

Tasty flavour pairings for potatoes you'll find in my recipes are; butter, hard and blue cheese, chilli, cream, onions, eggs, garlic, mushrooms, mustard, and parsley. Others to try include; all root veg, all greens, cumin, garam masala, leeks, rosemary, sage, tomato, and thyme.

RECIPE IDEA For the simplest potato wedges, toss cut wedges of skin-on potato with olive oil, salt, dried herbs, and chopped fresh garlic or dried garlic granules. Bake in a hot oven for around 45–50 minutes until crispy.

TOP TIP
Any moisture or light on the potato can encourage them to rot quicker. Potatoes keep best in a paper bag in a dark, dry, cool cupboard, rather than in the fridge or on an open shelf.

Roasted New Potato and
Green Bean Salad with Mint

No summer BBQ is complete without a potato salad, and this is my go-to.
I know, I know, waxy new potatoes are meant to be served boiled, but I
don't love the papery skins so prefer to roast until the skins are crispy yet
the insides remain soft.

I sometimes use thinly sliced shallots instead of spring onions, swap the
mint for watercress or the green beans for asparagus.

SERVES 2 AS A SIDE | TIME TO PREPARE – 40 MINUTES

400g/14oz baby or new potatoes, scrubbed clean and left whole if small enough or
   chopped into bite-sized pieces
1 tbsp olive oil
150g/5½oz green beans, end trimmed and cut in half or into 3 x 2.5cm/1inch pieces
2 spring onions, very thinly sliced on an angle
zest of 1 lemon
large handful of mint leaves (approx. 5g/⅛oz)
salt and pepper

FOR THE DRESSING
½ tsp wholegrain mustard
½ tsp honey
juice of half a lemon (approx. 1 tbsp)
3 tbsp olive oil

Preheat the oven to 200°C fan/220°C/450°F/gas mark 7. On a baking tray,
toss the potatoes with 1 tablespoon of olive oil and season with salt. Roast
for 20 minutes. Reduce to 180°C fan/200°C/400°F/gas mark 6 and cook for
another 15 minutes, until crispy on the outside and cooked through on the
inside. Remove from the oven and cool off for a short time, around 5 minutes.
Meanwhile, make the dressing. In a small bowl stir together the mustard,
honey, and lemon juice until combined. Whisk in the oil until emulsified.
Season with salt and pepper to taste. Set aside for the flavours to mingle.

Bring a small saucepan of salted water to the boil, then blanch the beans
for 2–3 minutes, until just al dente. Drain and rinse immediately under cold
water until cold to the touch. Shake off any excess water then leave to dry
on kitchen paper. To put the salad together, toss the cooked potatoes in a
medium-sized bowl with the beans, chopped spring onions, and enough
dressing to just coat. Season with lemon zest, then tear your mint leaves
and add to the bowl (they will go black more quickly if sliced). Transfer to
a serving platter or bowl to serve.

Stuffed Jacket Potato Skins with Stilton and Mushrooms

A classic, but with good reason, because they celebrate the simple joy of buttery, cheesy, mashed potato AND crispy skins in one bite. Look for varieties of white potato best for baking for perfectly fluffy insides. Although the hands-on time for this recipe is minimal, potatoes do take a long while to bake in the oven. If you're concerned about energy use, you could use a microwave or air fryer for the pre-bake. Alternatively, make use of the oven space and roast other veggies at the same time to use tomorrow. Serve with a side salad of dressed leaves and crunchy veg or slaw.

Try with sweet potato instead – reduce the cooking time depending on size.

SERVES 2 | TIME TO PREPARE – 1 HOUR 25 MINUTES

2 medium-large baking potatoes (approx. 300g/10½oz each)
olive oil
125g/4½oz chestnut mushrooms, thinly sliced
100g/3½oz Stilton cheese, or more to taste, crumbled
2 tbsp milk
2 tsp butter
1 tbsp finely chopped parsley
a pinch of cayenne pepper
salt and pepper

Preheat the oven to 180°C fan/200°C/400°F/gas mark 6. Prick the potatoes all over with a fork. Rub the skin with olive oil – around 1 teaspoon per potato should be enough. Sprinkle each with a little flaked salt. Bake on the wire rack of an oven shelf for 1 hour until the skin is crispy and the centre cooked through. Split the potato in half lengthways, let the steam dissipate and leave to cool until safe to handle.

Heat 1 tablespoon of oil in a frying pan over a medium heat and sauté the sliced mushrooms for 3 or so minutes until brown all over. Remove from the pan to cool.

Scoop out the potato flesh into a bowl, carefully, as to keep the skins intact. Mash with a fork, add in three-quarters of the cheese, the milk and butter, and whip together until smooth. Stir through the parsley, three-quarters of the mushrooms, and season to taste with salt, pepper, and cayenne pepper. Pile back into the potato shells, smooth over the top, then add the remaining mushroom slices and crumbled blue cheese on top. Transfer the stuffed skins to a baking tray and put back into the oven for 15–20 minutes, or until the cheese on top has melted and browned.

Leftover Roastie, Herb, and Gruyère Frittata

Anything goes when it comes to a frittata; vegetables for body, herbs or greens for flavour, eggs, cheese and a little dairy for richness. A successful frittata lies in the alignment of appropriate pan-size-to-egg ratio, hob and grill heat, and timings – mine are only a guide and I urge you to follow your instincts at each stage. For this recipe I use an oven-safe 20cm/8 inch frying pan which gives my ideal frittata depth of 3cm/1¼ inch. You can double up the recipe for a bigger pan, just adjust cooking times to suit.

Whenever I roast any variety of potato, including sweet potato, I always cook a few extra so that I can turn the leftovers into tomorrow's frittata. This cuts down on the frittata's cooking time as well as oven energy use.

SERVES 2 | TIME TO PREPARE – 30 MINUTES

1 tbsp olive oil
1 onion, or 2 banana shallots, finely sliced
5 eggs
2 tbsp Greek yoghurt (or the equivalent quantity of crème fraîche or double cream)
2–3 tbsp any finely chopped soft herbs (e.g. parsley, dill, tarragon, or chives)
50g/1¾ oz Gruyère or mature Cheddar cheese, grated
175g/6oz leftover roast potatoes, chopped into bite-sized pieces (approx. 2 medium-sized potatoes)
salt and pepper

Preheat the grill to medium-high. Heat 1 tablespoon of olive oil in a small frying pan over a low-medium heat, and sauté the sliced onion or shallots with a good pinch of salt for around 5–8 minutes until softened.

Meanwhile, in a small jug whisk together the eggs with the yoghurt, chopped herbs, and a handful of the cheese. Season with salt and pepper.

When the onions have softened, toss the chopped potatoes into the pan and mix in so everything is evenly distributed. Pour in the herby egg mix and cook for around 4–5 minutes, until the eggs are starting to set around the edges of the pan. Scatter over the remaining cheese and slide the pan under the grill. Cook for around 5–6 minutes until the top has set, and is lightly browned and puffed up.

Stick a knife in to check if the inside has cooked through, a little gooeyness is fine as the eggs will continue to cook in the residual heat of the pan. Stand for 5 minutes, then flip out the frittata onto a board. Slice into 4 deep wedges to serve.

The ever-dependable root vegetable, always there in times of comfort. From rösti to gnocchi, potato farls to vichyssoise, and of course crisps and chips, many cuisines celebrate potatoes.

Swede

WINTER

Swede – a person from Sweden or a wintry vegetable? Other names for swede include rutabaga, neeps, or Swedish turnip, the last of which is what we have now shortened to swede and explains how it got its name. Botanically speaking, this underground vegetable is from the brassica cabbage family, but in recipes is treated similarly to other roots. Swedes have an orange flesh and an ombre skin that fades from dark purple to yellow. Depending on how they're cooked, they have a sweet, nutty taste with just a hint of that sulphur we recognize from cabbage.

Although it can be grated and eaten raw, I think swede is best when cooked; boil, steam, stew, or roast. I have two Welsh influences on my swede cookery from my Welsh Grandma. The first is to boil, mash with carrot and butter, then season with nutmeg and white pepper. We called this 'potch'. The second is its inclusion in Welsh cawl – a brothy soup made from lamb neck and root veg. Along with carrots, parsnips, and potatoes, simmered swede gives a gentle comforting sweetness to the broth. Although creamy when puréed, I don't think swede's brassica tang is right for a blended soup. Swede can also be roasted if you prefer this root vegetable crispy.

Swedes need to be peeled – the older the swede, the thicker the skin. As per my advice for celeriac, you may find it easier to use a knife rather than a vegetable peeler. They can be hard to chop and it might, at times, feel like you're trying to slice through concrete. A sharp knife, patience, and a strong arm is required.

Tasty flavour pairings for swede you'll find in my recipes are; celery, Cheddar cheese, garlic, onions, potato and other root veg, and parsley. Others to try include; apple, carrot, cinnamon, cumin, ginger, honey or maple syrup, nutmeg, rosemary, and star anise.

RECIPE IDEA Combine mashed swede with potato and use as a pie topping.

TOP TIP I have not managed to include swede's close relation turnip in my top 40 vegetables, but they can be used similarly.

One Pot Swede, Chicken, and Quinoa Stew with Parsley Gremolata

Swede adds a surprisingly tasty sweetness to this chunky chicken stew and is a reminder that it is a vegetable that needn't be relegated. Chicken thighs are simmered with aromatics to make a quick broth, before being shredded and added back in with quinoa and some simmered vegetables. The method is based on a classic chicken soup I learnt to make at chef school and is my go-to when feeling under the weather.

Swede can be replaced with other root vegetables such as celeriac, potato, or parsnip.

SERVES 2 | TIME TO PREPARE – 1 HOUR

FOR THE BROTH
2 large or 3 small bone-in chicken thighs, skin removed
1 onion, skin left on, chopped into chunks
1 carrot, roughly chopped
1 celery stick, roughly chopped
1 bay leaf
2 sprigs of thyme
3 peppercorns

FOR THE SOUP
1 tbsp olive oil
1 onion, finely chopped
1 carrots, finely chopped
1 celery stick, finely chopped
1 garlic clove, finely chopped
1 tsp finely grated ginger
3 sprigs of thyme, leaves stripped
450g/1lb swede, peeled and diced into 1.5cm/⅝ inch cubes
50g/1¾oz quinoa, rinsed
juice of 1 lemon
a handful of parsley leaves, finely chopped
salt and pepper

FOR THE GREMOLATA
3 tbsp finely chopped parsley
1 plump or 2 small garlic cloves, finely chopped
zest of 1 lemon

For the broth, put the chicken thighs, onion, carrot, and celery into a large saucepan with the bay leaf, thyme, and peppercorns. Add enough water so the chicken is just covered (approx. 500ml/17fl oz). Bring to the boil, then reduce to a simmer and cook uncovered for 30 minutes, or until the chicken will easily come away from the bone to shred. Strain the mixture, reserving the stock. Discard the soggy veg and aromatics. Set aside the chicken to cool.

For the soup, put the saucepan back on the hob with 1 tablespoon of olive oil. Over a medium heat, sweat the finely chopped onion, carrot, and celery with a good pinch of salt for 5 minutes until it starts to soften. Add the garlic, ginger, thyme, and chopped swede, cover with a lid, and sweat for 5 minutes, stirring occasionally. Pour in the reserved stock and bring to the boil. Add the quinoa, reduce to a simmer, and cook with the lid on for another 15 minutes, or until the swede is tender and the quinoa cooked.

While the stew cooks, make the gremolata. Finely chop the parsley, garlic, and lemon zest together on your board. Shred the chicken with a fork and discard the bones.

When the quinoa has cooked, add the chicken back into the stew to warm through. Season to taste with salt, pepper, lemon juice, and add a little chopped parsley to break up the orange hue of the stew. Top up with water if you'd like a looser stew. Serve the warm stew with the gremolata sprinkled across the top.

Mixed Root Vegetable and Cheddar Bake

This method for baking layers of root vegetables bathed in stock is inspired by the French recipe for boulangère, with the not so French addition of Cheddar on top. It takes a while to slice and layer up the vegetables, but from then on you can let the oven take over and do the work. Serve as a vegetarian main for two, with a salad on the side, or as a side for 3–4.

Choose similar-sized root vegetables for this; I prefer swede, celeriac, and potato. As an alternative you could pair smaller potatoes, carrots, or parsnips.

SERVES 2 AS A MAIN | TIME TO PREPARE – 1 HOUR 30 MINUTES

750g/1lb 10oz root veg – a mixture of swede, celeriac, potato
1 onion, thinly sliced
10g/¼oz sage, half finely chopped
250ml/9fl oz chicken or vegetable stock
2 tsp butter, plus extra to grease the dish
40g/1½oz Cheddar cheese, grated
salt and pepper

Preheat the oven to 180°C fan/200°C/400°F/gas mark 6.

Peel the vegetables and slice with a knife, or using the thinnest setting of the mandoline into 2mm/⅛ inch discs. Cut the potatoes lengthways. If the celeriac and swede are large, cut them into half moons.

Prepare a baking dish (approx. 18 × 22cm/7 × 8½ inches in size), by greasing it with a little butter. Layer up alternating slices of potato, celeriac, and swede, overlapping them until you have filled one layer of the dish. Season with salt and pepper, and top with all of the sliced onion and the finely chopped sage. Add a second layer of alternating potato, celeriac, and swede, season, and tuck in the remaining sage leaves just under the vegetables so they don't burn. Pour over enough stock so that the dish is three-quarters full of liquid. Dot the butter over the dish, cover with foil, and bake for 45 minutes.

Remove the foil and bake uncovered for another 15 minutes to crisp up the top, then scatter over the cheese and bake for a final 20 minutes, or until the cheese is crispy and browned, and the veg is cooked through.

Swedes have an orange flesh and an ombre skin that fades from dark purple to yellow. Depending on how they're cooked, they have a sweet, nutty taste with just a hint of that sulphur we recognize from cabbage.

Sweet Potato

AUTUMN TO EARLY SPRING

A sweet potato is not a potato at all, it's actually a tuber. It is sweet though, the vegetable naming team got that bit right. These rugby-ball shaped roots have hugely risen in popularity in my lifetime, and we didn't have them at home in the Nineties. Who was behind their PR campaign? I have a feeling it was due to their new 'superfood' status, a label which we have all since realized was a made up term without scientific backing. Like all vegetables, they are nutritious and we welcome them as part of a diverse balanced diet.

The most widely available sweet potatoes have a dusky pinky-brown skin and creamy orange flesh. You may also occasionally find white fleshed sweet potatoes particularly in Afro-Caribbean shops, or the uniquely and amazingly coloured purple sweet potatoes. The density and flouriness of the flesh varies across the colour variations but all have a similar sweet creamy flavour. Sweet potatoes are sometimes called yams in the USA, but a yam is also an entirely different hairy tuber – don't let that confuse you as it did me.

Sweet potatoes are a versatile vegetable – they have suitability for, and excel under, a wide variety of cooking methods; roasting, baking whole, stuffing, steaming, boiling, braising, mashing, and puréeing into soup. They also make excellent chips, which are never as crispy as those made from white potatoes, but they do taste good.

The peel can be left on if roasting in wedges, but otherwise should be removed. I have discovered, since teaching family cooking classes, that sweet potatoes are always a hit with kids, but annoyingly trickier for them to chop. The safest way to chop this vegetable (that has a tendency to slip and roll over your board) is to split it in half lengthways using the bridge cut, then flip it over onto the flat edge you have just created, before continuing. This is a tip you can apply to most vegetables.

Tasty flavour pairings for sweet potato you'll find in my recipes are; allspice, butter, chickpeas, chilli, coriander, cumin, garlic, ginger, lemon, orange, and walnuts. Others to try include; beans, cinnamon, dill, honey, lime, parsley, pecans, rosemary, tahini, and tomatoes.

RECIPE IDEA Use a large grated sweet potato for a twist on rösti. Grate, sit with a pinch of salt for 10 minutes, then squeeze out excess water. Add a whisked egg, season, and shape into patties. Fry in oil for a few minutes each side until crispy and cooked through.

TOP TIP
Toss sweet potato chips or
wedges in polenta before roasting
to help keep them crispy.

Allspice Roasted Sweet Potato with Chickpeas and Tangerine

A dish for late wintertime, when sweet potato and citrus seasons collide. Warm roasted sweet potato wedges layered with chickpeas are refreshed by the tangy tangerine and citrusy crunchy toasted coriander seeds.

Swap the sweet potato for any other root vegetable or butternut squash.

SERVES 2 | TIME TO PREPARE – 40 MINUTES

500g/1lb 2oz sweet potatoes, skin-on and sliced into wedges
1 tbsp olive oil
½ tsp ground allspice
2 tangerines or 3 smaller clementines/satsumas
1 x 200g/7oz can chickpeas, drained and rinsed
2 heaped tbsp finely chopped parsley
1 tbsp coriander seeds
salt and pepper

FOR THE DRESSING
1 tbsp tangerine juice (from one of the above tangerines)
1 garlic clove, finely chopped
½ tsp finely grated ginger
½ tsp honey
2 tbsp olive oil

Preheat the oven to 200°C fan/220°C/425°F/gas mark 7. Toss the potatoes in a baking tray with 1 tablespoon of olive oil, the allspice, and season with salt. Roast for 30 minutes until the potatoes are cooked through and browned. Peel the tangerines and remove as much of the pith as you have patience for. Cut one in half and squeeze out 1 tablespoon of juice for your dressing. Slice the remaining tangerine into rounds and set aside. Make the dressing. In a small bowl, mix the tangerine juice, garlic, ginger, and honey, then whisk in the olive oil. Toss the chickpeas in the dressing, season generously with salt and pepper to taste, and add half of the chopped parsley. Leave to marinate while the potatoes finish.

Warm a frying pan to a high heat. Dry toast the coriander seeds until they just start to brown and are fragrant. Roughly bash with a pestle and mortar, leaving some seeds whole. Spread the potatoes onto a sharing platter, use a slotted spoon to remove the chickpeas from the dressing and scatter over the potatoes. Top with the sliced tangerine, drizzle over the remaining dressing, and finish with the coriander seeds and remaining parsley.

Spiced Sweet Potato Hash with Fried Eggs and Coriander Yoghurt

A hash for brunch is a good way to use up any type of potato. You might be expecting a hash to be crispy but in this version, potatoes are gently cooked with onions, a fragrant mix of spices, and just enough water to help them steam. Be careful not to overcook the potato to keep its shape.

Try this same recipe with a white potato.

SERVES 2 | TIME TO PREPARE – 30–35 MINUTES

FOR THE SWEET POTATO HASH

2 tbsp neutral oil, such as rapeseed or light olive oil
1 red onion, finely chopped
1 plump garlic clove, finely chopped
a skinny thumb-sized piece of ginger (approx. 10g/¼oz), peeled and finely chopped
½ tsp black mustard seeds
½ tsp ground cumin
½ tsp ground coriander
½ tsp ground turmeric
2 medium-sized sweet potatoes, peeled and chopped into 1cm/½ inch cubes
juice of 1 lime
2 tbsp finely chopped coriander
salt and pepper
4 fried eggs, to serve

FOR THE CORIANDER YOGHURT

4 tbsp Greek yoghurt
2 tbsp finely chopped coriander
1 garlic clove

Heat the oil in a medium pan over a medium heat. Sauté the onion until it starts to soften. Add the garlic, ginger, spices, and a good pinch of salt. Cook for a minute more, then add the sweet potatoes and 2 tablespoons of water. Cover and lower the heat. Cook for 20 minutes, until the potatoes are fork tender but not mushy. Stir every few minutes to prevent sticking, add more water if it dries out too much. Meanwhile, make the coriander yoghurt. Mix the Greek yoghurt and coriander in a small bowl, then finely grate in the garlic using a microplane, mix well, and refrigerate until ready to serve.

When the potatoes are tender, squeeze in the lime juice to the pan, stir through the chopped coriander and season to taste. Serve each plate topped with 2 fried eggs and drizzle over the coriander yoghurt.

Baharat Spiced Lamb Cutlets, Sweet Potato Purée, and Pomegranate Walnut Salsa

I love to make vegetable purées and use them where you might think of serving mash but want something more refined. This purée just has four ingredients; sweet potatoes, stock, butter, and salt. There's so much flavour from the sweet potatoes – that's all you need. The purée is paired with spiced lamb cutlets and a fruity-nutty-herby-chilli salsa to balance the sweetness in the potato. Serve with a pile of salad leaves.

If you don't eat red meat, or only want to eat it occasionally, swap the lamb for my Chickpea Stuffed Aubergine (*see* page 242), a cauliflower steak, or sumac roasted chicken leg. This purée method will also work with other vegetables like carrot or squash, you might just need to adjust the quantity of stock used to compensate for variances in water content.

SERVES 2 | TIME TO PREPARE – 40 MINUTES

FOR THE LAMB
2 garlic cloves, roughly chopped
½ tbsp baharat
1 tbsp olive oil
zest of 1 lemon
4 lamb cutlets or loin chops, best quality you can afford
salt and pepper

FOR THE SWEET POTATO PURÉE
400g/14oz sweet potato, peeled and chopped into large chunks
90ml/3fl oz vegetable stock
1 tbsp butter

FOR THE SALSA
40g/1½oz walnuts, finely chopped
seeds from half a medium pomegranate (approx. 60g/2¼oz)
20g/¾oz coriander, finely chopped
1 tbsp finely chopped mint leaves
½ small green chilli (approx. 1 tsp once finely chopped), or more to taste
2 tbsp olive oil
juice of 1 lemon

Using a pestle and mortar, pound the garlic with a pinch of salt, then add the baharat, oil, and lemon zest, and smoosh together into a paste. Rub the paste all over the lamb cutlets, avoiding the fatty rind if you can (to avoid it burning). If you have time, cover and leave the lamb to marinate in the fridge for a few hours. Bring to room temperature before cooking.

Make the sweet potato purée. Put the chopped potatoes into a medium saucepan, cover with water, and add a little salt. Bring to the boil and simmer for 12 minutes, until a knife glides through the potatoes with ease. Drain and put the cooked potatoes in a high-speed blender with the stock (or use a stick blender in the pan) and blitz until incredibly silky smooth. Return to the saucepan, add the butter, and season to taste. The purée should be thick enough to hold form on the plate, if too runny, simmer to reduce, if too thick, add more stock. Set aside while you prepare the rest of the dish.

While the potatoes simmer, make your salsa. Mix together the chopped walnuts, pomegranate seeds, coriander, mint, chilli, and olive oil. Add lemon juice to taste. Season and set aside while you cook the lamb.

Heat a heavy-bottomed frying or griddle pan over a medium-high heat. You won't need any oil. Using tongs, hold the cutlets together and cook on their fatty rind for around 4 minutes to render the fat. Check the cutlets frequently to make sure the heat is just right and not burning. Flop them down to cook for 3–4 minutes on each side until charred (this is for medium-rare – I recommend lamb pink in the middle). Transfer the cutlets to a board, and cover with foil to keep them warm while they rest for 4 minutes (half their cooking time). While the lamb rests, heat your sweet potato purée back up so that it is piping hot – be careful it can be volcanic.

Plate up individual servings starting with a pool of sweet potato purée, the salsa, and then top with the lamb cutlets, propped up against each other to create height on the plate for dramatic effect.

SQUASHES

In this chapter, you'll find the summer squash courgette, familiar butternut, and the myriad of weird and wonderful thicker skinned winter varieties such as crown prince, onion, and delicata. As well as having to look up how to spell the official Latin name for these vegetables – *cucurbitaceae* – it doesn't roll off the tongue too easily, so I prefer the informality of squashes.

Courgette and Summer Squash
214 – 221

Butternut Squash
222 – 229

Winter Squash
230 – 237

Courgette and Summer Squash

SUMMER

Courgette's most comfortable spot is hanging out in a Mediterranean recipe with its seasonal pals tomato and aubergine. There is more flavour from the deep green edible skin than the bland soft flesh and edible seeds, so careful consideration of preparation and cookery methods is required. The green courgettes most likely to be in your kitchen are the 'defender' variety, although there are many more green, as well as yellow, skinned varieties, which are interchangeable across recipes. Look out for the small, round globe courgettes, which are excellent for stuffing, or the squat, flying saucer lookalike 'patty pan' summer squash. Or the longer curved 'tromboncino', which could pass as an orchestral instrument – funnily enough, it's named after the trombone. I am not a fan of the larger marrow, hence its absence from this chapter, but a reminder that it exists.

All courgettes and summer squashes can be eaten raw. Charred on a hot cast-iron griddle pan is best, but stuffed, slow cooked, stewed, puréed into soups, or grated and formed into fritters are also good ways to prepare courgettes. Courgettes can be roasted in chunks but I don't believe this brings out their best side.

A vegetable peeler or mandoline is a helpful kitchen tool for the courgette and will enable you to shave all varieties into long ribbons or carpaccio-style circles of varying thickness for marinating raw or searing on a hot griddle pan. To enjoy these ribbons raw, marinate in olive oil, lemon juice and salt for at least 30 minutes to soften.

All courgette plants produce edible flowers. They either grow straight from the vine (male) or are attached to the courgette fruit (female). Flowers can be stuffed and cooked, or torn and added raw to salads or on top of pizza.

Tasty flavour pairings for courgette you'll find in my recipes are; basil, butter, feta cheese, Parmesan cheese, chilli, dill, garlic, lemon, mustard seeds, parsley, pine nuts, and tomatoes. Others to try include; aubergine, ricotta, mozzarella, pasta, peppers, saffron, sage, and yoghurt.

RECIPE IDEA For an outrageously quick summer supper, soften courgette ribbons in butter, add Parmesan, season, and toss with cooked stuffed tortellini.

> **TOP TIP**
> Some recipes might tell you to salt grated courgettes to help get rid
> of their excessive wateriness. You can do this, but I find the salt isn't
> necessary, and squeezing alone will be fine for smaller quantities.

Charred Courgettes, Quinoa, Soft Herbs, and Feta

Just-off-the-griddle warm courgettes, fragrant herbs, soft quinoa, and creamy salty feta; I adore this summer dish. I recently came to the conclusion that slightly thicker oval slices, rather than skinny ribbons of courgettes, are both easier to manoeuvre on the griddle and better at holding their shape once turned through the rest of the ingredients, so now recommend this.

Try this recipe with any variety of courgette. For a colour variation, try mixing one yellow and one green courgette.

SERVES 2 AS A MAIN | TIME TO PREPARE – 30 MINUTES

500g/1lb 2oz (approx. 2 medium) courgettes
olive oil
150g/5½oz quinoa, rinsed
300ml/10fl oz cold vegetable stock
30g/1oz mixed soft herbs (a combination of 2–3 from parsley, coriander, mint, dill, and basil), finely chopped
zest and juice of ½ lemon
100g/3½oz feta cheese, crumbled
2 tbsp toasted pine nuts or pumpkin seeds
salt and pepper

Slice your courgettes into 5mm/¼ inch slices on a 30-degree angle to create ovals. Transfer to a bowl and toss with 2 tablespoons of olive oil. Set aside. Place the quinoa and stock in a medium-sized saucepan that you have a lid for. Bring to the boil, cover, turn to a low heat (you need a very gentle bubble – I recommend moving to your smallest hob), and cook for 18–20 minutes, by which time the stock should be absorbed and the quinoa soft. Turn off the heat and let sit for 5 minutes with the lid on to absorb any remaining moisture. Transfer to a large mixing bowl to cool.

Towards the end of quinoa cooking time, heat up your griddle pan to medium-high. Working in batches, fry the slices for around 3 minutes on each side, or until charred and cooked through. Season the cooked courgettes with a little salt. When the quinoa has cooled a little, toss through the chopped herbs and grate over the lemon zest. Juice half of the lemon and add that into the quinoa too, along with 2 tablespoons of olive oil, and stir well to combine. Season to taste. To serve, plate up the quinoa and layer over the warm charred courgettes. Top with the crumbled feta and toasted pine nuts.

Courgette 'Smoosh' on Toast with Halloumi, Honey, and Chilli

This unctuous green smoosh is an ideal toast topper as an alternative to avocado. Here, I serve it with pan-fried halloumi, honey, and chilli, but as with avocado, there are far more iterations to be enjoyed...

To transform the smoosh into a pasta sauce, loosen it with a little pasta water and add Parmesan. Cooked pancetta or peas are good additions. A batch of smoosh will provide enough for two recipes – so try them both!

SERVES 2, PLUS A LITTLE LEFT OVER | TIME TO PREPARE – 50 MINUTES

FOR THE COURGETTE SMOOSH
750g/1lb 10oz (approx. 3 medium) courgettes, coarsely grated
1½ tbsp butter
olive oil
1 onion, finely chopped
1 garlic clove, finely chopped
juice of 1 lemon
salt and pepper

TO SERVE
½ x 225g/8oz block of halloumi cheese, sliced into 4 slices
2 slices of bread
honey
chilli flakes

Place the grated courgettes in a sieve over a bowl. Give them a good squeeze to remove as much water as you have patience for. Meanwhile, over a low heat melt the butter and 1 teaspoon of olive oil in a frying pan big enough to host all of the courgette. Add the onions, season with a pinch of salt, and cook for 10 minutes until completely softened. Add the garlic and cook for a further minute before stirring in the grated courgette. Turn up the heat to medium-high and cook, stirring intermittently, for around 20 minutes, until the courgette has reduced and completely broken down into a smoosh that is thick enough to spread. Add a little lemon juice (start with half a lemon) for freshness and season to taste. If not eating straight away, cool and store in an airtight container in the fridge for up to 5 days.

In a heavy-bottomed frying pan or griddle pan, heat 1 tablespoon of olive oil to a medium-high heat and fry the halloumi on each side for 2–3 minutes until nicely browned. Generously heap the courgette smoosh on toasted bread, top with the halloumi, a drizzle of honey, and a sprinkle of chilli flakes.

Round Courgettes Stuffed with Bulgur Wheat, Tomato, and Capers

I first cooked this recipe whilst working on a retreat in rural south west France. I was meant to be stuffing regular courgettes, but was seduced by the idea of something different when I found round globe courgettes at the local market. Once you've scooped out the courgettes, keep the little hats, they help the flavours to mingle together during the bake. Serve with roasted potatoes and a sliced tomato salad.

You can also use this stuffing for regular courgettes. Halve and scoop out the seeds and enough flesh to create a cavity, then follow the method as below. The stuffing will crisp a little in the oven, with no protective courgette 'hat', which is absolutely fine.

SERVES 2 | TIME TO PREPARE – 45 MINUTES

40g/1½oz bulgur wheat
2 medium-sized round courgettes or 4 smaller ones (approx. 280g/9¾oz each)
olive oil
1 small onion, finely chopped
1 celery stick, finely chopped
1 garlic clove, finely chopped
2 medium-sized tomatoes, cut in half, seeds scooped out and flesh diced
½ tsp fresh or dried thyme
½ tsp dried oregano
a pinch of chilli flakes
2 tbsp capers
1 tsp balsamic vinegar
1 heaped tbsp finely chopped parsley
Parmesan cheese
salt and pepper

Preheat the oven to 180°C fan/200°C/400°F/gas mark 6.

First prepare your bulgur wheat. Place in a small heatproof bowl, submerge the grains with just a shallow layer of boiling water, then cover the bowl with a plate. Leave for up to 20 minutes, by which time all the water should have been absorbed, and the grains tender but not mushy. Fluff up with a fork and set aside.

Meanwhile prepare the courgettes. Slice off the tops to make little hats. Scoop out enough of the flesh to leave a cavity to stuff, leaving a 5mm/¼ inch border. Rub the insides and outsides of the courgettes with olive oil – you'll need around 1 tablespoon for this. Place upside down on a baking tray along with the lids and bake for 20 minutes. Remove from the oven until cool enough to handle. Drain off any escaped liquid.

While the courgettes are baking make your sauce. Over a medium-low heat, warm 1 tablespoon of olive oil in a small saucepan. Sauté the onion and celery with a pinch of salt for 8–10 minutes until fully softened. Add the garlic, diced tomatoes, thyme, oregano, chilli flakes, and 2 tablespoons of water. Bring to a gentle bubble and cook over a medium heat for around 10 minutes, or until the tomato flesh has broken down. Remove from the heat and mix in the bulgur, capers, balsamic vinegar, and parsley. Season to taste.

Stuff the courgettes with the bulgur filling until fit to burst. Top with a heavy dusting of finely grated Parmesan, pop the lids back on, and return to the oven for 10–15 minutes, until piping hot and the courgettes are tender. Serve warm.

Griddled Patty Pan Carpaccio with Tarragon Vinaigrette

Sunshine circles of griddled yellow patty pan summer squash served with the punchy flavours of tarragon and grainy mustard. An excellent side dish to anything summery; meat, fish, or plant based. If you don't have a griddle pan, then treat yourself to one – they are fairly inexpensive and it will become one of your most used kitchen pans.

If you can't get hold of a patty pan, try this recipe with regular green or yellow courgettes.

SERVES 2 AS A SIDE | TIME TO PREPARE – 10 MINUTES

1 medium-sized yellow patty pan squash (approx. 150–175g/5½–6oz)
olive oil
¼ tsp wholegrain mustard
zest and juice of ½ lemon
1 tbsp finely chopped tarragon, plus a few extra leaves, to garnish
4 anchovies from a tin in olive oil (optional)
salt and pepper

Slice the patty pan into 3mm/¼ inch circles, either by hand or using a mandoline on the smallest setting. If the seeds get in the way, pull them out as you go. Put the slices into a bowl and toss with 2 tablespoons of olive oil, to coat well.

Make the dressing. In a small bowl, mix together the mustard, lemon juice and zest, and 1 tablespoon of olive oil until well combined, then stir through the chopped tarragon. Season to taste.

Heat a cast-iron griddle pan to medium-high. Work in batches and char the oiled slices of patty pan for around 30 seconds on each side, until the flesh softens and griddle lines appear. Plate up the cooked patty pan on a large plate, overlapping the cooked slices a little until you cover the plate. Season with salt.

Drizzle just enough dressing over the patty pan plate to lightly cover. Add a few extra sprigs of tarragon and the anchovies as a garnish, if you like.

Pea and Goat's Cheese Stuffed Courgette Flowers with Honey

In Italy, courgette flowers are usually stuffed with ricotta and deep fried with a crispy batter, which is how I once had them in a restaurant in Sorrento. In my home kitchen, I prefer to bake them. You miss out on the crispy coating but stuffed courgette flower recipes are really all about the filling anyway – here a delicious combination of peas, soft goat's cheese, and zingy lemon. After you've drizzled over the sweet honey, a handful of seasoned diced chopped tomatoes with a drizzle of olive oil makes an additional fresh and summery garnish.

If the flower has been harvested attached to a baby courgette, keep it intact and increase the cooking time to 12–15 minutes.

SERVES 2 (2 FLOWERS EACH) | TIME TO PREPARE – 30 MINUTES

85g/3oz frozen peas, defrosted with boiling water from the kettle and drained
60g/2¼oz soft goat's cheese
a handful of chives and mint (approx. 2 tsp), finely chopped
zest of ½ lemon
4 good-looking courgette flowers, suitable for stuffing
olive oil
drizzle of honey
salt and pepper

Preheat the oven to 180°C fan/200°C/400°F/gas mark 6.

Pulse the defrosted peas in a food processor until roughly broken down, a little texture is good. Add to a small bowl with the goat's cheese and use a fork to mash everything together into a paste. Stir in the chopped herbs and lemon zest, and season to taste.

Gently pull back the petals, being careful not to tear them, and pop out the stamen to create room for your filling. Spoon a tablespoon of filling into each flower cavity and twist the loose ends of the flowers together to seal. Place onto a lined baking tray, drizzle with olive oil, and bake in the oven for 8–10 minutes, or until the flowers are lightly browned.

Carefully transfer to a serving plate and generously drizzle honey over the stuffed flowers. Eat immediately.

Butternut Squash

AUTUMN

Sweet, nutty butternut is the most widely available of the winter squashes and British supermarkets are rarely without it, often stocking imported ones throughout the year. Although, I do think we should save it for autumn, when butternut's warm orange flesh mirrors the colour of falling leaves.

Butternut squash is best cooked. Roasting intensifies butternut's natural sweetness, and is always my go-to cooking method over boiling or steaming, even if the end destination is a soup or stew. Roast in wedges or cubes then add to a salad, risotto, or quiche, layer into a gratin, or pair with autumnal spices and blitz into a soup. Braised or simmered, there are tagines, curries, and stews to be explored. Mashed squash can provide a tasty filling for large ravioli-style pasta and must be served with buttered sage.

Preparing this rollable cylinder of a vegetable requires a sharp knife and a confident hand, but, with guidance, anyone can do it without ending up in A&E. First split the squash into two pieces, separating the seed-containing round end and the cylindrical piece. This will be the most difficult chop. Now you've got multiple flat surfaces to steady yourself for the next cuts. Remove the stalk and tip, peel off the skin (if doing so) with a sharp peeler, and break down into cubes or wedges depending on your recipe. Scoop out the seeds. To peel or not to peel butternut squash is a very good question. The skin is technically edible, but leaving it on depends on your recipe, as well as personal preference. If your roasted squash cubes are destined for a stew or risotto, floating bits of peel are obviously not very desirable. But, if you roast the cubes or wedges until the flesh is soft and the skin a little crispy and toss through a warm autumnal salad, it's fine.

Don't discard the seeds, save for snacking. Rinse to remove any stringy flesh, toss with salt and rosemary, and bake at 180°C fan/200°C/400°F/gas mark 6 for 5–10 minutes until crispy.

Tasty flavour pairings for squash you'll find in my recipes are; butter, blue cheese, chilli, coconut milk, coriander, garlic, ginger, lemon, lime, onions, prosciutto, parsley, pasta, and sage. Others to try include; bitter leaves, ricotta, soft cheese, chickpeas, cinnamon, cream, leeks, rosemary, and spinach.

RECIPE IDEA For an easy gratin, roast slices of squash until soft, then layer with softened onions and béchamel sauce. Top with sage breadcrumbs mixed with Parmsean and bake until golden.

TOP TIP
To save the faff of peeling, cut the squash in half and bake for 60–90 minutes at 180°C fan/200°C/400°F/gas mark 6 until it collapses and the flesh is soft. Once cool enough to handle, scoop out the edible parts to use.

Squash and Blue Cheese Risotto with Crispy Prosciutto

Creamy sweet squash, tangy blue cheese, and salty prosciutto complement each other in this comforting bowl of risotto – it's the first thing I want to make each autumn. It's quite enough on its own, but lovely with a few salad leaves on the side.

You can use any variety of squash for this risotto. Ideally you will need a squash you can both mash to stir through the cooked risotto, and leave in larger pieces to use as a garnish. If you are using a squash with a skin that is edible, leave it on for the garnish. For a vegetarian option leave out the crisped ham.

SERVES 2 | TIME TO PREPARE – 45 MINUTES

1 small butternut squash (approx. 850g/1lb 14oz), peeled and diced into
   2cm/¾ inch cubes (approx. 600g/1lb 6oz, once peeled and diced)
olive oil
4 slices (60g/2¼oz) prosciutto crudo
1 small onion or banana shallot, finely diced
1 garlic clove, finely chopped
150g/5½oz arborio risotto rice
125ml/4fl oz white wine
850ml/1½ pints warm chicken stock or vegetable stock
50g/1¾oz blue cheese, such as Stilton, Roquefort or gorgonzola
1 tbsp butter
salt and pepper

Preheat the oven to 180°C fan/200°C/400°F/gas mark 6.

Toss the peeled and chopped squash onto a baking tray in a single layer with 1 tablespoon of olive oil and season with salt. Roast for 25–30 minutes, until it will easily mash with the back of a fork.

Meanwhile, heat 1 tablespoon of olive oil in a wide, deep frying pan over medium heat. Lower in the slices of prosciutto (you may need to do this in batches) and cook for 2–3 minutes, until they crisp up. Remove using tongs and set aside. Leave any rendered fat in the pan and top up with olive oil so that you have around 1 tablespoon of fat in the pan. Over a low-medium heat sauté the chopped onions with a pinch of salt for 5–8 minutes until softened. Add the garlic, cook for a further minute, then stir in the rice. Turn up the heat and pour in the wine. Cook until almost all of the wine has evaporated.

Lower the heat a little and start adding the warm stock, one ladleful at a time – wait for each ladleful of stock to be absorbed before adding the next. Continue this for the next 20–22 minutes, maintaining the heat at a gentle bubble, until the rice is al dente. You may not need all the stock.

When the squash is soft, divide it into two piles. Mash half with the back of your fork. Stir this into the risotto while the rice is in its final stage of cooking to give your risotto base an orange hue.

To finish the dish, turn off the heat, add the crumbled blue cheese and butter into the risotto pan, and cover with a lid. Rest for 2 minutes. Stir in the remaining squash cubes, season the risotto to taste, and plate up with the crispy ham on top.

Pithivier with Butternut Squash, Curly Kale, Mozzarella, and Sun-dried Tomato

A pithivier is a French enclosed circular pie. It looks fancy, but with the saviour of shop-bought puff pastry it is relatively simple. You will only need the cylinder end of the squash for this – choose one with a diameter of roughly 8–10cm/3¼–4 inches. Keep the rest of the squash wrapped in the fridge for up to a week, or cube and roast for tomorrow's salad. Serve with steamed broccoli or a light green salad.

You could replace the squash in this recipe with a similar sized disc of celeriac or beetroot wedges; use a total of 350g/12oz of vegetable across the two pies.

SERVES 2
TIME TO PREPARE – 1 HOUR 10 MINUTES (MOST OF THAT IS HANDS-OFF OVEN TIME)

2 x 2.5cm/1 inch thick discs of butternut squash sliced from the cylinder end of a
    medium-sized squash, peeled
olive oil
1 garlic clove, finely chopped
40g/1½oz curly kale, stripped from stalk and roughly chopped
1 x 320g/11½oz sheet ready rolled puff pastry, brought to room temperature
4 tsp sun-dried tomato paste
100g/3½oz ball mozzarella cheese, sliced into 6 pieces
1 egg yolk, lightly whisked
salt and pepper

Preheat the oven to 180°C fan/200°C/400°F/gas mark 6.

Rub the squash discs all over with a little olive oil and season. Place on a baking tray and bake in the oven for 40 minutes, until a knife will easily glide through the centre. Remove from the oven and slide the squash onto a cooling rack to cool down. Raise the temperature of the oven to 200°C fan/220°C/425°F/gas mark 7.

Meanwhile, prepare the rest of your filling. Add ½ tablespoon of olive oil to a frying pan over a medium heat and briefly sauté the chopped garlic to soften. Add the chopped kale along with 1 tablespoon of water and cook for 1–2 minutes, until just wilted. Set aside to cool.

Unroll the sheet of puff pastry and use a bowl or plate as a guide to cut your pastry circles. The two circles for the base should have a diameter at least 2cm/1 inch bigger than your butternut squash discs. The other two circles for the top need to be 1cm/½ inch bigger than the pastry bases.

Transfer the smaller discs to a lined baking tray. Place the butternut squash discs in the centre of the smaller circles and top each with 2 teaspoons of sun-dried tomato paste, three slices of mozzarella, and the cooked kale. Wet the edges of the pastry base with a little water, then place the larger pastry circle on top of the filling to create a dome shape. Squidge the edges together, then use a small knife to make a tiny hole at the top. Gently score curves around the pie from the centre hole towards the edges (don't go through the pastry) to create the classic pithivier look. Brush the pastries all over with the whisked egg yolk.

Bake the pithiviers in the oven for 25 minutes until the pastry is browned and crispy all over, and the base is firm and crusty when tapped.

Roasted Butternut Squash with Buckwheat, Harissa, and Pomegranate

Heady with harissa and bejewelled with pomegranate, this warm golden salad pops up on my retreat catering menus every autumn. There, I serve a large platter alongside a tart bowl of hummus and leafy salad, but at home I'd just serve a bowl of this with crumbled feta. Cooking buckwheat for a marinated salad is different to how a packet might tell you to – it's important the grains keep their shape rather than go to mush. The method I use is similar to how you cook pasta and it's imperative that the buckwheat is drained well before it's completely soft. You can swap the buckwheat for any other grain, just adjust the cooking method accordingly.

This recipe will work with any of the firm winter squashes that keep their shape once cooked. I also like it with onion squash – leave the skin on and slice in crescent moons.

SERVES 2 | TIME TO PREPARE – 40 MINUTES

1 small butternut squash (approx. 850g/1lb 14oz), peeled and diced into
   2cm/¾ inch cubes (approx. 600g/1lb 6oz once peeled and diced)
1 tbsp olive oil
150g/5½oz raw buckwheat groats, rinsed
1½ tbsp rose harissa paste
15g/½oz dill or coriander or a mixture, finely chopped
60g/2¼oz pomegranate seeds (approx. ½ a medium pomegranate)
zest and juice of ½ lemon
salt and pepper

Preheat the oven to 180°C fan/200°C/400°F/gas mark 6. Toss the squash on a baking tray in a single layer with 1 tablespoon of olive oil and season with salt. Roast for 25–30 minutes, until fork tender and charred on the edges. Meanwhile, cook and cool the buckwheat. Bring 1 litre/1¾ pints of water and 1 teaspoon of salt to the boil in a medium saucepan. Pour in the buckwheat and bring back to the boil. Turn down to a simmer and cook for 12 minutes, until just soft enough to eat but not mushy. Drain the buckwheat, rinse well under cold water and shake off the excess water. To dry out fully, spread out on kitchen paper or a dry clean tea towel on top of a cold baking tray.

In a large bowl, mix the cooked buckwheat groats with the rose harissa paste. Make sure the grains are well coated. Fold through the warm squash, chopped herbs, three-quarters of the pomegranate seeds, and lemon zest and juice. Taste to adjust the seasoning, adding more harissa for extra spice. Pile up on a platter or in individual bowls and scatter over the remaining pomegranate.

Butternut squash is best cooked. Roasting intensifies butternut's natural sweetness, and is always my go-to cooking method over boiling or steaming, even if the end destination is a soup or stew.

Winter Squash

There are over 100 varieties of winter squash. You won't always find a wide variety in the supermarket, but on veg patches, in farmers markets and veg boxes, you may discover something new. I couldn't possibly include every winter squash in this book – I'm not sure I have tried all of them myself yet – but the varying style of recipes should help you out with whatever squash you stumble upon. Many have multiple names, so if you find one that looks familiar, but you don't recognize the name this might be why.

Some of my favourite varieties to look out for are crown prince, kabocha, onion squash (also called red kuri), delicata, acorn, and carnival. Avoid cooking with Halloween pumpkin – it's fabulous for carving but can be flavourless. Many of the smaller knobbly gourds are best left as table decorations as the flesh can be quite stringy. A general rule of thumb is that the larger ones are best for puréeing or roasting in wedges and the smaller ones for stuffing. Crown prince (blue skinned), kabocha (green, teal, or orange skin varieties), onion (red skin), are all larger, firmer squashes with creamy orange flesh and nuttier notes. While they differ in firmness of flesh a little, you should be able to switch them in and out of recipes (as well as those for the butternut) that call for roasting or puréeing.

The smaller squashes like acorn and carnival, are perfect for stuffing. Slice off the top to create a lid and scoop out the seeds to create a cavity. Stuffings can be made from legumes, grains, or minced meat, combined with aromatics (onion, leek, garlic), spices for flavour, and something wet to bring it together (stock, chopped tomatoes, coconut milk). Delicata, with its yellow and green skin and deep yellow flesh, sits somewhere between the two – I think of it as a firmer courgette. Cut into rings and remove the seeds. It looks stunning in a warm autumnal salad (*see* page 236).

Take care when preparing these squashes, the larger ones can be beastly in size. Use a sharp chef-style knife to cut in half through the root, remove the seeds, then slice into wedges. Never peel before chopping. You can always remove the skin after cooking, when it has softened, if you'd rather not eat it.

Tips on flavour pairings are the same as Butternut Squash on page 222.

RECIPE IDEA For an easy salad, roast crescent moons of squash in olive oil and salt until tender, and toss with purple chicory leaves. Drizzle over a sweet balsamic vinegar dressing, and top with feta and toasted hazelnuts.

Crown Prince Squash, Cannellini Beans, and Chilli Sage Butter

The simple beauty of serving a seasonal ingredient with flavours that go well together. Roasted wedges of golden crown prince drizzled with fragrant butter take pride of place on top of the quick-cook bean equivalent of a creamy risotto. Serve with bread to wipe the buttery bowl clean.

Try with any of the larger squashes that can be sliced and roasted.

SERVES 2 | TIME TO PREPARE – 35 MINUTES

FOR THE SQUASH
½ crown prince squash (700–800g/1lb 9oz–1lb 12oz), scrubbed clean, sliced into
   3cm/1¼ inch wedges and seeds removed
1 tbsp olive oil
salt and pepper

FOR THE DISH
50g/1¾oz butter
10 fresh sage leaves
½ tsp chilli flakes
1 plump or 2 small garlic cloves, finely sliced
1 x 400g/14oz can cannellini beans, drained and rinsed
175ml/6fl oz vegetable stock
salt and pepper

Preheat the oven to 200°C fan/220°C/425°F/gas mark 7. Place the squash wedges in a single layer on a baking tray, toss with 1 tablespoon of olive oil, and season. Roast for 30 minutes, turning over halfway to ensure an even colour, until lightly browned and soft enough for a knife to glide through.

When the squash is almost ready, prepare the rest of the dish. Melt half of the butter in a frying pan over a medium-high heat, until frothy. Add the sage leaves and the chilli flakes, and cook for 45 seconds, until the sage is just starting to darken. Pour into a small ramekin and set aside.

Put the frying pan back on the heat. If a few chilli flakes remain in the pan, leave them there, they'll add flavour to the beans. Add the remaining butter to the pan and, once frothy, add the garlic and toss for 30 seconds. Add the drained beans and stock. Use the back of your spoon to gently crush some of the beans to release some of their starch to create a creamy sauce. Cook for 2–3 minutes until it has reduced to a loose risotto consistency and is piping hot. Season to taste. Loosen with water if you'd like saucier beans. Plate up the beans, stack the squash wedges on top, and pour over the butter to serve.

Any Squash, Coconut, and Lime Soup

This silky soup recipe will work with butternut or any of the winter squashes. The flavour will differ between the squash so when 'seasoning to taste' you'll need to practise your flavour balancing skills. Lime will help cut through sweetness, whilst honey or a pinch of sugar will counteract any bitterness. Serve with hunks of warm bread for dunking.

SERVES 2–3 | TIME TO PREPARE – 1 HOUR 15 MINUTES

1 squash (approx. 1.3kg/3lb before carving)
2 tbsp neutral oil (light olive oil, rapeseed or coconut oil)
1 onion, thinly sliced
2 garlic cloves, finely chopped
thumb-tip-sized piece of ginger, peeled and finely chopped
1 x 200ml/7fl oz can coconut milk
250ml/9fl oz vegetable stock
juice of 1–2 limes
chilli flakes
salt and pepper

Preheat the oven to 180°C fan/200°C/400°F/gas mark 6.

Carefully cut the squash into half or quarters (it's fine to leave the seeds where they are). Place cut side up on a baking tray, drizzle over 1 tablespoon of oil, season with salt, and roast in the oven for 1 hour or until the flesh is completely soft. Rest until cool enough to handle, then use a spoon to scrape out and discard the seeds, and carefully scoop out all of the flesh to use.

While the squash is cooling, start on the soup base. Heat 1 tablespoon of oil in a medium-large saucepan over a low heat. Add the sliced onions and a pinch of salt, and sauté for 10 minutes until fully softened. Add the garlic and ginger, and cook for a further minute. Add in the cooked squash flesh, coconut milk, and stock. Simmer for 5–10 minutes to mingle the flavours.

Blend in a high-speed blender or with a hand blender until silky smooth. Season with salt, pepper, and plenty of zingy lime juice to taste. Ladle into bowls and sprinkle over chilli flakes to serve.

Whole Baked Squash Filled with Comté and Chive Macaroni Cheese

Who needs a ceramic baking dish when you can use a squash shell as an edible dish? A smaller onion, acorn, or carnival squash is a good size for stuffing. Even the smaller squashes vary in size so if you end up with too much filling, pile it into a ramekin or small baking dish and cook alongside the main event. If you can't find French Comté cheese, substitute with Swiss Gruyère or a strong mature Cheddar. Serve with a side salad.

If you'd like to make this more extravagant, add in a handful of raw peeled prawns (85g/3oz) to the macaroni mix as you pile it into the squash shells.

SERVES 2 | TIME TO PREPARE – 1 HOUR

1 medium-sized squash (approx. 700g/1lb 9oz), split in half through the stalk, seeds
   scooped out
2 tsp butter
90g/3¼oz dried elbow macaroni or other similar small-shaped pasta
60g/2¼oz Comté cheese, grated, plus extra for the topping
2 tbsp finely chopped chives
25g/1oz fresh breadcrumbs
salt and pepper

FOR THE BÉCHAMEL SAUCE
15g/½oz butter
15g/½oz plain flour
1 tsp Dijon mustard
250ml/9fl oz semi-skimmed milk

Preheat the oven to 180°C fan/200°C/400°F/gas mark 6.

Prick the inside of the squash halves all over with a fork, season, and add the butter into the cavity. Place on a baking tray and roast in the oven for 30–35 minutes, or until a knife glides easily through the squash flesh. Five minutes into the cooking time, when the butter has melted, swirl it around so it drips into the fork marks and flavours the squash.

Meanwhile, cook the macaroni. Bring a medium-sized saucepan of salted water to boil. Cook for 6 minutes (or according to packet instructions) until just al dente. Drain, reserve a few tablespoons of the cooking water, and set aside.

Make the béchamel sauce. Melt the butter in a medium-sized saucepan over a medium heat. Add the flour and stir constantly for 2 minutes as it thickens to a doughy paste – this is your roux. Add the Dijon mustard, then slowly add the milk, stirring constantly with a wooden spoon, so that the roux loosens into a thick sauce. Bring to a simmer, stirring regularly, then cook on a low-medium heat for 5–10 minutes, or until thickened – it should coat the back of a spoon. Add the Comté, half of the chopped chives, and season to taste (if you want to add more cheese, now is the time). Add the cooked macaroni into the sauce, loosen with a couple of tablespoons of the reserved pasta water for a consistency of double cream.

Prepare the breadcrumb topping by mixing together the breadcrumbs with the remainder of the chopped chives.

When the squash has finished its pre-roast, remove from the oven and pile the macaroni cheese filling across the two halves. Scatter the chive breadcrumbs across the top of the squash, top with a little more cheese, and return to the oven to bake for a final 10–15 minutes, or until the cheese has melted and browned.

Warm Delicata with Black Rice, Cavolo Nero, and Za'atar Dressing

I like to prepare delicata squash by cutting it into thick rounds, so you're left with a stunning set of yellow hoops. These contrast with black rice and deep green cavolo nero for a recipe that gives all the shades of autumn. There are a number of varieties of black rice, so please check the suggested cooking time of whichever you're using. The top of this dish can always be enhanced by a little feta.

Any of the squashes that can be roasted will work in this recipe, but you'll miss out on the hoop effect.

SERVES 2 | TIME TO PREPARE – 45 MINUTES

1 delicata squash (approx. 500g/1lb 2oz), sliced into 1–2cm/½ –¾ inch rounds, seeds
   scooped out
1 tbsp olive oil
3 sprigs of fresh thyme, leaves stripped from the stalk
125g/4½oz black rice, rinsed well
4 leaves of cavolo nero, stems removed, and thinly shredded
1 tbsp toasted pumpkin seeds
salt and pepper

FOR THE DRESSING
1 tsp honey
1 garlic clove, finely chopped
2 tsp red wine vinegar
1 tsp za'atar, plus extra for garnishing the dish
2 tbsp olive oil

Preheat the oven to 180°C fan/200°C/400°F/gas mark 6.

Place the squash pieces in a single layer on a baking tray. Toss with 1 tablespoon of olive oil, the thyme leaves and season with salt. Roast in the oven for 30–35 minutes, until tender, and the flesh is starting to caramelize.

Cook the rice with timings according to variety and packet instructions, taste test well before the cooking time is up, the rice should be cooked through, al dente, but not mushy. Drain and give a good shake, to remove the excess cooking water.

Meanwhile, make up the dressing and prepare the cavolo nero. In a small bowl or jar, stir together the honey, garlic, vinegar, and 1 teaspoon of the za'atar to combine. Add in the oil then whisk (or add the jar lid and shake) together to emulsify. Season with salt and pepper to taste.

Place the shredded cavolo nero in a bowl large enough to mix the entire salad, add 1 teaspoon of the dressing. Using your hands, massage the oil and salt into the cavolo nero for around one minute to soften the fibres in the kale. While the rice is still warm, add to the bowl with the cavolo nero. Pour over three-quarters of the remaining dressing, making sure all the grains of rice are well coated. Taste and adjust seasoning.

Plate up the rice and cavolo nero on a serving platter and top with the cooked squash pieces. Drizzle the remaining dressing over the squash pieces, then garnish with a generous scattering of za'atar and the toasted pumpkin seeds.

SUMMER VEGETABLES

A glorious group of vegetables that
keep us longing for hot summer days.
Biologically speaking, aubergines, peppers,
and tomatoes are nightshades, cucumber
is a member of the cucurbit family and
sweetcorn kernels are seeds of a grass.
There is a saying that things that grow
together, go together, so they're going
together here in this chapter.

Aubergine

SUMMER

These glossy purple-skinned vegetables with a mild tasting soft flesh, suck up oil and flavour like a sponge. Quite unlike its nightshade relatives (tomato, pepper, and potatoes) in texture and flavour, but a perfect recipe partner for them. Popular in the Mediterranean, you'll also find aubergine in recipes across Asia and particularly South East Asia, its native home. If aubergines are undercooked they can be bitter, or if overcooked, the slimy texture can be off-putting. Like Goldilocks' porridge, it needs to be cooked just right.

In addition to the dark purple aubergine, there are speckled skin 'graffiti' varieties, or some in various shades of purple in regular or rounded bulb shapes. The earliest version of an aubergine was small, white, and similar in appearance to an egg, hence the name eggplant in some English speaking countries. My experience of cooking these different varieties is that, once the aubergines have been cooked, they all taste much the same. Look out for baby aubergines; they're usually imported to the UK from Kenya. Use in curries or stuff them, Gujarati-style, with peanut and coconut.

Cooking methods that suit aubergine are frying, braising, stewing, or roasting. Aubergines work well in curries and various stewed sauces like caponata, ratatouille, or pasta alla Norma. Slices of aubergine lend themselves to griddling, layering into a bake, or rolling into a tube around a creamy filling (*see* Aubergine Rolls, page 244), or aubergine halves themselves can be stuffed. In the Japanese dish nasu dengaku, halves or wedges are smothered in sticky sweet miso glaze, which is absolutely divine. Aubergine flesh can also be puréed. In baba ganoush, the whole aubergine is blistered over a flame for smokiness and the soft flesh scooped out and smooshed together into a dip with garlic, tahini, olive oil, and lemon juice. Aubergines are soft and relatively easy to slice. The peel is edible and is left on for cooking in most instances. The stalk isn't edible, but if you are serving an aubergine half, slice through it and leave it attached, or it looks a bit odd.

Tasty flavour pairings in my recipes are; ricotta cheese, Parmesan, chilli, chickpeas, garlic, ginger, lemon, onions, parsley, pomegranate, soy sauce, tahini, tomatoes, thyme, and yoghurt. Others to try include; breadcrumbs, cinnamon, honey, lamb, lentils, miso, mustard, pasta, peppers, and rosemary.

RECIPE IDEA Add texture to soft roasted aubergine by tossing in a polenta crust before baking. Split into quarters, dust with an equal mix of 15g/½oz quick-cook polenta, 15g/½oz plain flour, and season. Drizzle with olive oil and bake at 180°C fan/200°C/400°F/gas mark 6 for 45 minutes. Serve with a squidge of honey.

TOP TIP
For what it's worth, the current widely accepted advice across the
culinary world is that there is no longer a need to salt aubergines to
extract their bitterness, which marvellously cuts down on their prep time.

Chickpea Stuffed Aubergine with Tahini Yoghurt

These lightly spiced chickpea stuffed aubergines, swimming in a pool of tahini yoghurt, and topped with pomegranate seeds (or molasses out of season) are a dazzling vegetarian centrepiece. I have often served this dish for my retreat clients, especially in Italy and the south of France, where the aubergines are both flavourful and ginormous. If you happen to find ginormous aubergines, half per person is probably enough. A simple side salad (try the Fennel Harissa on page 68) is all that's needed to turn this into a complete meal.

Not another vegetable from this chapter, but surprisingly, this recipe method also works with sweet potatoes. Choose rugby-ball shaped sweet potatoes around 300g/10½oz each.

SERVES 2 | TIME TO PREPARE – 55 MINUTES

FOR THE AUBERGINES
2 medium-sized aubergines
olive oil
1 banana shallot or ½ onion, finely chopped
1 garlic clove, finely chopped
1 tsp ground cumin
1 tsp ground coriander
¼ tsp ground allspice
1 x 400g/14oz can chickpeas, drained and rinsed
juice of ½ lemon
1 heaped tbsp finely chopped parsley
handful of fresh pomegranate seeds or a light drizzle of pomegranate molasses
salt and pepper

FOR THE TAHINI YOGHURT
200g/7oz Greek yoghurt
1 tbsp tahini
zest and juice of ½ lemon

Preheat the oven to 200°C fan/220°C/425°F/gas mark 7.

Slice the aubergines in half lengthways, straight through the stalk. Use a sharp knife to score a 5mm/¼ inch border around the edge of the aubergine. Rub the skin and flesh with around 1 tablespoon of olive oil and place flesh-side down on a lined baking tray. Roast in the oven for 40 minutes, or until the flesh is completely soft and gives way when squeezed at the deepest point. Remove from the oven and wait until cool enough to handle. Reduce the oven temperature to 180°C fan/200°C/400°F/gas mark 6.

Scoop out the aubergine flesh inside of the scored border, work carefully so you don't tear the skins. Shred the aubergine flesh with two forks and set aside with the skins for now.

Make the filling. Heat 1 tablespoon of olive oil in a large frying pan over a low heat and sauté the shallot with a pinch of salt until softened (8–10 minutes). Add the garlic and the spices, cooking until fragrant, then add the chickpeas and shredded aubergine flesh. Mix well and cook for a couple of minutes to help any excess water from the aubergine evaporate. Add the lemon juice, most of the parsley and season to taste with salt, pepper, and olive oil. Pile the mixture back into the aubergine skins, doming it on top, transfer back on the lined baking tray, lightly drizzle with olive oil, and bake for 10 minutes for the filling to set in the skins and to warm through.

Make the tahini yoghurt by whisking together the Greek yoghurt with the tahini and the lemon zest and juice until completely smooth. Season to taste.

To serve, spread the tahini yoghurt over one serving platter or 2 individual plates and top with the stuffed aubergine. Garnish with the remainder of the chopped parsley and a scattering of pomegranate seeds, or a light zig-zag drizzle of pomegranate molasses.

Baked Aubergine Rolls
with Ricotta and Harissa

This is a tasty summer aubergine bake that provides stiff competition for the classic parmigiana. Rolls of partially baked softened aubergine are stuffed with a harissa-spiked ricotta filling, nestled tightly into a dish, baked with a passata sauce, and topped with Parmesan. You'll need at least 10 aubergine rolls to feed 2 people, and the slices with skin on one side can be used too, just roll them with the skin on the inside. Serve with some fresh green leaves.

The rolls can also be made from thickly sliced ribbons of courgette. Adjust cooking times to suit.

SERVES 2 | TIME TO PREPARE – 1 HOUR 5 MINUTES

2 medium aubergines, stalk removed and sliced lengthways
    into 10–12 x 1cm/½ inch slices
olive oil
400g/14oz passata
a pinch of caster sugar
2 garlic cloves, finely chopped
3 sprigs of thyme, leaves stripped
250g/9oz ricotta, drained
1 tbsp rose harissa paste
zest of 1 lemon
40g/1½oz Parmesan cheese, finely grated
1 tbsp toasted pine nuts (optional)
1 tbsp finely chopped parsley (optional)
salt and pepper

Preheat the oven to 200°C fan/220°C/425°F/gas mark 7.

Brush the aubergine slices all over with olive oil (approx. 2 tablespoons) and place on a lined baking tray in a single layer. Season with salt. Bake for 20–25 minutes, until lightly browned and soft enough to roll without breaking. Flip over halfway. Cool for 5 or so minutes, until safe to handle.

While the aubergine cooks make the tomato sauce. Pour the passata into a saucepan, add a pinch of sugar, the chopped garlic and thyme, and 1 tablespoon of olive oil. Simmer gently on the hob for 10–15 minutes, until reduced a little and thickened. Season to taste.

In a small bowl whisk together the ricotta with the rose harissa paste, lemon zest, and 1 tablespoon of the grated Parmesan cheese. Season to taste.

When the aubergine has cooled, lay the slices across a chopping board. Dividing equally, drop dollops of the spiced ricotta at the wider end of the aubergine. Roll up the aubergine and nestle in two tight rows inside a baking dish (approx. size 18 x 22 cm/7 x 8½ inches), with the join of the aubergine hiding underneath.

Pour over the tomato sauce, drizzle over a little olive oil, then sprinkle over the rest of the Parmesan. Bake in the oven for 20 minutes until the cheese is golden. Add an optional scattering of toasted pine nuts and parsley. Allow to stand for 5–10 minutes before serving.

Aubergine and Tenderstem Broccoli Tray Bake with Peanut Butter Sauce

Peanut butter straight from the jar and spread onto buttery toast is a morning favourite, but add it to a few simple store cupboard ingredients and watch it transform into a sweet, tangy, salty sauce. The sauce accompanies layers of roasted aubergine and broccoli, ribbons of crunchy carrot, and sliced spring onion, all prepared and served in one tray. If you are extra hungry, serve with a portion of cooked rice.

This same tray bake template will work with sweet potato instead of aubergine, and other varieties of broccoli. Adjust cooking times to suit.

SERVES 2 | TIME TO PREPARE – 40 MINUTES

2 aubergines, sliced lengthways into quarters
light olive oil
1 small red chilli
2 garlic cloves
1 thumbnail-sized piece of ginger, peeled
200g/7oz Tenderstem broccoli
1 medium carrot, shaved into ribbons with a peeler
1 spring onion, thinly sliced on an angle
1 tbsp finely chopped coriander
salt

FOR THE PEANUT BUTTER SAUCE
1½ tbsp smooth peanut butter
1 tbsp maple syrup
1 tbsp soy sauce
juice of ½ lime, other ½ cut into wedges to serve

Preheat the oven to 200°C fan/220°C/425°F/gas mark 7.

Place the aubergine quarters into a large baking tin, so that they are in 1 layer. Toss with 2 tablespoons of light olive oil, season with salt and roast for 20 minutes.

Meanwhile, make your peanut butter sauce. In a small bowl whisk together the peanut butter, maple syrup, soy sauce, and the lime juice until completely smooth. If your peanut butter is thick, you may need to loosen the sauce with a little water. Add a teaspoon at a time until you get a sauce that drips from the spoon. Season to taste and set aside.

Remove the seeds from the chilli, then finely chop half of it alongside the garlic and ginger together on your chopping board.

After the aubergine has had 20 minutes, and on its way to softening, pull out the tray. Reduce the oven temperature to 180°C fan/200°C/400°F/gas mark 6. Toss the broccoli with 1 tablespoon of oil and spread out across the top of the aubergine. Sprinkle over the garlic, ginger, and chilli, and give the tray a good shake to distribute. Roast for a final 15 minutes until the broccoli is browned and crispy, and the aubergine tender.

To finish the dish, drizzle the peanut butter sauce across the top of the veg and scatter over the carrot ribbons, spring onion, and coriander. For extra heat, garnish with the remainder of the chilli, finely sliced. Serve the tray straight to the table with the spare lime half cut into wedges.

Cucumber

Cucumbers are a member of the cucurbit family, a distant relation of summer and winter squash, as well as melons. These watery, mild tasting, crunchy vegetables have a thin, edible, deep-green skin, and small seeds. Heritage varieties usually have a thicker ridged skin, larger seeds, and a more pronounced 'cucumber' flavour. Mini-sized Persian cucumbers are less watery and can be pickled whole or diced into crisp salads. Other regional varieties are far less common away from a cucumber enthusiast's home-grown patch, but fun to try if you find them or they pop up in your veg box. I once struck lucky with a lemon-coloured cucumber. A bite-sized, crunchy cucamelon is a cross between a watermelon and a cucumber – it's great in a cocktail.

Cucumbers are usually eaten raw but they needn't just be a crudité. I was partial to a tuna and cucumber sandwich in my school lunch box for the majority of my school days – the added crunch broke up the heaviness of tuna doused in mayonnaise. I'm now more likely to be encouraging you to pickle a cucumber, blend it into a gazpacho, grate it to add to a cooling tzatziki, or dice it into a Greek, Shirazi, or kachumber salad. In all these salads from warmer climes, cucumber is combined with tomato, onion, herbs, and an oil or vinegar/citrus dressing for a cooling effect.

Leave the peel on a regular cucumber for colour, flavour, and fibre. I sometimes remove the watery middle of a cucumber along with its seeds to keep a salad crisp for longer; slice a cucumber in half lengthways, then scoop out a seed channel with a teaspoon. You can then slice into long strips and dice, or slice into half moons. A fun and tasty preparation technique for cucumbers is smacking. This Chinese technique for bashing cucumbers until the skin splits, breaks the skin and flesh in a way a knife could never. Why? It creates jagged edges for a marinade to cling to. Find my Smacked Cucumbers with Sea Bass and Vermicelli Noodles on page 250. I predict charred cucumbers to be the next trend.

Tasty flavour pairings you'll find in my recipes are; chilli, coriander, cumin, dill, garlic, lemon, mint, parsley, and soy sauce. Others to try include; feta, blue cheese, lettuce, salmon, sesame, tarragon, tomatoes, and yoghurt.

RECIPE IDEA Grate half a cucumber into a sieve and mix with a pinch of salt, come back in five minutes and squeeze out any excess water. Mix with a small pot of Greek yoghurt, a finely chopped clove of garlic, and a handful of shredded mint for a simple, cooling tzatziki-style sauce.

Smacked Cucumbers with Sea Bass and Vermicelli Noodles

If you've had a bad day, then taking a rolling pin to a cucumber is just the ticket. Cucumber juice may fly across the kitchen, so be careful! The marinade for the smacked cucumbers has a bit of sweetness, saltiness, and chilli, and acts like a quick pickle. The cucumbers are fantastic as a side dish in their own right. For a fresh and light summer supper, I pair them with quick-to-cook sea bass and vermicelli noodles. The cucumber marinade seeps into the noodles to flavour them too.

Make this recipe with regular cucumbers or a few smaller Persian ones.

SERVES 2 | TIME TO PREPARE – 35 MINUTES

FOR THE CUCUMBER
1 large cucumber
1 garlic clove, finely grated or finely chopped
1 tbsp soy sauce
1 tbsp maple syrup
1 tbsp rice vinegar
a pinch of chilli flakes, or more to taste

FOR THE REST OF THE DISH
2 x 50g/1¾oz nests of vermicelli rice noodles
2 sea bass fillets
2 tbsp neutral oil
2 tbsp roasted salted peanuts
a handful of coriander or mint (or both) leaves, left whole or chopped if large
salt and pepper

First prepare the cucumbers. Smack the cucumber all over using a rolling pin, until the skin starts to split. Chop the split cucumber into bite-sized pieces, and pop into a suitable sized bowl. Add in the garlic, soy sauce, maple syrup, rice vinegar, and chilli flakes, and toss to coat. Leave to marinate for at least 30 minutes, stirring regularly to ensure every bit of cucumber gets a good bath in the marinade.

Meanwhile, soak the noodles in a bowl of boiling water for 3 minutes, covering with a plate (or according to packet instructions). Drain and cool under the cold tap and leave to drip dry in a sieve, shaking off any excess water.

Prepare the fish; make 3–4 slashes in the skin, pat dry with kitchen paper, and season both sides with salt and pepper. Heat 2 tablespoons of oil in a large non-stick pan over a medium-high heat. Lower the 2 fish fillets skin-side down into the oil and hold down for 5–10 seconds to stop the sides curling up. After 2 minutes, the skin should be crisped up and the fish will easily come away from the pan. Flip over and cook for a further minute until the flesh is opaque.

Plate up on a sharing platter or on individual plates. Start with the noodles, then add the cucumber, including drizzling over any leftover marinade. Top with the cooked sea bass and garnish with the peanuts and herb leaves. Add extra chilli for a spicier hit.

Cucumber and Nectarine Tabbouleh-style Salad

A tabbouleh is first and foremost a herb salad – a full-on 'parsley is like lettuce to me' salad. This results in the freshest flavours, and yet, it's the kind of salad that holds well in the fridge for a couple of days. This is a retreat menu classic for me and I love to play around with variations on the expected Lebanese-style parsley, mint, tomato, and bulgur wheat combo, depending on what's best in season (perhaps even using kale for an autumn tabbouleh). Cooling cucumber adds to the freshness, as does freshly chopped, sweet stone fruit, which share some similar flavour properties to tomatoes.

For a variation, replace the cucumber or nectarine with tomatoes, as per the original salad. You can also substitute the bulgur for other grains but you will need to adjust the cooking method accordingly.

SERVES 2–4 AS A SIDE | TIME TO PREPARE – 25 MINUTES

60g/2¼oz bulgur wheat
50g/1¾oz parsley, stalks and leaves finely shredded
25g/1oz dill, stalks and leaves finely shredded
1 large cucumber, halved, seeds scooped out and diced
2 nectarines, finely diced
2 spring onions, finely sliced
1 garlic clove, finely grated or chopped
½ tsp ground cumin
½ tsp ground coriander
zest and juice of 1 lemon
2 tbsp olive oil
salt and pepper

First prepare the bulgur wheat. Place in a small heatproof bowl. For this amount of bulgur, cover with 1–2cm/½–¾ inch of freshly boiled water from the kettle, cover the bowl with a plate, and leave for up to 20 minutes, by which time all the water should have been absorbed (if not, then drain). Fluff up into individual grains with a fork and leave to cool.

While the bulgur soaks, prepare the rest of the ingredients. Place the shredded herbs, chopped cucumber, nectarines, spring onion, and garlic into a medium-sized bowl.

Add the cooled bulgur to the vegetables, sprinkle over the cumin, coriander, lemon zest and juice, and 2 tablespoons of olive oil, and season well. Stir well so everything is well combined and adjust seasoning to taste.

Leave the peel
on a regular
cucumber for
colour, flavour, and
fibre. I sometimes
remove the watery
middle of a
cucumber along
with its seeds
to keep a salad
crisp for longer.

Pepper

SPRING TO EARLY AUTUMN

From the mild bell pepper to the fiery scotch bonnet, all peppers are rated by their spiciness using the exponential Scoville scale – the Richter scale of the food world. This section features mostly zero-rated vegetable-sized peppers, rather than the smaller chilli peppers we only use a tiny amount of for their flavour and heat.

Bell peppers come in a complete traffic light set of colours – green, yellow, and red. Green peppers are unripe red peppers and are a little bitter and acidic in flavour. You get a good flavour balance when green and red peppers are used in combination in a stir fry, otherwise choose red, amber, or yellow if you enjoy the sweeter life. Elegant Romano peppers are even sweeter and have a long tapered body, which is great for stuffing (*see* Stuffed Peppers, page 260). Blistered Padrón peppers are a must for any tapas meal – these smaller green peppers are typically mild but you will get the odd one that is loaded with the kind of spice that will leave you with tears streaming out of your eyes.

Peppers can be eaten raw – dice for a salad or a salsa. When cooked, their natural sweetness intensifies – and this is the best way to eat peppers – roast, stir fry, stew, griddle, grill, BBQ, char on an open flame, or thread on a skewer alongside courgettes and halloumi. Once cooked, pepper flesh can be peeled and blended into a roasted pepper sauce (*see* page 258), or add to dips such as hummus or Lebanese muhamara with walnuts and pomegranate molasses.

Bell pepper seeds aren't spicy but it's best to remove them along with the core and the bitter white pith. To prepare a pepper, slice off the stalk and base end to leave you with a cylinder. Slice down the side and open out the pepper, removing the core and seeds as you go. Lie flat on your chopping board with the inside facing up, then slice out any remaining bits of pith. Slice your deseeded pepper flesh into chunks or julienne (cut into long, thin strips), and then dice.

Tasty flavour pairings for peppers you'll find in my recipes are; almonds, courgettes, feta, cumin, garlic, mint, paprika, parsley, polenta, and tomatoes. Others to try include; aubergine, basil, mozzarella, oregano, pine nuts, rocket, sweetcorn, and watercress.

RECIPE IDEA Roast, grill, or griddle chunks of peppers in olive oil until charred. Peel, then dress with chopped garlic, olive oil, balsamic vinegar, and garnish with pine nuts and rocket leaves for a tasty side.

TOP TIP
You can buy jars of roasted peppers that have already been skinned.
These provide a handy shortcut for any roasted pepper recipe.

Pepper, Walnut, and Pomegranate Stew with Griddled Polenta Wedges

Blistered peppers, chopped tomatoes, and smoky paprika are ingredients I use frequently together in a breakfast shakshuka, but even I'm getting bored of this recipe. With the addition of walnuts, and pomegranate molasses, inspired by their use together in the Persian fesenjan stew, it's something just different enough to try with peppers. The polenta wedges served with the stew take a bit of prepping ahead as the polenta needs to set for at least 30 minutes before you can slice it. If you don't have a griddle pan you can brush them with olive oil and bake in a 180°C fan/200°C/400°F/gas mark 6 oven for 25 minutes until crisp.

You can make this stew with any variety of peppers, or try mixing in some courgette.

SERVES 2 | TIME TO PREPARE – 50 MINUTES

FOR THE POLENTA
olive oil
500ml/17fl oz vegetable stock
100g/3½oz quick cook polenta
1 tsp finely chopped or dried rosemary or thyme

FOR THE STEW
1 tbsp olive oil
1 small red onion, thinly sliced
2 peppers (red, yellow, or orange), thinly sliced
1 garlic clove, finely chopped
1 tsp smoked paprika
1 tsp ground cumin
½ tsp pul biber
1 x 200g/7oz can chopped tomatoes
1 tbsp pomegranate molasses
50g/1¾oz walnuts, toasted and finely chopped
2 tbsp finely chopped soft herbs (e.g. mint and/or parsley)
juice of ½ lemon
salt and pepper

TO SERVE
a sprinkle of crumbled feta cheese (optional)

First make your polenta. Oil a 1kg/2lb 4oz bread loaf tin ready for the polenta. Pour the stock into a saucepan, bring to the boil, then reduce to a simmer. Pour in the polenta in a steady stream, and cook for 2–3 minutes, whisking continuously, until the polenta has thickened into a thick paste. Stir in the rosemary and season generously with salt and pepper. Spread the polenta paste over the oiled tin – it should be around 2cm/¾ inch deep. Leave to set for 30 minutes at room temperature. Refrigerate once cool if not using immediately.

Make the stew. Heat 1 tablespoon of olive oil over a low-medium heat in a wide, deep frying pan. Sauté the onions with a pinch of salt for around 5 minutes until starting to soften. Turn up the heat and add the peppers, cook stirring regularly for around another 5 minutes, until the skin blisters. Turn the heat back down, and add the garlic and spices, cook briefly, then tip in the can of chopped tomatoes, half fill the empty can with water (100ml/3½fl oz) and add that in too. Lastly, add the pomegranate molasses and toasted chopped walnuts. Bring to a simmer, and leave to lightly bubble away and thicken for 15–20 minutes. Add a splash of water if it gets too dry. Stir through the chopped herbs and season to taste with lemon juice, salt, and pepper.

While the stew simmers, cook your polenta. Flip the set polenta out of the tin, slice into two squares, and then four triangles. Heat a griddle pan to medium-high and brush the triangles all over with olive oil. Cook the polenta wedges for 5–6 minutes each side, until browned on the outside and cooked through on the inside. Only turn once for perfect griddle lines.

To serve, divide the stew between two wide pasta bowls, top with the polenta wedges, and if using, a little crumbled feta cheese.

Blistered Padrón Peppers, Prawns, Crispy Potatoes, and Roasted Red Pepper Sauce

All the best flavours from Spanish tapas-style dishes, brought together into one dish. My roasted pepper sauce is inspired by the Catalan recipe for romesco, and I have not met anyone who hasn't fallen in love with it on first taste. I like mine punchy with red wine vinegar, which compliments the creamy potatoes. Serve with a leafy side salad, and a little bread to mop up the sauce, if you don't quite manage to do that with the potatoes.

If you can't find Padrón peppers, include another vegetable instead – blistered asparagus or green beans would be my pick.

SERVES 2 | TIME TO PREPARE – 1 HOUR

FOR THE ROASTED PEPPER SAUCE
2 medium red bell peppers
3 tbsp olive oil
1 heaped tbsp blanched or flaked almonds
1 garlic clove, finely chopped
1 tbsp red wine vinegar
1 tbsp finely chopped parsley
½ tsp smoked paprika
a pinch of cayenne pepper, or more to taste

FOR THE DISH
400g/14oz baby potatoes, skin on and sliced into thick rounds (approx. 8mm/⅜ inch)
olive oil
125g/4½oz Padrón peppers
175g/6oz raw king prawns
1 garlic clove, thinly sliced
1 tbsp finely chopped parsley
juice of ½ lemon
salt and pepper

Preheat the oven to 200°C fan/220°C/425°F/gas mark 7.

Place the whole bell peppers on a rack in the top of your oven. Roast for 35–40 minutes, until blackened and the flesh has softened all over.

Spread out your cut potatoes in one layer on a baking tray, toss with 1 tablespoon of olive oil and season with salt. Roast in the oven below the peppers for 25 minutes until crispy and cooked through.

When the peppers are blackened, transfer to a small bowl and cover with clingfilm, to make them sweat off their skins. Leave the peppers to sit in the bowl for around 10 minutes until they are cool enough to touch. Peel off the skin and discard along with the seeds. Use a high-speed blender or hand blender with a beaker to blend together the pepper flesh with 3 tablespoons of olive oil, the almonds, chopped garlic, red wine vinegar, chopped parsley, smoked paprika, and cayenne pepper until really smooth. Season to taste with salt and pepper and don't be afraid to add more vinegar for punch. Taste test by dipping in a cooked potato. Set aside.

Finally, cook the Padrón peppers and prawns. Heat 1 tablespoon of oil in a medium-sized frying pan over a high heat. Toss in the Padrón peppers and cook tossing frequently, for around 3–4 minutes until blistered all over and starting to collapse. Move the peppers to one side of the dish, add a little extra oil into the pan if the peppers have soaked it all up. Drop in the prawns and garlic, and cook for around 2 minutes, until pink and cooked through. Toss the peppers and prawns together. Take off the heat, add the parsley, squeeze over the juice of half a lemon, and season to taste.

Plate up on 2 individual dinner plates. Start with a circle of the red pepper sauce, top with the potatoes, then the Padrón peppers and prawns.

Romano Peppers Stuffed with Courgette, Rice, and Walnuts

I've cooked these stuffed peppers in Portugal, Italy, France, and all over the UK, and rarely have a problem finding the beautiful Romano peppers. The filling and stuffing can be done in advance – get ahead is my motto! You can use a variety of rice to stuff the peppers but you want one that will hold its shape after being boiled, like basmati, wild rice, or a whole grain variety such as black or Camargue rice. Adjust the cooking time to suit. Serve alongside roasted potatoes and a sliced tomato or green salad.

Regular bell peppers can also be used for this recipe. Shave a little off the bottom so that they stand up on the plate.

SERVES 2 | TIME TO PREPARE – 50 MINUTES

50g/1¾oz rice, well rinsed
1 courgette (approx. 200g/7oz), coarsely grated
2 large Romano (pointed) peppers
25g/1oz walnuts, roughly chopped
1 tbsp sultanas
1 garlic clove, finely chopped
1 heaped tbsp finely chopped dill
1 tbsp olive oil
zest and juice of ½ lemon
salt and pepper

Preheat the oven to 180°C fan/200°C/400°F/gas mark 6. Cook the rice according to type. Drain and cool. While the rice cooks, place the grated courgettes in a sieve over a bowl then give them a good squeeze to remove as much water as you have patience for. Set aside.

Cut the tops off the peppers, carefully remove the seeds and any membrane from the insides with a sharp knife, retain the tops. If the peppers you have look a bit narrow to stuff from the stalk end, you can slice the pepper open from the stalk down to the tip. If so, you should cover the peppers with foil halfway through baking, to avoid a crispy filling.

Mix the cooked rice with the courgettes, walnuts, sultanas, garlic, dill, olive oil, and lemon zest and juice. Season the filling to taste. Stuff the peppers until almost overflowing then transfer to a lined baking tray. Prop the lids by the peppers (if using bell peppers, put the lids on top) and bake in the oven for 25 minutes, or until the pepper flesh has softened and is slightly charred. Serve warm.

Blistered Padrón peppers are a must for any tapas meal – these smaller green peppers are typically mild but you will get the odd one that is loaded with the kind of spice that will leave you with tears streaming out of your eyes.

Sweetcorn

LATE SUMMER TO EARLY AUTUMN

Sweetcorn is maize, a grass crop, and the ears it produces, packed full of sweet kernels, get starchier the older they get – don't forget this is a crop that also produces the corn-based products cornflakes, polenta and cornflour. There is a time and place for canned and frozen sweetcorn – any month either side of August and September – but there is really nothing like the taste of fresh, in season, crisp, sweet, sweetcorn.

If you look into heritage varieties you will find sweetcorn ears with purple, red, or multi-coloured kernels. I'm not a huge fan as I find it a bit bland, but there is also baby sweetcorn, which is best used in stir fries.

Sweetcorn can be boiled or steamed, grilled, griddled, or roasted. The cob can either be cooked whole, or you can remove the kernels before cooking them. Boiling the corn will give you softer kernels, adding the direct heat of the oven, grill, or BBQ will caramelize the natural sugars in the corn, giving you crispiness. Once you have your cooked kernels, they can be puréed into creamed corn or a chowder, added to salsas and salads, or bound together with an egg and flour and fried into fritters.

If you source corn whilst wrapped up in its natural husk, leave it wrapped up until you use it, to prolong its freshness. When ready to use, peel back the layers of the husk and pull away the threads. Sweetcorn is often sold trimmed or in stubbier cobettes, which does save on the practically impossible task of cutting it in half for smaller portions. If you'd like to remove the kernels prior to cooking, even off the base of the corn if not already flat, hold it up straight with the flat base on your chopping board, then use a sharp knife to slice downwards removing the kernels as you go. Turn and repeat until you're left with a naked husk. See the Sweetcorn Ribs recipe on page 266 for advice on how to prepare this latest trend.

Tasty flavour pairings for sweetcorn you'll find in my recipes are; butter, chilli, coriander, garlic, ginger, lime, paprika, salmon, spring onions, sweet potato, and tomato. Others to try include; cream, dill, eggs, pasta, peppers, potatoes, rosemary, and sage.

RECIPE IDEA For an easy fritter, combine blanched and cooled kernels with sliced spring onion, coriander, egg, and a little gram flour to bind. Season or add spices. Fry heaped tablespoon dollops in a decent amount of oil for 2–3 minutes on each side, until browned.

TOP TIP
Under the 'three sisters' crop system devised by Native Americans, corn, squash, and beans are grown together. These companion plants support each other whilst growing, and provide an all-round source of nutrition.

Roasted Sweetcorn, Sweet Potato, and Salmon Tray Bake

A deliciously easy all-in-one tray bake recipe with only a chopping board, mixing bowl, and baking tray to wash up. Rounds of sweet potato are roasted until soft, then joined by juicy kernels of corn and smoky-sweet-lime marinated salmon fillets. The traybake is finished out of the oven with sweetcorn's pals tomatoes, spring onions, and coriander.

For a variation, use thin slices of squash as a substitution for the sweet potato, or add a handful of green beans instead of the sweetcorn kernels.

SERVES 2 | TIME TO PREPARE – 45 MINUTES

2 sweet potatoes (approx. 450g/1lb), peeled and sliced into discs 5mm/¼ inch thick
olive oil
2 corn on the cob, husk removed (if present) and kernels sliced off
125g/4½oz cherry tomatoes, quartered
2 spring onions, finely sliced
1 tbsp chopped coriander
juice of ½ lime
salt

FOR THE SALMON
2 salmon fillets (approx. 125g/4½oz each)
juice of ½ lime
½ tbsp maple syrup or honey
1 garlic clove, finely chopped
¼ tsp ground cumin
¼ tsp smoked paprika

TO SERVE
a drizzle of Greek yoghurt or sour cream

Preheat the oven to 180°C fan/200°C/400°F/gas mark 6.

Toss the sweet potato slices onto your baking dish in a single layer (just overlapping is fine) with 1 tablespoon of olive oil and season with salt. Pop into the oven for 25 minutes.

Meanwhile, prepare your marinade for the salmon. Dab the salmon fillets dry with kitchen paper and put in a medium-sized bowl. Squeeze over the lime juice, ½ tablespoon of olive oil, the maple syrup, garlic, cumin, smoked paprika, and season with salt. Mix well to ensure the salmon flesh and skin are covered in the marinade. Set aside to marinate.

Toss the sweetcorn kernels in 1 tablespoon of olive oil and season. When the sweet potato has had 25 minutes, or has softened and is starting to brown, remove from the oven, scatter over the sweetcorn, and place the salmon fillets and any spare marinade on top, with the skin facing up. Return to the oven for a final 12 minutes, or until the salmon is opaque and cooked through.

Remove the tray from the oven and carefully lift off the salmon. Toss the chopped cherry tomatoes, spring onions, and coriander onto the baking dish and give everything a good shake. Squeeze over the remaining lime. Taste and adjust seasoning. Divide the vegetables between two dishes and top with the salmon, and a drizzle of Greek yoghurt or sour cream.

Sweetcorn Ribs with Flavoured Butter Variations (Miso, Chilli, and Lime, Garam Masala)

Sweetcorn ribs became popular because of social media, I even jumped in on the trend myself. The bad news is that even with practice and confident knife skills, they are a pain to chop. The good news is that the sweetcorn doesn't taste any different when chopped as a rib, and you're very welcome to leave the cobs whole. I have tried par-boiling the cobs to make them easier to cut. Around 8 mins is just enough, but since by this point they're already ready to eat, it somewhat negates the baking in the oven bit.

Any of these flavoured butters will make your cooked veggies taste sublime. Stir through cooked peas, steamed greens, or roasted cauliflower.

SERVES 2 | TIME TO PREPARE – 25–35 MINUTES

2 corn on the cob
1 tbsp olive oil
salt
1 tbsp finely chopped coriander or parsley

MISO BUTTER
1 tbsp butter, at room temperature
½ tbsp white miso paste
1 tsp honey

CHILLI LIME BUTTER
1½ tbsp butter, at room temperature
zest of 1 lime
¼ tsp dried chilli flakes
salt

GARAM MASALA BUTTER
1 tbsp butter, at room temperature
1 garlic clove
a thumb-tip-sized piece of ginger, peeled
1 tsp garam masala
salt

Preheat the oven to 180°C fan/200°C/400°F/gas mark 6.

To make the ribs, stand the corn up on its flat end, and using a very sharp chef's knife, split it down the middle into two pieces. Keeping the split corn standing, split each of the halves into a further 2 pieces so that you have 4 'ribs'. Alternatively, skip this part and leave your cobs whole.

Place the ribs on a baking tray, drizzle over 1 tablespoon of olive oil, and season with salt. Give everything a good shuffle to distribute the oil. Bake the ribs in the oven for 20 minutes, or the whole corn for 30 minutes, until the edges are starting to char and the corn easily comes off the cob when pulled with your fingers.

While the sweetcorn bakes, make your choice of butter. Using a pestle and mortar, smoosh together your ingredients of choice into a soft spreadable paste.

For the miso butter, adjust the quantity of miso to taste, as types of miso will vary in flavour.

For the garam masala butter, combine the garlic, ginger, and salt, before adding the butter.

Brush the flavoured butter over the sweetcorn as soon as it comes out of the oven and scatter over the chopped herbs. Wait for it to cool off a touch before eating, unless you want a burnt tongue.

Tomato

SUMMER TO EARLY AUTUMN

What is it about homegrown tomatoes that just, well, taste better? Perhaps it's the timing of plot to plate, the fact they're left on the vine to develop longer, or maybe it's just the taste of smugness. If you've ever tasted a fruity, juicy tomato whilst on holiday in the Mediterranean, you'll know that sunshine and heat grows better tomatoes – it's for this reason the best tomatoes in the UK are grown on the sunny Isle of Wight. There are so many varieties, an entire chapter could be dedicated to them. I generally find supermarket salad tomatoes an utter disappointment, so if I must, I choose small cherry tomatoes, which are the sweetest, or average-sized salad vine tomatoes. Both are good for salads and cooking. Gigantic beefsteak varieties – look out for the heritage variety 'marmande' – are best for raw salads. Don't forget canned tomatoes, which keep the tomato dream alive all year round; I always add a pinch of sugar and cook for longer than you might expect, to do away with the 'tinny' flavour. As with fresh, quality matters.

Tomatoes can be eaten raw, roasted, simmered slowly in oil (this is called a confit), stewed, grilled, blistered in a hot pan, stuffed, or puréed. No Michelin stars for this one, but my Dad, who barely knew where our kitchen was, had a specialty dish of homegrown tomatoes, sliced, microwaved, and served warm sloshed over buttered toast. Let me know if you try it. If your kitchen knife isn't sharp enough to cut a tomato skin, it's a good hint it needs sharpening. A serrated knife can be useful to pierce through the skin. For larger tomatoes, you may wish to slice out the core but there's really no need to fish out the seeds. To peel a tomato, make a small cross in the bottom of the fruit, blanch the tomato in hot water for a minute, chill in ice-cold water until cool to the touch, and peel – great if you have a tomato glut, but in this book I make use of those already peeled and in a tin. If it's just the unpeeled raw flesh you're after, you can grate a whole tomato – the flesh will pass through the grater and the skin left in your hand. This tomato pulp can be served with olive oil on garlic rubbed toast for a simple *pan con tomate*.

Tasty flavour pairings you'll find in my recipes are; balsamic vinegar, basil, capers, chilli, dill, garlic, legumes such as beans and lentils, onions, oregano, and parsley. Others to try include; aubergine, mozzarella, cucumber, fennel, nectarines and peaches, peppers, strawberries, and yoghurt.

RECIPE IDEA Slice heritage tomatoes, drizzle over extra-virgin olive oil, add flaky sea salt, wafer thin rings of shallot, torn basil, and a spoon of capers for a deliciously simple side dish that tastes of summer.

Slow Roasted Confit Tomato, Chickpea, and Hake Tray Bake

To confit is to cook something slowly in fat, it works marvellously with tomatoes in olive oil. Add just enough oil for the tomatoes to paddle, rather than drown in, alongside chickpeas, then bake a fillet of hake on top for an all-in-one tray bake. Serve with bread or couscous to mop up the juices, and perhaps a handful of salad leaves.

Use a variety of colour and sizes of tomatoes for this dish. A mix of whole cherry tomatoes and quartered larger vine tomatoes is ideal. For a variation, substitute some or all of the tomatoes with peppers or aubergines for a full-on summer vegetable party.

SERVES 2 | TIME TO PREPARE – 1 HOUR

400g/14oz mixed tomatoes, smaller ones left whole, larger ones halved or quartered
1 x 400g/14oz can chickpeas, drained and rinsed
3 garlic cloves, bashed and peeled
1 tbsp tomato purée
½ tsp each of dried or fresh oregano and thyme leaves
a pinch of dried chilli flakes
6 tbsp olive oil
2 skinless hake or cod fillets (approx. 125g/4½oz each)
2 tbsp finely chopped soft herbs (e.g. dill or parsley)
½ lemon, sliced into 2 wedges
salt and pepper

Preheat the oven to 150°C fan/170°C/315°F/gas mark 2½. In a baking dish (sized approx. 30 x 24cm/12 x 9½ inches), add the tomatoes, chickpeas, garlic, tomato purée, oregano, thyme, chilli flakes, and season with salt and pepper. Pour over the olive oil and give the dish a good shuffle so that everything is well combined. Roast in the oven for 45 minutes or until the smaller tomatoes have collapsed and the larger ones are starting to char. Stir halfway through.

Remove from the oven and turn up the oven to 180°C fan/200°C/400°F/gas mark 6. Mash the garlic cloves into the oil and give the ingredients a stir. Season both sides of the fish with salt and pepper, make two wells in the tomatoes, and nestle in both pieces of fish. Scoop up a little of the oil from the baking dish and drizzle over the fish. Put the dish back into the oven and bake for 8–10 minutes, or until the fish is no longer opaque and is cooked through. A thicker fillet may take longer. When ready, sprinkle over the chopped herbs and squeeze the lemon wedges over the fish. Taste the saucy tomatoes and adjust the seasoning if needed. Serve straight to the table.

Cherry Tomatoes with
Puy Lentils, Capers, and Dill

I came up with this recipe whilst cooking on an early summer retreat near Sorrento in southern Italy a few years ago. The tomatoes were so incredible, I found myself continually searching for new ways to incorporate them into meals to keep the guests happy. They needed barely more than a helping hand from olive oil, salty capers, and dill to complement their flavour. The recipe followed me back home to London, and here I regularly make this with raw cherry tomatoes or best of the season larger tomatoes on the vine, to try and replicate the taste of the Italian sun-drenched tomato.

For a variation, substitute the tomatoes with roasted peppers or aubergines.

SERVES 2 AS A MAIN, 4 AS A SIDE | TIME TO PREPARE – 40 MINUTES

100g/3½oz puy lentils, rinsed
1 bay leaf
2 tbsp olive oil, plus more to drizzle
1 tbsp balsamic vinegar
1 plump garlic clove, finely chopped
3 tbsp capers
300g/10½oz cherry tomatoes, halved, or large tomatoes sliced into wedges
25g/1oz bunch of dill, fronds finely chopped
a handful of basil leaves
salt and pepper

First cook your lentils. Place lentils in a saucepan with 300ml/10fl oz water (3 x the lentil weight) and a bay leaf. Bring to the boil then reduce to a gentle simmer. Cover and cook for 22 minutes, until the lentils are soft enough to eat but retain some bite in the centre. Turn off the heat, sit for 5 minutes, then drain, shaking off as much excess water as possible. Discard the bay leaf.

In a medium-sized bowl, toss the warm lentils with the olive oil, balsamic vinegar, garlic, and capers, then allow the lentils to cool off so they're no longer steaming before stirring in the fresh tomatoes and dill. Season to taste with salt and pepper.

Plate up on a serving platter and finish with a few basil leaves and another drizzle of olive oil.

Cherry Tomato, Prawn, and Butter Bean Mauritian-inspired Rougaille with Coriander Flatbreads

I've been lucky to spend some time travelling in Mauritius with my school friend Myra and her Mauritian family, and have since been inspired to explore the unique blend of ingredients used in Mauritian cuisine at home. A *rougaille* is a staple tomato-based sauce with garlic, thyme, chilli, and ginger – a result of Indian and French influences on the island. In Mauritius, I've eaten it restaurant-style with seafood or fish, home-cooked by Myra's aunties, and as part of a street food snack inside a soft roti with butter beans. In my sauce, inspired by all of these, I combine all the spices you'd expect to find, add butter beans and prawns, and make the bulk of the sauce from fresh cherry tomatoes, which cook down really quickly if you don't mind the skins. These soft flatbreads are very different from Mauritian roti but do an excellent job of mopping up the sauce.

Try making a *rougaille* with fresh larger tomatoes instead – you'll need to remove the stalks and seeds.

SERVES 2 | TIME TO PREPARE – 35 MINUTES

1 tbsp rapeseed or light olive oil
1 small or ½ large onion, finely chopped
2 garlic cloves, finely chopped
a skinny thumb-sized piece of fresh ginger, peeled and finely chopped
3 sprigs of thyme, leaves stripped
a pinch of chilli flakes
300g/10½oz cherry tomatoes, quartered
1 tbsp tomato purée
165g/5¾oz raw king prawns
1 x 200g/7oz can butter beans, drained and rinsed
2 tbsp finely chopped coriander
juice of ½ lemon, or more to taste
salt and pepper

FOR THE FLATBREADS
125g/4½oz strong white bread (or plain) flour
1 tbsp finely chopped coriander
½ tsp baking powder
¼ tsp salt
125g/4½oz Greek yoghurt

First make your flatbread dough. Combine the flour, chopped coriander, baking powder, and salt in a small bowl. Stir in the yoghurt using a fork, then go in with your hands to bring it together into a dough. Briefly knead on the kitchen worktop, then place back in the bowl, cover, and rest for 15–30 minutes.

While the dough rests, cook your *rougaille*. Heat 1 tablespoon of oil in a large, lidded frying pan over a low-medium heat. Sauté the onion with a pinch of salt for 5–8 minutes (the longer the better), until softened. Add the garlic, ginger, thyme leaves, and chilli flakes, and cook for a minute more, then stir in the quartered cherry tomatoes, tomato purée, and 4 tablespoons of water. Let it start to bubble, then cover and continue to cook over a low-medium heat for around 6–8 minutes, until the tomatoes start to break down and the sauce thickens. Drop in the raw prawns and butter beans, and cook for a final 4 minutes, until the prawns are cooked through and pink. Sprinkle in the chopped coriander and season to taste with lemon juice, salt, and pepper.

While the *rougaille* bubbles, roll out and cook the flatbreads. Lightly flour your surface, divide the dough into 2, then roll each out thinly to around 3mm/⅛ inch thick. Heat a heavy-bottomed frying pan to a high heat. Add one of the flatbreads into the dry pan, turn down the heat a little, and cook for roughly 90 seconds on each side, or until they're browned, starting to puff up, and there's no raw dough. Repeat with the second flatbread and keep them both warm, wrapped in a clean tea towel, while you finish the *rougaille*.

Serve the flatbreads alongside the prawns, with a chopped crunchy salad on the side.

Conversion Charts

WEIGHT

METRIC	IMPERIAL
5g	⅛oz
10g	¼oz
15g	½oz
25/30g	1oz
35g	1¼oz
40g	1½oz
50g	1¾oz
55g	2oz
60g	2¼oz
70g	2½oz
85g	3oz
90g	3¼oz
100g	3½oz
115g	4oz
125g	4½oz
140g	5oz
150g	5½oz
175g	6oz
200g	7oz
225g	8oz
250g	9oz
280g	9¾oz
300g	10½oz
325g	11½oz
350g	12oz
375g	13oz
400g	14oz
425g	1lb
500g	1lb 2oz
550g	1lb 4oz
600g	1lb 5oz
650g	1lb 7oz
700g	1lb 9oz
750g	1lb 10oz
800g	1lb 12oz
850g	1lb 14oz
900g	2lb
950g	2lb 2oz
1kg	2lb 2oz
1.25kg	2lb 12oz
1.3kg	3lb
1.5kg	3lb
1.6kg	3lb 8oz
1.8kg	4lb
2kg	4lb 8oz
2.25kg	5lb
2.5kg	5lb 8oz
2.7kg	6lb
3kg	6lb 8oz

LIQUID MEASURES

METRIC	IMPERIAL	SPOONS/CUPS
5ml		1 tsp
15ml		1 tbsp/ 3 tsp
30ml	1fl oz	2 tbsp
60ml	2fl oz	4 tbsp
90ml	3fl oz	6 tbsp
125ml	4fl oz	½ cup
150ml	5fl oz	⅔ cup
175ml	6fl oz	¾ cup
200ml	7fl oz	
225ml	8fl oz	1 cup
275ml	9fl oz	
300ml	10fl oz	1¼ cup
325ml	11fl oz	
350ml	12fl oz	1½ cups
375ml	13fl oz	
400ml	14fl oz	1¾ cups
450ml	15fl oz	
475ml	16fl oz	2 cups
(US : 1 pint = 16fl oz)		
500ml	17fl oz	
575ml	18fl oz	
600ml	1 pint	2½ cups
(UK: 1 pint = 20fl oz)		
750ml	1¼ pints	3 cups
900ml	1½ pints	3½ cups
1 litre	1¾ pints	4 cups
1.2 litres	2 pints	5 cups
Or 1 quart		
1.5 litres	2½ pints	
1.7 litres	3 pints	
2 litres	3½ pints	

DRY MEASURES

	METRIC	IMPERIAL	SPOONS/CUPS
Breadcrumbs, dried	140g	5oz	1 cup
Breadcrumbs, fresh	55g	2oz	1 cup
Butter	25g	1oz	2 tbsp
	50g	2oz	4 tbsp
	115g	4oz	½ cup
	225g	8oz	1 cup
Cheese, cottage cream, curd	225g	8oz	1 cup
Cheese, Cheddar, Parmesan, grated	115g	4oz	1 cup
Cornflour	140g	5oz	1 cup
Courgette, grated	200g	7oz	1 cup
Flour, plain	140g	5oz	1 cup
Mushrooms, sliced	55g	2oz	1 cup
Hazelnuts, peanuts	115g	5½oz	1 cup
Oats, rolled	85g	3oz	1 cup
Olives, stone in	175g	6oz	1 cup
Onions, chopped	150g	5½oz	1 cup
Peas, frozen	115g	4oz	1 cup
Long-grain uncooked rice	200g	7oz	1 cup
Short-grain uncooked rice	215g	6¾oz	1 cup
Caster sugar	200g	7oz	1 cup
Sultanas	175g	6oz	1 cup

UK–US Cooking Terms

Aubergine – eggplant
Beetroot – beet
Borlotti bean – cranberry bean
Broad bean – fava bean
Butter bean – lima bean
Cannellini bean – white bean/white kidney bean
Celeriac – celery root
Chickpea – garbanzo bean
Chicory – endive
Chilli flakes – crushed red pepper/red pepper flakes
Coriander – cilantro
Courgette – zucchini
Cream (single/double) – cream (light/heavy)
Flour (plain) – Flour (all purpose)
French beans – string/green beans
Grill – boil/broiler
Jacket potato – baked potato
Jerusalem artichoke – sunchoke
Milk (semi-skimmed) – milk (two-percent)
Pepper – bell pepper
Prawn – shrimp
Puy lentils – French green lentils
Rapeseed (oil) – canola
Rocket – arugula
Spring onions – green onions/scallions
Swede – rutabaga
Sweetcorn – corn/maize
Tenderstem broccoli – Broccolini
Tomato purée – tomato paste
Toastie – grilled cheese

Further Reading and Resources

ON THE WEB

BBC Good Food Seasonal Calendar
  bbcgoodfood.com/seasonal-calendar
Eat the Seasons
  eattheseasons.co.uk

BOOKS

Jane Grigson's Vegetable Book
  Jane Grigson (Penguin Books, 1980)
The Flavour Thesaurus
  Niki Segnit (Bloomsbury, 2010)
The Flavour Thesaurus: More Flavours
  Niki Segnit (Bloomsbury, 2023)
The Flavor Bible
  Karen Page and Andrew Dornenburg (Little, Brown and Company, 2008)

VEG BOX SCHEMES IN THE UK

Better Food Traders
  A network of independent veg box schemes and retailers –
    betterfoodtraders.org
Abel & Cole
  abelandcole.co.uk
Riverford
  riverford.co.uk
Oddbox
  oddbox.co.uk

Index

Acknowledgements

Firstly, my thanks go to Lucy, Kiron, Alice, and the whole team at Pavilion for commissioning and producing this book and helping me bring my decade long dream of writing a cookbook to fruition. Thank you too, to Freya for producing the most beautiful illustrations that somehow make veg seem more fun.

Testing 100 recipes for a cookbook is no mean feat, and when I sent out a plea for help, I couldn't quite believe how many of you volunteered! An enormous thank you to Aaron, Ali, Alice, Ann, Bec, Ceri, Clare, Deb, Elef, Emma, Fran, Gemma, Hayley, Jacqui, Janine, Jennifer, Jessie, Judith, Kelly, Lucy, Luna, Magdalena, Mel, Michaela, Molly, Myra, Paul, Pip, Pippa, Rachel D, Rachel Q, Rebs, Rhian, Rich, Richard, Roland, Roz, Tasha. Whether you helped with 1 or 10 (!) recipes, thank you so much for taking my recipes into your home kitchens and for providing such useful feedback – this book is all the richer for it.

To everyone who I have ever cooked for on a retreat or supper club, taught in a cooking class, or has followed my recipes online since the early blogging days or more recently, your hunger has encouraged me to keep the creativity going, thank you.

To the Guild of Food Writers, for your professional support in particular your Futures Fund grant, and Mentorship Scheme which gifted me the wisdom of Judy Ridgway to inspire me to get those all-important first words of a proposal down on paper, thank you Judy.

To all my colleagues at the Garden Museum, thank you for your endless support for my work, and this book, and especially to Matt for introducing me to Lucy.

To my friends at Encore Choir and Lambeth Wind Orchestra – you don't know how much singing, playing and hanging out with you at rehearsals and beyond helped to keep me sane while this book was being produced.

To Uncle Wyn and Aunty Lucia for giving me advice on Italian recipes and always offering me an Italian place to escape.

To my gorgeous circle of girlfriends. Thank you for cheerleading me, always.

And, finally to my family. Thank you to my sister Rhian and brother Richard for your love and always being there, no matter what, and to Mum and Dad, who I miss, and I know would be proud of me – whilst equally surprised that this is what I ended up doing with my life.

About the Author

Ceri Jones trained as a Natural Chef in Berkeley, California. Her cooking has always had a focus on health and community, and she has carved out a niche cooking on wellness retreats around the world. Ceri is currently Food Educator at the Garden Museum in London, where she has pioneered one of the first museum food learning programmes in the country, inspiring people to cook with, learn more about, and enjoy eating plants. Above all, Ceri is passionate about empowering people with the skills they need to elevate their home cooking and inspires people to expand their knowledge of ingredients, their recipe repertoire and improve their practical know-how to give them the confidence to make the most out of and truly enjoy every ingredient on their plate. This is her first book.

To find out more about Ceri, visit **www.cerijoneschef.com**
@cerijoneschef

Pavilion
An imprint of HarperCollins*Publishers* Ltd
1 London Bridge Street
London SE1 9GF

www.harpercollins.co.uk

HarperCollins*Publishers*
Macken House
39/40 Mayor Street Upper
Dublin 1
D01 C9W8
Ireland

10 9 8 7 6 5 4 3 2 1

First published in Great Britain by Pavilion
An imprint of HarperCollins*Publishers* 2024

ISBN 978-0-00-860393-9

This book is produced from independently certified FSC™ paper
to ensure responsible forest management.

For more information visit: www.harpercollins.co.uk/green

Publishing Director: Stephanie Milner
Commissioning Editors: Kiron Gill, Lucy Smith
Editor: Anna Glover
Editorial Assistant: Shamar Gunning
Design Manager: Laura Russell
Senior Designer: Alice Kennedy-Owen
Production Controller: Grace O'Bryne
Illustrator: Freya Elise Kemp
Cover Designer: Bess Daly
Proofreader: Katie Hardwicke
Indexer: Vanessa Bird

Printed and bound in the UK